Experiencing Globalization

Experiencing Globalization

Religion in Contemporary Contexts

Edited by
Derrick M. Nault, Bei Dawei, Evangelos Voulgarakis,
Rab Paterson and Cesar Andres-Miguel Suva

ANTHEM PRESS
LONDON · NEW YORK · DELHI

Anthem Press
An imprint of Wimbledon Publishing Company
www.anthempress.com

This edition first published in UK and USA 2014
by ANTHEM PRESS
75–76 Blackfriars Road, London SE1 8HA, UK
or PO Box 9779, London SW19 7ZG, UK
and
244 Madison Ave. #116, New York, NY 10016, USA

First published in hardback by Anthem Press in 2013

British Library Cataloguing-in-Publication Data
A catalogue record for this book is available from the British Library.

Library of Congress Cataloging-in-Publication Data
The Library of Congress has catalogued the hardcover edition as follows:
Experiencing globalization : religion in contemporary contexts /
edited by Derrick M. Nault ... [et al.].
p. cm.
Proceedings of a conference held in Mar. 2010 at National Chung
Cheng University.
Includes bibliographical references.
ISBN 978-0-85728-559-1 (hardcover : alk. paper)
1. Globalization–Religious aspects–Congresses. 2.
Asia–Religion–Congresses. I. Nault, Derrick M.
BL65.G55E97 2013
201'.7–dc23
2012036395

ISBN-13: 978 1 78308 323 7 (Pbk)
ISBN-10: 1 78308 323 9 (Pbk)

This title is also available as an ebook.

TABLE OF CONTENTS

PREFACE

The essays in this volume were originally presented at a conference held at National Chung Cheng University in Jiayi, Taiwan in March 2010 entitled *(En)countering Globalizations: Religion in the Contemporary World*. Convened by the Asia Association for Global Studies (AAGS), a scholarly organization based in Tokyo, the conference gathered scholars from Asia, the Middle East, Europe and North America to examine the impact of globalization on contemporary religious life.

Many individuals helped to make the event a success. Though he was unfortunately unable to attend due to illness, Dr Hans Peter Liederbach (Kwansei Gakuin University, Japan), the former president of AAGS, provided the original idea for the conference. Dr Mark Juergensmeyer (University of California, Santa Barbara), noted expert on religious violence, conflict resolution and South Asian religion and politics, delivered an insightful and captivating keynote address on religious challenges to the secular state. Dr Jou-juo Chu (National Chung Cheng University, Taiwan) and her on-site conference organizing team of students did an exceptional job of welcoming, entertaining and assisting guests. Last but not least, the conference would not have been possible without the enthusiastic participation of some 120 presenters and attendees hailing from 12 different nations.

For the publication of this volume, the contributors are indebted to Tej P. S. Sood and the Anthem Press team for their suggestions, guidance and expertise.

Derrick M. Nault
University of Calgary

Chapter 1

INTRODUCTION

Bei Dawei
Hsuan Chuang University, Taiwan

Evangelos Voulgarakis
Independent Scholar, Taiwan

Derrick M. Nault
University of Calgary, Canada

Globalization

Centuries hence, when future historians look back upon our era, surely globalization will stand out as one of its defining trends. Technological advances have resulted in ever-accelerating levels of travel, trade and communication. Human ties (e.g., cross-border marriage and adoption) and population movements have followed, challenging various regional and cultural identities. Transnational institutions and agreements have gained new importance. Integration into global markets has brought routine contact with "foreigners," whether in the form of competition or alliance, and imitation is widespread. Elements of a common culture can be identified in our business practices, choice of languages, clothing and hairstyles, consumer products, entertainment, education, military affairs and politics, among other spheres. We may even speak of a certain "global consciousness," a reflexive awareness of our growing interconnectedness.[1]

Scholars and public intellectuals disagree as to how far back to trace this process. Thomas Friedman (1999, 2005) focuses primarily on the end of the Cold War, and the technological and managerial developments of the 1990s. Benjamin Barber (1992) looks to the post-World War II rise of multinational corporations and international trade regimes (such as the Bretton Woods institutions and the various common markets). Paul Hirst and Grahame Thompson (1996) liken this to earlier cycles of internationalization, such as the period between 1870–1914. William H. McNeill (1963) emphasizes the period of European industrialization and colonialism from 1750 to 1950. Immanuel Wallerstein (1974, 1980, 1989) begins with the great age of European exploration and the intercontinental maritime empires established in its wake. Janet Abu-Lughod (1991) and Jack Weatherford (2004) hail the contributions of the thirteenth-century *pax Mongolica*. Others nominate the Umayyad and Abbasid Caliphates (e.g., Stearns, Adas, Schwartz and Gilbert 2004), or earlier land-based Eurasian empires associated with the Silk Road. Andre Gunder Frank and Barry K. Gills (1991, 1993) suggest a figure of "five thousand years" ago, referring to trade ties between the Sumerian and Harappan civilizations. Daniel Quinn (1992) and Jared Diamond (1997) point to the development of mass agriculture some 10,000 years ago. Finally, James Harrod (2006) refers to "periods of globalization" during the Lower Paleolithic, between 1.9 and 1.6 million years ago, in which Olduwan industries (and presumably also the hominins themselves) spread out from Africa across Asia via the Indian Ocean Rim.

Of course there is some merit to each of these starting points, at least within specifically defined contexts, and there have been numerous attempts at periodization (some by the same authors). Here we may usefully resort to David Held's distinction between "thick" globalization (characterized by high extensity, intensity, velocity and impact) and several earlier forms. For example, the ancient Silk Road (which combined high extensity with low intensity, velocity and impact) would be an example of "thin" globalization (Held, McGrew, Goldblatt and Perraton 1999; see also Nye 2002). At any rate, the present momentum—for better or worse, and regardless of the system's ultimate success or failure—is clearly in the direction of thickness. Less amenable to reconciliation are the questions of whether our era is unique, or part of some larger economic or historical cycle; and whether neo-liberal economic policies will, or should, prevail under the New World Order.

However periodized or conceptualized, that globalization is a contested process is demonstrated through the spectrum of "anti-globalist" figures, which extend from the far left (the "Black Bloc") to the far right (Marine Le Pen), and encompasses environmentalists, labor organizers, anarchists (David Graeber and John Zerzan fill several of these roles), indigenous rights activists, conspiracy theorists (Theodore Kaczinsky, David Icke), dissident economists (Joseph Stiglitz, Susan Strange), postmodern cultural critics and miscellaneous others. Noam Chomsky himself protests the nomenclature:

> The dominant propaganda systems have appropriated the term "globalization" to refer to the specific version of international economic integration that they favor, which privileges the rights of investors and

lenders, those of people being incidental. In accord with this usage, those who favor a different form of international integration, which privileges the rights of human beings, become "anti-globalist." This is simply vulgar propaganda. (Cited in Matejcic 2005, par. 6)

By way of illustration, Chomsky complains that the world press routinely describes the World Social Forum—a diverse, international group with global aims—as "anti-globalist," in apparent contrast with the (far less representative) participants in the annual World Economic Forum at Davos, Switzerland.

It is often observed that globalization has resulted in countervailing, atomistic forces of "glocalization," regionalism, subcultural identity and individualism. Globalized cultural products have aroused a reaction among nationalists of various stripes, their eagerness made "more keen when confronted with the media assault of Western music, videos and films that satellite television now beams around the world, and which threaten to obliterate local and traditional forms of cultural expression" (Juergensmeyer 2001, 66). Such modernizing leaders as Jawaharlal Nehru, Gamal Abdel Nasser and Shah Reza Pahlavi all faced a backlash of this nature, with varying results. In the United States we might point to the overlapping subcultures of white supremacists, neo-militias and tax protesters who mistrust the federal government and, in some cases, fear world government. Many such groups point to globalization as the reason for their political and social reclusiveness, though their precise motivations range from conspiracy theories to a desire for exclusivity (Abanes 1996; Heller 1995). The ethical questions involved are fascinating. For example, the ideologies of white nationalists—who are active and networked in numerous countries—can be difficult to distinguish from other groups seeking ethnic-based nations or autonomous homelands (although no one would confuse the late Eugene Terre'Blanche with the Dalai Lama).

Attempting to make sense of the above, global studies is an emerging interdisciplinary field with globalization as its object of study. To be sure, not everyone admits the legitimacy of this body of discourse. Indeed, globalization as a subject has been dismissed as "folly" (Rosenberg 2002), "global babble" (Abu-Lughod 1997) and "globaloney" (Veseth 2006), and a catch phrase meaning "anything, everything and nothing" (Munck 2000, 84). Yet in view of the enormous differences between life today and twenty years ago (let alone the Lower Paleolithic), surely such changes are deserving of scholarly attention, if still imperfectly understood.

Religion

The meaning and scope of "religion" is unclear to specialists, or at least not yet a matter of general agreement (e.g., Greil and Bromley 2003).

The boundaries of the field (if not its very core) are challenged by the difficulty of distinguishing, for example, a traditional religious leader from a traditional chieftain; a religious practice from mere etiquette; or religious cosmology from primitive science (noting that many aspects of our present scientific worldview are likely to be remembered as quaint and culture-bound). Wilfred Cantwell Smith (1962) and Jonathan Z. Smith (1982) argue that the very category of "religion" is a social construct illegitimately generalized from the example of Christianity. The world abounds with cults and ideologies that might be deemed in some sense religious-like, but whose details do not quite resemble those of the Abrahamic religions. Chinese "religions," for example, rarely provide their adherents with a multi-generational group identity (many Chinese people profess uncertainty as to whether they even have a religion, or what it should be called), but are better described as personal interests, family customs or community activities. As for Chinese group identity, this is more usually drawn from a shared sense of history, culture and politics (including Confucianism as well as several modern state or party affiliations). Whether these are *ipso facto* religious in nature is difficult to say. Structural functionalist approaches (e.g., Émile Durkheim, Bronislaw Malinowski) classify institutions according to their social roles, whereas "substantive" approaches (e.g., Clifford Geertz, Melford Spiro) focus on content, such as ritual or supernatural beliefs. We may also distinguish "inclusivists" from "exclusivists," depending on their willingness to acknowledge the religious character of such borderline cases as atheism, the "civil religion" or football.[2]

As tempting as it may be to dismiss the concept of religion as meaningless, there are equally good grounds for assuming it to be basic to human nature, along with other forms of behavior that seem to define us as a species. (For a discussion of chimpanzee religion, see Harrod (forthcoming).) That is to say, every society we know anything about, past or present, has something like a religion, or so the argument goes. Perceiving evolutionary utility behind this apparently universal phenomenon, Pascal Boyer (2002) proposes that we possess an intuitive sense of what might make a plausible religious belief (in the sense that we can imagine some religion, somewhere, believing in it), and which of his various hypothetical examples could not possibly function as such. Perhaps the solution is to say that while many aspects of "religion" are indeed universal, their fusion into a single category is artificial and culture-bound. Timothy Fitzgerald (2003) suggests that "[i]t may not be a coincidence that *anthropologists* who discuss religion are *less* likely to become submerged by conceptual problems that the category typically induces than are those who come from religious studies" (par. 10). Fitzgerald for his part sees the sacred/secular distinction as a Western projection, at least as applied to Japanese weddings.

Even if we resist the total conflation of the sacred with the profane, that "religion" tends to mirror the ordinary world seems clear enough. Concepts of supernatural beings generally reflect the lifestyles of the societies positing them. Hunting cultures conceive of spirits associated with animals and nature (such as the worldwide prehistoric figure of the Master of the Animals). Agricultural civilizations worship pantheons whose political structure, gender roles and division of labor are thought to resemble their own. Gods and goddesses of fertility, war and weather are common. In this light, we should expect to find various trends associated with globalization reflected in contemporary religious developments. For example, it may not be coincidence that interest in ESP has grown in tandem with improvements in communications technology. (One nineteenth-century American Spiritualist newspaper was entitled *The Spiritual Telegraph*.)

The history of the "great" religions is intimately bound up with globalization in its various phases. Several (Hinduism, Buddhism, Zoroastrianism, Christianity, arguably Judaism) coalesced in the context of centralizing states or empires, developed a distinct identity in contrast to local rivals, then spread beyond their parent region along the great trade routes. Islam initially gained strength on the periphery, along the trade routes between India, Ethiopia and Byzantium, and only later entered the centers of power. The history of European colonialism is intertwined with that of Christian mission, while capitalism owes much to the "Protestant work ethic" as posited by Weber. Of course, other religions have sent their missionaries and traders, as a glance at the demography of Southeast Asia will reveal. Examples of cross-fertilization are plentiful and extend to the most rarefied levels of scholastic philosophy (as in the interreligious disputations of ancient India and the medieval West) and spiritual practice (e.g., mutual influences among mantra recitation, *dhikr* and monologistic prayer).

A century ago Franz Cumont (1906) offered the following analogy for the situation of religion during the Hellenistic age:

Let us suppose that in modern Europe the faithful had deserted the Christian churches to worship Allah or Brahma, to follow the precepts of Confucius or Buddha, or to adopt the maxims of the Shinto; let us imagine a great confusion of all the races of the world in which Arabian mullahs, Chinese scholars, Japanese bonzes, Tibetan lamas and Hindu pundits would be preaching fatalism and predestination, ancestor-worship and devotion to a deified sovereign, pessimism and deliverance through annihilation—a confusion in which all those priests would erect temples of exotic architecture in our cities and celebrate their disparate rites therein. Such a dream, which the future may perhaps realize, would offer a pretty accurate picture of the religious chaos in which the ancient world was struggling before the reign of Constantine. (196)

His fellow Mithraism specialist David Ulansey (2000), noting that Cumont's wildest flight of fancy has more or less come true, wonders whether some new mystery may yet arise—perhaps by means of that new *oikomene*, the Internet—to ape the transformation of ancient Christianity into a trans-imperial symbolic system. One is reminded of science-fiction writer Philip K. Dick who, in his VALIS series as well as in his gnostic memoir *Exegesis*, considers the contemporary world as the archetypal recapitulation of ancient Rome. Lest this suggest a doomed repetition of history, Kathryn Babayan (2002) identifies a strain of Iranian *ghulat* movements that interpreted the cyclical time characteristic of Persian cosmology, in an "alchemical" sense "leading to metamorphosis, with the spirit enhanced each time it incarnates into new and purer forms" (xv).

Today, most religions boast some sort of international presence, whether as a consequence of historic expansion and migration, or in the form of diasporas. While it is still possible to find world maps color-coded to reflect the majority religion of each region, the limits of such a project are obvious in view of globalization. Arjun Appadurai (1996) instead proposes to map "(a) ethnoscapes, (b) mediascapes, (c) technoscapes, (d) finanscapes, and (e) ideoscapes" onto a Lacanian "social imaginary" (33). In such a fashion we can begin to make sense of something like the Foundation for the Preservation of the Mahayana Tradition (FPMT), an international network of Gelugpa dharma centers headquartered in Portland, Oregon, but founded by Tibetan and Sherpa monks in India and Nepal (one of whom has apparently reincarnated as a Spaniard), and whose funding comes disproportionately from ethnic Chinese communities in East/Southeast Asia.[3]

In his essay "Defining Religion: A Pluralistic Approach for the Global Age," Frank J. Lechner (2003) points out that

> "religion" can be source, component, or affected party. Religion has been a source of globalization by creating transnational or inter-state relations, by stimulating and endorsing the expansion of such relations, and by articulating a distinctive awareness of the world as a whole. Religion has been a component of globalization insofar as religions themselves have spread globally, built global institutions, and aspired to being global actors. Religion has been affected by globalization since worldwide social and cultural conditions have changed the conditions for its flourishing, relativized the identities of religious groups, and involved religion in addressing the problems of the world as such. (72)

For example, the Catholic Church has been a *source* of globalization thanks to its role in the development of international law. (The contributions of certain modern philosophers, such as Jacques Maritain or Pierre Teilhard de Chardin, might also be mentioned.) It has been a *component* of globalization in the sense that its institutions are found throughout the world. It plays the role of an *affected party*, for example, in the current pedophilia scandals, in which globalized communication has proved decisive in determining the public response. Lechner goes on to itemize various theories on the nature of globalization and the conceptions of religion that result from them for each of these three categories.

Religions have responded to globalization in various ways. The casual observer may think first of the world's various fundamentalisms,[4] some of them (but by no means all) associated with political violence. At the time of writing, American news sources are reporting on an anti-government conspiracy by the Hutaree militia, an armed Christian millenarian group based in Adrian, Michigan. Middle East scholar Juan Cole (2010) likens its theology to that of the Mahdi Army of Muqtada al-Sadr. Both groups have been mobilizing angry, unemployed young men to fight the Antichrist and his globalist minions (including religious minorities—American Muslims, Iraqi Christians—who are presumed to side with the enemy), with the ultimate aim of establishing a religious state. Writes Cole (2010): "The Hutaree fear the United Nations, as the Mahdi Army fears the US occupation. Both groups are victims of a neo-liberal world order that uses and discards working people, while protecting and cushioning the super-rich." The list of violent fundamentalisms might be extended indefinitely, to include other religious groups (e.g., ultra-Orthodox Israeli settlers, anti-Tamil Sinhalese Buddhist *sangha*, proponents of Hindutva or Khalistan) with varying degrees of power in their host societies. Some are "have-nots" acting out of frustration; some could fairly be described as "haves" seeking to preserve their good fortune; many simply amount to competing identity groups with incompatible aspirations. The familiar complaint that religion is being unfairly blamed for conflicts of a more worldly nature returns us to the question of what, if anything, is meant by the word "religion."

Other groups welcome globalization. According to the Baha'i religion, our era is witnessing the gradual emergence of a world civilization under a common government—a development Baha'is believe represents the will of God. "The earth is but one country," proclaimed their nineteenth-century Iranian founder, "and mankind its citizens" (Baha'u'llah 1976, 250). By now their ranks have expanded to include members from nearly every conceivable ethnic group, offering an example in microcosm of the global society whose appearance they foresee. It is useful to explore to what extent these expectations are *sui generis*, as Baha'i literature often claims. In some respects the project calls to mind Osama bin Laden's aspiration to reestablish an Islamic caliphate with authority over a swathe of Muslim countries, if not the whole world.

(For a discussion of the globalist credentials of al-Qaeda—an organization that might be otherwise expected to be "against" globalism—see the opening pages of Streger 2009.) We hasten to add that the Baha'i vision differs by being pacifistic, to some extent pluralistic, and uncertain as to whether the future world will fall under the control of the Universal House of Justice (their Supreme Soviet) or merely partake of a Baha'i ethos. Another, more welcome parallel might be with the Catholic understanding of the Kingdom of God, conceived as a gradually unfolding divine reality made manifest in the world through individual believers, the Church and, ultimately, Christ. Like the Baha'i social teachings, much Catholic theology prescribes correctives to current neo-liberal social trends. However, few Catholics would suppose the Millennium to be immanent, except as manifest in the Church's institutions (which are designed with practicality, not prophecy in mind).

Blavatskean Theosophy shares the Baha'i pretension that subsumes all religions under a common ideological superstructure. (All religions possess a core of truth, we are told, which the new revelation clarifies and updates.) For that matter, a number of New Religious Movements[5] (e.g., Caodaism, Yiguandao, Oomoto) offer similarly integrative theologies, though these often turn out to be primarily concerned with a specific culture (here the Vietnamese, Chinese and Japanese, respectively). Subud, a twentieth-century Javanese *kebatinan* (mystical) movement that has acquired an international following, conceives of its *latihan kejiwaan* (spiritual exercise) as the life-force behind all religions which, when properly cultivated, is capable of transforming the world. Finally, the Unification Church intends to establish the literal Kingdom of God on Earth, a one world theocratic government ruled by "Lord of the Second Advent" Sun Myung Moon and his wife. This too is a kind of globalism, though it differs from more typical neo-liberal or leftist interpretations. The Baha'is anticipate the selection of a universal language; the Moonies specify this will be Korean, while Oomoto supports Esperanto.

Most typical than either the resisters or enthusiasts are the numerous religious groups which view globalization as neither good nor bad in itself, but simply the way things are, and adjust themselves to whatever international considerations happen to be present. For example, a number of conservative US Episcopal churches, complaining of liberalism on the part of their national body, have sought alternative episcopal oversight from elsewhere in the Anglican Communion (often Africa or South America), while hoping to retain ties with the Archbishop of Canterbury. Another example would be the movement associated with Turkish Muslim theologian M. Fethullah Gülen, whose followers manage an international network of schools and businesses without, however, ever really transcending their Turkish identity. Imitation and convergent evolution are widespread, as illustrated by the "Protestant

Buddhism" of Anagarika Dharmapala (after Gananath Obeyesekere) or the "Islamic Calvinism" of the Gülen movement (after a 2005 ESI report).

In modern-day religious belief, identity and participation are increasingly matters of choice rather than duties prescribed by society. We may "roll our own" blends, as New Age spiritual seekers and neo-pagan revivalists are known to do; or if we patronize existing service-providers, the fact that they must compete in a religious economy affects the very nature of the church–parishioner relationship. (An apocryphal tale has it that a church-shopping Generation X couple, on being told why a particular church was the One True Church, responded with "That's great, but do you have a basketball league?") Rodney Stark and William Sims Bainbridge (1985, 1987) are two major theorists who explore how religious movements evolve in this milieu. They distinguish, for example, between audience cults (such as readers of a popular book on UFOs), client cults (such as the customers of a fortune teller) and full-blown cult movements (Stark and Bainbridge 1985, 169), all of which flourish or perish according to whether their promised rewards ("compensators") are thought sufficiently attractive and credible. A certain amount of cynicism can be detected on the part of religion providers and customers alike. Increasing levels of attention and allegiance go to para-church groups or Internet communities, even as the category of "Spiritual but Not Religious" (SBNR) gains prominence.[6] All of this reminds us of the difficulties involved in defining religion.

On that note, we cannot resist mentioning the plethora of ostensibly religious groups (often Internet-based) that, on inspection, turn out to be satirical spoofs (see Cusack 2010): the Discordian Society, the Church of the SubGenius, Campus Crusade for Cthulhu, Elvis worship, Landover Baptist Church, Join Me (Danny Wallace), the Jedi census campaign … the list is endless. And no debate on God's existence would be complete nowadays without reference to the Flying Spaghetti Monster or the Invisible Pink Unicorn. As Freud says, many a truth is spoken in jest.

One of the most interesting developments has been the rise of inter-religious dialogue, held through a variety of institutes, symposia and fairs.[7] Of these, the most notable is the Parliament of the World's Religions, founded in 1993 as a centenary revival of the 1893 World Parliament of Religions in Chicago (the prototype of all these events). Traditional themes include harmony, tolerance and pluralism. Diana L. Eck, director of the Pluralism Project at Harvard University, explains that

> pluralism is not diversity alone, but *the energetic engagement with diversity*. Diversity can and has meant the creation of religious ghettoes with little traffic between or among them. Today, religious diversity is a given, but pluralism is not a given; it is an achievement. Mere diversity without real

encounter and relationship will yield increasing tensions in our societies. (Eck 2008, par. 2)

Russell T. McCutcheon (2003) takes Eck to task for inconsistency, since she prescribes openness to people and groups who are committed to different values, yet rails against "exclusivists, extremists, and tribalists" who are not so tolerant as she is (153–9, especially 158). Understandably, diversity and pluralism can also be perceived as threats leading to the disastrous loss of identity. John Hick (1980) reports that inter-religious friendships led him to doubt the exclusive truth of Christianity—a rather old-school conflict that underscores the potential of globalization to erode beliefs as well as borders (17).

An oft-heard premise of interfaith work is that one ought to show respect and friendliness towards other religions, while remaining faithful to one's own. This sort of pluralism may not be sustainable for more than a generation or so. Tsem Tulku Rinpoche (2010) describes the relationship between his Uncle Naran, a Mongolian Buddhist, and Aunt Honey, a Russian Catholic, who were the very model of pluralistic tolerance. Each respected the other's religion and maintained separate bedside altars, but their two daughters came to identify with both religions simultaneously. At the clergy level, several priests of the US Episcopal Church have gotten into trouble for appearing to follow more than one religion at the same time. William Melnyk was defrocked for moonlighting as a druid priest; Ann Holmes Redding, for converting to Islam (she felt there to be no contradiction between the two faiths); and Kevin Thew Forrester failed to win election as bishop largely because of controversy over his practice of Zen meditation (which he insisted was not a religion). Of course these examples assume a norm of exclusivity, in which syncretism or multiple identification must be concealed.

In the long run, it seems inevitable that religious cultures will converge—we simply cannot live alongside one another without becoming part of one another's lives. How this can be reconciled with group claims of uniqueness (or superiority) is difficult to predict. While the human tendency to organize ourselves into competing identity groups appears universal, religion does not necessarily need to take part in this (as Chinese culture demonstrates). It is tempting to imagine our descendants regarding the scriptures of all religions as parts of a single tradition, as we do with the disparate books of the Bible or the classics of philosophy. (Consider, for example, the *Orange Catholic Bible* from Frank Herbert's *Dune* books, or the voluminous commentaries of Osho.) In that spirit, we note that religiously motivated non-violence has a complex intellectual history, involving Jainism, Quakerism, the Doukhobors, Thoreau, Tolstoy, Gandhi, Martin Luther King and the (fourteenth) Dalai Lama. More likely, religion will continue to reflect the competitive and opportunistic nature of our species, though this need not result in destructive confrontations. We may at least hope for rules of conduct to be enforced and for occasional manifestations of goodwill (however motivated), though still in a wider context of religious exclusivity and competition.

About this Book

The intersection of religion and globalization has been discussed in a number of works, beginning (appropriately enough) with Peter F. Beyer's *Religion and globalization* (1994). While this is a monograph, books with multiple contributors comprise the majority. By now many of these have become dated—none more abruptly than Hopkins et al. (2001), published the day after the 9/11 attacks—though the historical approach of Esposito, Fasching and Lewis (2007) effectively insulates it from obsolescence. Most such collections are limited in scope, perhaps inevitably so. However, the 25 articles in Beyer and Leaman (2007) display enormous depth and diversity of coverage, while Csordas (2009) is noteworthy for its focus on less-studied regions (for example, there is a chapter on Papua New Guinea and two on the Yoruba). Linquist and Handelman (2011), which is otherwise standard in approach, includes such original themes as Buddhism and shamanism in Siberia, and the interplay between religion and politics in East Timor and Spain. In general, editors face a choice between attempting systematic coverage (which often means hewing to a rather predictable menu of topics, whether in terms of major world religions or perennial hotspots), or adopting a more random mix, in line with the interests and expertise of prospective contributors. In view of the vastness and complexity of the topic, there is surely room for any number of additional studies, representing various approaches.

The chapters in this volume emerged from a March 2010 conference of the Asia Association for Global Studies (AAGS), held at National Chung Cheng University in Jiayi, Taiwan, entitled *(En)countering Globalizations: Religion in the Contemporary World*. It is therefore appropriate that Taiwan is well-represented in the present compilation, which includes chapters on Chinese Buddhism, folk Daoism and aboriginal religion. (Other articles discuss Hinduism, Christianity, Islam and miscellaneous New Religious Movements.) As for the rest of Asia, the reader will also find topics relating to India, Japan and Bahrain. But "Asia" in the name of the Association only indicates our location, and is not meant as a topical restriction. Accordingly, several papers take a wider, perhaps more "global" view.

Adam Smith, the founder of modern economics and the subject of the first chapter, was by profession a "moral philosopher"—essentially, a theologian. Christian Etzrodt further identifies him as a "Neo-Calvinist in the Presbyterian tradition," and discerns a religious motivation behind his formulation of classical economics theory in *The Wealth of Nations* (1776). For example, Smith described free trade as beneficial, not because he understood the law of comparative advantage, but because competitive markets would encourage such well-known Calvinist values as hard work and "asceticism" (i.e., savings and investment), even among non-Calvinists. Etzrodt sees the resulting periods of British, American and globalist domination as phases of an ongoing process of "Calvinization" (analogous with americanization or westernization), whose religious character explains much of the resistance globalization has encountered from rival value-systems (whether Lutheran or Salafi *jihadi*). Along the way, Etzrodt ventures his own theory of globalization which—addressing an old controversy—acknowledges the advance of technology to be linear, but proposes another category of "idealistic" causes (such as Calvinism) more cyclical in nature.

A far more radical critique is raised by the American ecological writer Daniel Quinn, who argues civilization as we know it to be unsustainable due to population pressures. His writings, principally *Ishmael* (Quinn 1992), are of interest to the New Age and anarcho-primitivist movements. Bei Dawei considers the religious dimensions of Quinn's worldview. Briefly, Quinn blames a lifestyle/cultural complex associated with the so-called "Agricultural Revolution" for a vicious cycle in which food surpluses cause population growth among agriculturalists, and hence further food surpluses, in a process which has already resulted in mass species extinction as well as the displacement and destruction of countless "other cultures." Since this cannot continue indefinitely, we face a choice between total civilizational collapse and the development of stable, sustainable lifestyles. A former Trappist postulant, Quinn now names "animism" (after E. B. Tylor, *Primitive Culture* (1871)) as his religion, and criticizes the world's better-known faiths for mirroring and perpetuating the expansionist, absolutist beliefs of their host societies. While he does not discuss "globalization" by name, the global scope of the problem is obvious, with the result that a certain global consciousness becomes necessary if we are to leverage our doom into a mere decline.

Although the antiquity of *yajña*, or Vedic sacrifice, rivals that of civilization itself, this family of Hindu rituals has evolved more than is commonly recognized, and now finds itself subject to the forces of globalization. Silke Bechler discusses the ways in which the practice of *yajña* has been transformed—especially in the Indian diaspora, where it often becomes a "highly stage-managed public spectacle or even a festival" complete with corporate sponsorship, media attention, charitable projects and cultural shows. Important changes include the loss of regional and sub-ethnic variations in ritual performance; an emphasis on the celebration of Indian culture and identity; and widened participation to allow, for example, ordinary worshippers to make offerings into the fire (an act once conducted strictly by priests), or even participation by Westerners. Finally, technological advances have led to new ritual possibilities, such as conducting *homa* (offerings of ghee into the household fire) through the Internet, either virtually or by proxy.

Religion is often perceived as a conservative force, especially in relation to gender roles. Whether feminine imagery of the divine encourages greater esteem for ordinary women is a matter of some dispute. Using a comparative approach, Evangelos Voulgarakis finds that neither the Greek Orthodox exaltation of the Virgin Mary, nor the Greek neo-pagan appropriation of Athena, nor the Buddhist veneration of the Bodhisattva Guanyin reflects a particularly feminist orientation. Rather, these patriarchal institutions resort to feminist rhetoric in order to adapt to the demands of a globalized audience, conceding few substantive reforms. The Orthodox hierarchy—traditionally involved in state affairs and generally characterized by nationalism and a strong mistrust of Western influences—recoils from ordaining women, often citing feminist-sounding concerns. The Greek neo-pagans are united chiefly by their shared opposition to monotheism and the Greek Orthodox Church, and strict, absolutist criteria as to who ought to be regarded as a "real Greek"; they are led exclusively by men, even as they celebrate the supposedly egalitarian practices of the ancients. Guanyin (who in Asian contexts is routinely invoked in support of traditional, male-oriented family values) is depicted in the West as a symbol of such characteristic Western concerns as individualism and self-assertion. More importantly, these groups' treatment of feminine symbols reflects their true attitudes toward religious pluralism which, despite pluralist etiquette, they perceive as the imposition of an inescapable globalization. Voulgarakis's analysis might easily be extended to other holy females such as Muhammad's daughter Fatima in the Shia tradition (see Corbin 1977), Tahirih for the Baha'is or the Tibetan tutelary deity Dorje Phagmo and her associated *tulku* lineage (Diemberger 2007).

Girardo Rodriguez Plasencia describes the spiritual atmosphere of Japan's Mt. Ikoma (642 m), near the city of Osaka. Mt. Ikoma is home to the Ishikiri healing shrine (Shinto), Shigisan and Hōzanji temples (Shingon Buddhist), various sites associated with legendary ascetics Kūkai and En-no-Gyōja (respectively, the founders of Shingon and the Shugenodō tradition of mountain worship), the largest concentration of Korean temples in Japan (eclectic, but including Korean shamanism) and, most recently, an assortment of health spas and spiritual centers such as the Kundalini Yoga Center (Sikh, associated with Yogi Bhajan and the 3HO). Rodriguez situates these latter activities within the global interest in what Shimazono Susumu calls "new spirituality movements and cultures" (NSMC, *shinreisei undō bunka*). This encompasses—wholly or partly—several overlapping subcategories: the New Age Movement, a primarily

Western phenomenon that has also entered Japan to some extent; an analogous Japanese phenomenon referred to as the "spiritual world" (*seishinsekai*) or more recently, as "spirituality" (*supirichuariti*, an English loanword); and some but not all New Religious Movements, including the Japanese new religions (*shinshūkyō*). In contrast with the situation in the West, where the New Age Movement exists in tension with traditional Judeo-Christian religiosity, NSMC activities enjoy more interaction with traditional Japanese religions, leading Inoue Nobutaka to perceive a "neo-syncretism" between them. The result on Mt. Ikoma is a peculiarly Japanese yet to some degree internationalized blend of activities, from waterfall austerities to fasting *dojos*, aimed at "the unity of mind, body, and spirit" and "the sacralization of nature and the self."

Magdalena Karolak and Nikodem Karolak explore the parallels between religious populism, including support for fundamentalist religious parties, in Poland and Bahrain. In both countries, this religious phenomenon has appeared in tandem with changing socio-economic conditions and is associated with the rhetoric of moral revolution aimed at subordinating the state system to religion. Perennial emphases include traditional gender roles, xenophobia and opposition to vice (as defined by local religious mores). Where Polish religious parties appeal to "Catholic solidarity" and Polish nationalism against various perceived enemies, their Bahraini counterparts speak of Islamic values in much the same elevated way (notwithstanding the political divide between that country's majority Shia community and ruling Sunni elite). Voter support for such parties has recently dropped in Poland as well as Bahrain as a result of scandal, with its inevitable suggestion of hypocrisy, and a perceived weakness on economic issues. The exception is al-Wefaq, which benefits from its status as the voice of Bahrain's Shia opposition. As Europe struggles with economic integration, and the Arab world with protest movements aimed at democratic reforms, one wonders (with an eye to the relative success of Turkey's AK Party) how the rhetoric of moral reform can combine with the need for compromise.

Liao Pei-Ru discusses Taiwan's Tzu Chi (*Ciji*: "Compassion Relief") Foundation, a Buddhist organization founded by the celebrated nun Zhengyan (also spelled "Cheng Yen"), now active in numerous countries. One of several large Buddhist organizations in Taiwan, and the island's largest charity, Tzu Chi has been a subject of several recent monographs (e.g., DeVido 2010; Huang 2009; Jones 1999; Madsen 2007). Liao analyzes a prime-time serial drama produced by the organization's TV channel, Da Ai, for its themes. That drama, *Xigu Ama* (literally "Silicon Valley Grandma," but translated as *Love from the Valley*), is based on the eventful life of Hsiu-Chin Lin-Wang (1917–2003) (also written as "Lin Wang Xiuqin") who would ultimately found a chapter of Tzu Chi in San Jose, California. The drama is noteworthy not only for its insights into the institutional culture of Tzu Chi, but also for its presentation of Taiwan history, local religion and women's roles. In the wider context of religious television, Liao examines how the Da Ai network revolutionizes yet strengthens the transmission of an otherwise traditionally Confucian outlook and identity to a particular segment of Taiwan's population. Her focus is on identity and social engagement as mobilized by the communications media of an international organization that is simultaneously local, as well as authoritarian and culturally exclusive. The issue of to what degree the result should be regarded as "feminist" is a complex one, and calls to mind the wider controversy between apologists for a feminist reading of Buddhism (Gross 1993; Klein 1996; Kwok 2000; Paul 1985) and doubters of same (Cabezon 1991; Collet 2006; Faure 2003).

In 2009, two international sporting events held in Taiwan—the World Games in Kaohsiung and the twenty-first Deaflympics in Taipei—staged opening and closing ceremonies which burlesqued the island's folk religion. Imitating traditional Daoist temple processions, in which giant Chinese gods (actually human-occupied puppets) stride through the streets on inspection, the shows featured playful, manga-fied versions of the god-puppets disco-dancing and riding motor-scooters. Thzeng Chi Hsiung and Tsai Chin Chia discuss the origins, context and meaning of these *Dianyin Santaizi* troupes (from the name of the god Santaizi, or "Third Prince," plus *dianyin*, or "electronic music," i.e., techno dance music). The effect is regarded not as sacrilege, but as a natural extension of Santaizi's character as a *deus ludens*. Still, the god is transported from the realm of the sacred to that of the secular, where it becomes a symbol of the *Taike* ("Taiwan hick") style. A related phenomenon is the use of comicized god-images in advertising, or as toy figurines. Note that Taiwan society is pervaded by the images of globalized "cartoon" (actually multimedia) characters like Doraemon and Hello Kitty, which future archeologists may assume to be our gods.

Many legal regimes expect claimants to indigenous or aboriginal status to maintain distinctive cultural practices (although this requirement is not usually applied to other forms of ethnicity). Tiaukhai Iunn analyzes the efforts of Taiwan's Siraya to win government recognition[8] through such manifestations of ethnic consciousness as language revival, and the reconstruction of their traditional religious ritual in honor of the (originally monotheistic, and possibly female) deity Alid. Of several extant versions of the Alid ritual, Iunn accepts the version of Tham-khian to be the most authentic, rejecting the Kabuasua form (the current favorite) as too sinicized. Sinicization affects not only the style of worship, but also theology, since hybrid forms tend not to accept Alid as the only god, or even as the highest god. In this light, perhaps the Siraya Presbyterians—who refer to the Christian God as Alid—are more faithful to the traditions of their ancestors. This tension between Austronesian, Chinese and Christian cultural elements marks what would otherwise be a controversy among putative Taiwanese aborigines as an issue in globalization. Analogous debates can be heard among indigenous peoples around the world. Incidentally, the seventeenth-century encounter of the Siraya with the Dutch VOC was a major turning point in the history of Taiwan, whose very name is derived from a Siraya toponym.

The articles in this collection are thus highly innovative and interdisciplinary, as befits the combination of globalization (traditionally the domain of economists, sociologists and political scientists) with religious studies (a field incorporating the methodologies of history, anthropology and philological/textual criticism). Most approach religion from the perspective of lived experience, examining how religions spread across borders and emerge in new contexts in hybrid form, how various religious elements are transformed and diffused by globalization and how religion satisfies the psychological and social needs of believers and practitioners. A number of ancillary issues are explored in detail, among them the interrelationships between worldview, social behavior and group identity; and whether it makes sense to speak of "old" and "new" religious traditions, as opposed to a constantly evolving religious landscape in which continuity blends with innovation. Such queries are no mere academic exercises, but practical necessities in view of the inescapability of social change. Every society eventually faces the transience of its own axioms before the inescapable interplay of identity and diversity, competition and cooperation, exclusivity and accommodation. Whatever one makes of the symbols, rituals, sacred places, cultural artifacts, political and economic systems, and philosophies presented in this volume, they at least represent a full range of religious phenomena in a world poised between the centrifugal and centripetal forces of globalization.

Notes and References

1 For a short, readable introduction to globalization, see Monierre (2009).
2 For further discussion of such borderline cases, see various issues of the *Journal of the Centre for the Study of Implicit Religion and Contemporary Spirituality* (CSIRCS) (http://www.implicitreligion.org/journal.htm). McCutcheon (2003) explores the reasons why the concept of what he calls "*sui generis* religion" has retained its power in academic circles.
3 For information on the FPMT, erstwhile participant Bei Dawei directs readers to its article on the English-language Wikipedia, which he periodically edits, and which contains an extensive bibliography.
4 Some writers (notably Esposito 1992) warn against using the term "fundamentalism" to describe such diverse movements. Others (notably Marty and Appleby 1991) perceive significant commonalities.
5 For a global overview of New Religious Movements, see Clarke (2006). The publications of CESNUR (Massimo Introvigne), the Institute for the Study of American Religion (J. Gordon Melton) and INFORM (Eileen Vartan Barker) are inescapable, as are the

journals *Nova Religio* (since 1997) and the *International Journal for the Study of New Religions* (since 2010). One might also name the International Cultic Studies Association and its journal, *Cultic Studies Review* (since 2002).

6 The origins of the phrase are murky but predate Robert Fuller's eponymous book (2001). The specific wording (and its acronym) seems to have standardized gradually over the past decade.

7 For an overview of inter-religious dialogue organizations, see Braybrooke (1980), Judge (1993, 1994), and various issues of the (online) *Journal of Inter-Religious Dialogue* (http://irdialogue.org).

8 In 2010, Siraya activists joined other plains aborigines in petitioning UN Special Rapporteur James Anaya to investigate the refusal of Taiwan's government to recognize their tribes (Loa 2010).

Abanes, R. 1996. *Rebellion, Racism and Religion: American Militias*. Westmont: InterVarsity Press.

Abu-Lughod, J. 1991. *Before European Hegemony: The World-system AD 1250–1350*. Oxford: Oxford University Press.

Abu-Lughod, J. 1997. "Going Beyond Global Babble." In *Culture, Globalization and the World System. Contemporary Conditions for the Representation of Identity*. Ed. by Anthony D. King. Minneapolis: University of Minnesota Press, 131–8.

Appadurai, A. 1996. "Disjuncture and Difference in the Global Cultural Economy." In A. Appadurai. *Modernity at Large: Cultural Dimensions of Globalization*. Minneapolis: University of Minnesota Press, 27–42. Online: http://www.intcul.tohoku.ac.jp/~holden/MediatedSociety/Readings/2003_04/Appadurai.html (accessed January 12, 2010).

Babayan, K. 2002. *Mystics, Monarchs, and Messiahs: Cultural Landscapes of Early Modern Iran*. Cambridge, MA: Harvard University Press.

Baha'u'llah. 1976. *Gleanings from the Writings of Baha'u'llah*. Wilmette: Baha'i Publishing Trust. Online: http://reference.bahai.org/en/t/b/GWB/gwb-117.html (accessed February 3, 2010).

Banchoff, T., ed. 2008. *Religious Pluralism, Globalization, and World Politics*. Oxford: Oxford University Press.

Barber, B. 1992. "Jihad vs. McWorld." *Atlantic Monthly*. March. Online: http://www.theatlantic.com/magazine/archive/1992/03/jihad-vs-mcworld/3882/ (accessed February 13, 2010).

Beyer, P. F. 1994. *Religion and Globalization*. Thousand Oaks: Sage.

Beyer, P. F. and L. G. Beaman, eds. 2007. *Religion, Globalization, and Culture*. Leiden: E. J. Brill.

Boyer, P. 2002. *Religion Explained: The Evolutionary Origins of Religious Thought*. New York: Basic Books.

Braybrooke, M. 1980. *Interfaith Organizations, 1893–1979: An Historical Directory*. New York: Edward Mellon Press.

Cabezon, J. I., ed. 1991. *Buddhism, Sexuality, and Gender*. Albany: State University of New York Press.

Clarke, P. 2006. *New Religions in Global Perspective: A Study of Religious Change in the Modern World*. London: Routledge.

Cole, J. R. I. 2010. "Alleged Christian Terrorists Said to Target Moderate American Muslims." *Informed Comment*. March 3. Online: http://www.juancole.com/2010/03/alleged-christian-terrorists-said-to.html (accessed March 22, 2010).

Collet, A. 2006. "Buddhism and Gender: Reframing and Refocusing the Debate." *Journal of Feminist Studies in Religion* 22, no. 2 (January): 55–84.

Corbin, H. 1977. *Spiritual Body and Celestial Earth: From Mazdean Iran to Shi'ite Iran*. Princeton: Princeton University Press.

Csordas, T., ed. 2009. *Transnational Transcendence: Essays on Religion and Globalization*. Berkeley: University of California Press.

Cumont, F. 1906. *The Oriental Religions in Roman Paganism*. Chicago: Open Court Publications. Online: http://www.gutenberg.org/ebooks/22213 (accessed August 3, 2012).

Cusack, C. M. 2010. *Invented Religions: Imagination, Fiction, and Faith*. Farnham: Ashgate.

DeVido, E. A. 2010. *Taiwan's Buddhist Nuns*. Albany: State University of New York Press.

Diamond, J. M. 1997. *Guns, Germs, and Steel: The Fates of Human Societies*. New York: W. W. Norton and Co.

Diemberger, H. 2007. *When a Woman Becomes a Religious Dynasty: The Samding Dorje Phagmo of Tibet*. New York: Columbia University Press.

Eck, D. L. 2008. "What Is Pluralism?" *Pluralism Project*. Online: http://www.pluralism.org/pluralism/what_is_pluralism.php (accessed January 26, 2010).

Esposito, J. L. 1992. *The Islamic Threat: Myth or Reality?* Oxford: Oxford University Press.

Esposito, J. L., D. J. Fasching and T. Lewis, eds. 2007. *Religion and Globalization: World Religions in Historical Perspective*. Oxford: Oxford University Press.

ESI Report. 2005. "Islamic Calvinists: Change and Conservatism in Central Anatolia." Online: http://www.esiweb.org/index.php?lang=enandid=224 (accessed February 23, 2010).

Faure, B. 2003. *The Power of Denial: Buddhism, Purity, and Gender*. Princeton: Princeton University Press.

Fitzgerald, T. 2003. "'Religion' and 'the Secular' in Japan: Problems in History, Social Anthropology, and the Study of Religion." *Electronic Journal of Contemporary Japanese Studies*. Online: http://www.japanesestudies.org.uk/discussionpapers/Fitzgerald.html (accessed February 3, 2010).

Frank, A. G. 1998. *ReORIENT: Global Economy in the Asian age*. Berkeley: University of California Press.

Frank, A. G. and B. K. Gills, eds. 1993. *The World System: Five Hundred Years or Five Thousand?* London: Routledge.

———. 1991. *5000 Years of World System Theory: The Cumulation of Accumulation*. Boulder: Westview Press.

Friedman, T. L. 2005. *The World is Flat: A Brief History of the Twenty-First Century*. New York: Farrar, Straus and Giroux.

———. 1999. *The Lexus and the Olive Tree: Understanding Globalization*. New York: Farrar, Straus and Giroux.

Fuller, R. C. 2001. *Spiritual but not Religious: Understanding Unchurched America*. Oxford: Oxford University Press.

Graeber, D. R. 2004. *Fragments of an Anarchist Anthropology*. Chicago: Prickly Paradigm Press. Online: http://www.prickly-paradigm.com/paradigm14.pdf (accessed January 3, 2010).

Gross, R. M. 1993. *Buddhism after Patriarchy: A Feminist History, Analysis, and Reconstruction of Buddhism*. Albany: State University of New York Press.

Harrod, J. (Forthcoming). "The case for chimpanzee religion." *Journal for the Study of Religion, Nature, and Culture* vol. and no. TBA. Online: http://www.originsnet.org/publications.html (accessed January 3, 2010).

_____. 2006. "Periods of Globalization Over 'the Southern Route' in Human Evolution (Africa, Southwest Asia, South Asia, Southeast Asia and Sahul and the Far East): A Meta-review of Archaeology and Evidence for Symbolic Behavior." *Mother Tongue: Journal of the Association for the Study of Language in Prehistory* 11: 23–84. Online: http://www.originsnet.org/southernrt.pdf (accessed February 6, 2010).

Held, D., A. McGrew, D. Goldblatt and J. Perraton. 1999. *Global Transformations: Politics, Economics, and Culture*. Palo Alto: Stanford University Press.

Heller, S. 1995. "Home Grown Extremism." *The Chronicle of Higher Education*. May 12. A10–A11, A18.

Hick, J. 1980. *God Has Many Names*. Philadelphia: Westminster Press.

Hirst, P. and G. Thompson. 1996. *Globalism in Question: The International Economy of the Politics of Governance*. Cambridge: Polity Press.

Hopkins, D. N. et al., eds. 2001. *Religions/Globalizations: Theories and Cases*. Durham, NC: Duke University Press.

Huang, C. J. 2009. *Charisma and Compassion: Cheng Yen and the Buddhist Tzu Chi Movement*. Cambridge, MA: Harvard University Press.

Icke, D. V. 2007. *The David Icke Guide to the Global Conspiracy*. Isle of Wight: David Icke Books.

Jones, C. B. 1999. *Buddhism in Taiwan: Religion and the State, 1660–1990*. Manoa: University of Hawai'i Press.

Judge, A. 1994. "Learnings for the Future of Inter-faith Dialogue, Part II, Insights Evoked by Intractable International Differences." *Transnational Associations* 1 (1994): 15–22. Online: http://www.laetusinpraesens.org/docs/diaparl2.php (access February 17, 2011).

_____. 1993. "Learnings for the Future of Inter-faith Dialogue, Part I, Questions Arising from the Parliament of the World's Religions (Chicago)." *Transnational Associations* 6 (1993): 345–54. Online: http://www.laetusinpraesens.org/docs/diaparl.php (access February 17, 2011).

Juergensmeyer, M. 2001. "The Global Rise of Religious Nationalism." In *Religions/ Globalizations: Theories and Cases*. Ed. by D. N. Hopkins, L. A. Lorentzen, E. Mendieta and D. Batstone. Durham, NC: Duke University Press, 66–83.

Kaczynski, T. J. 1995. "Industrial Society and Its Future (a.k.a. The Unabomber Manifesto)." Published simultaneously in *New York Times* and *Washington Post*. September 19.

Klein, A. C. 1996. *Meeting the Great Bliss Queen: Buddhists, Feminists, and the Art of the Self*. Boston: Beacon Press.

Kwok Pui Lan. 2000. *Introducing Asian Feminist Theology*. Cleveland: Pilgrim Press.

Linquist, G. and D. Handelman, eds. 2001. *Religion, Politics, and Globalization: Anthropological Approaches*. Oxford: Berghahn Books.

Loa Iok-sin. 2010. "Pingpu Activists Ask UN Assistance in Aboriginal Claim." *Taipei Times* 1. May 6. Online: http://www.taipeitimes.com/News/front/archives/2010/05/06/2003472328 (accessed February 17, 2011).

Madsen, R. 2007. *Democracy's Dharma: Religious Renaissance and Political Development in Taiwan*. Berkeley: University of California Press.

Marty, M. E. and R. S. Appleby, eds. 1991. *Fundamentalisms Observed*. Chicago: Chicago University Press.

Matejcic, S. 2005. Untitled interview with Noam Chomsky. *Galerija Rigo*. Online: http://www.galerija-rigo.hr/?w=izlozbeandg=4andid=102andsl=147 (accessed February 6, 2010).

McCutcheon, R. T. 2003. *Manufacturing Religion: The Discourse on Sui Generis Religion and the Politics of Nostalgia*. Oxford: Oxford University Press.

McCutcheon, R. T. 2003. "The category 'religion' and the politics of tolerance." In *Defining Religion: Investigating the Boundaries between the Sacred and the Secular.* Ed by A. L. Greil and D. Bromley. Amsterdam: Elsevier.

McNeill, W. H. 1963. *The Rise of the West: A History of the Human Community.* Chicago: University of Chicago Press.

Monierre, C. 2009. "Global Society, Global Sociology." Online: http://globalsociology. pbworks.com/Global-Society%2C-Global-Sociology (accessed February 3, 2010).

Munck, R. 2000. "Labour in the Global: Challenges and Prospects." In *Global Social Movements.* Ed. by R. Cohen and S. M. Rai. London: Athalone Press, 83–100.

Nobutaka, I. 2000. *Contemporary Japanese Religion.* Tokyo: Foreign Press.

Nye, J. S. 2002. "Globalization versus Globalism." *The Globalist.* April 15. Online: http:// www.theglobalist.com/StoryId.aspx?StoryId=2392 (accessed February 9, 2011)

Paul, D. Y. 1985. *Women in Buddhism: Images of the Feminine in the Mahayana Tradition.* Berkeley: University of California Press.

Quinn, D. 1992. *Ishmael: An Adventure of the Mind and Spirit.* New York: Bantam.

Rosenberg, J. 2002. *The Follies of Globalization.* London: Verso.

Scholte, J. A. 2005. *Globalization: A Critical Introduction.* New York: Palgrave Macmillan.

Smith, J. Z. 1982. *Imagining Religion: From Babylon to Jonestown.* Chicago: University of Chicago Press.

Smith, W. C. 1962. *The Meaning and End of Religion.* Philadelphia: Fortress Press.

Soros, G. 2002. *George Soros on Globalization.* New York: Public Affairs.

Stark, R. and W. S. Bainbridge. 1987. *A Theory of Religion.* New York: Lang.

_____. 1985. *The Future of Religion.* Berkeley: University of California Press.

Stearns, N., M. B. Adas, S. B. Schwartz and M. J. Gilbert, eds. 2004. *World Civilizations: The Global Experience.* 4th edn. Harlow: Pearson Longman.

Stiglitz, J. E. 2002. *Globalization and Its Discontents.* New York: W. W. Norton.

Streger, M. B. 2009. *Globalization: A Very Short Introduction.* Oxford: Oxford University Press.

Tsem Tulku Rinpoche 2010. "Ingredients for a Successful Relationship. (Dharma Talk Given at a Wedding in Kuala Lumpur.)" Online: http://blog.tsemtulku.com/tsem-tulku-rinpoche/2010/04/ingredients-for-a-successful-relationship-rinpoche-on-how-to-stay-married.html (accessed February 7, 2010).

Ulansey, D. 2000. "Cultural transition and spiritual transformation: From Alexander the Great to cyberspace." In *The Vision Thing: Myth, Politics, and Psyche in the World.* Ed. by T. Singer. London: Routledge, 213–31. Online: http://www.well.com/~davidu/cultural.html (accessed February 4, 2010).

Veseth, M. 2006. *Globaloney.* Lanham: Rowman and Littlefield.

Wallerstein, I. M. 1989. *The Modern World System, Vol. III, The Second Great Expansion of the Capitalist World-Economy, 1730–1840s.* San Diego: Academic Press.

_____. 1980. *The Modern World System, Vol. II, Mercantilism and the Consolidation of the European World-Economy, 1600–1750.* San Diego: Academic Press.

_____. 1974. *The Modern World System, Vol. I, Capitalist Agriculture and the Origins of the European World-Economy in the Sixteenth Century.* San Diego: Academic Press.

Weatherford, J. 2004. *Genghis Khan and the Making of the Modern World.* New York: Three Rivers Press.

Zerzan, J. 1994. *Future Primitive and Other Essays.* New York: Autonomedia.

Part One

RELIGION IN GLOBAL AND TRANSCULTURAL PERSPECTIVE

Chapter 2

ADAM SMITH AND THE NEO-CALVINIST FOUNDATIONS OF GLOBALIZATION

Christian Etzrodt
Akita International University, Japan

Introduction

At the beginning of the twenty-first century a shift occurred from the political conflicts that characterized the Cold War period to the religious conflicts of the post-9/11 era. These latter religious confrontations appeared at a time when many people expected the world to become more and more integrated. In the 1990s, the process of globalization seemed to be unstoppable, but the situation changed in 2001 with the destruction of the World Trade Center. The sudden radicalization of the Islamic world was quickly interpreted as a religiously motivated rejection of the process of globalization. However, it could be argued that such an interpretation obscures the fact that globalization is itself the result of a religious doctrine. This chapter analyzes the impact of religion itself on the process of globalization, especially the connection between the liberalization of world markets and the universalization of Western values. It begins with a definition of the term "globalization," turns to a discussion of the causes of globalization and then offers a short description of the historical development of globalization. Finally, the origin of the idea of free trade is linked to the work of Adam Smith and his neo-Calvinist religious beliefs. From here it is argued that free trade, rather than representing a concept of secular origins, was from the beginning a tool to motivate all non-believers and sinners in the world to follow God's universal rules.[1]

Defining "Globalization"

As researchers do not agree on the meaning of "globalization," their analyses lead to very different conclusions depending on the definition they have chosen.

It is therefore necessary to state how the word "globalization" is used in this chapter. Jan Arte Scholte's (2005) summary of the most often used definitions of the term offers a good starting point for this discussion (16–17). Scholte identifies five notions of the concept. The first he calls *internationalization*, which is based on the idea of increasing cross-border activities, especially in the sense of "growing flows of trade and capital investment between countries" (Hirst and Thompson 1996, 48). Closely related to this is the second interpretation of globalization as the *liberalization* of world markets. Liberalization here means the lifting of national governments' restrictions on movements of goods and capital "in order to create an 'open', 'borderless' world economy" (Scholte 2005, 16; cf. Sander 1996, 27). The third definition of globalization is associated with *universalization*, a homogenization of cultural values worldwide that leads to "a planetary synthesis of cultures" (Reiser and Davies 1944). Closely related to this conception is the fourth definition of globalization as *westernization* or *americanization* (Taylor 2000). This perspective emphasizes the export of Western or American values (individualism) and institutions (capitalism and democracy) to the rest of the world. Furthermore this process can be also described negatively as imperialism in the sense of McDonaldization (Barber 1996; Gowan 1999; Ritzer 1993; cf. Schiller 1991). The fifth approach, linking globalization with respatialization, is unimportant in this paper and will not be discussed.[2]

The first four definitions based on the ideas of internationalization, liberalization, universalization and westernization refer to the two main classes of phenomena discussed in the sociology of globalization: the globalization of the economy and the globalization of culture (Sklair 2007, 234). Definitions of globalization as internationalization and liberalization are related to the economic dimension, whereas universalization and westernization are linked to the cultural dimension (see Table 1). Furthermore, the concepts of internationalization and liberalization can be regarded as two different descriptions of the same process. Internationalization in the sense of increasing international trade and foreign direct investment is a *neutral description of the effects* of the economic dimension of globalization. However, international trade and foreign direct investment can only grow if national governments' restrictions on transferring goods and capital between countries are removed. Otherwise, rational economic actors would not engage in these activities as they would be too costly. Therefore, liberalization is a *description of the cause* of internationalization. A similar argument can be applied to the definitions of globalization as universalization and westernization or americanization. Universalization in the sense of a homogenization of cultures is a *neutral description of the effect* of the cultural dimension of globalization. However, this concept does not say anything about which culture will become the new global standard. This information is provided by the definitions based on

Table 1. Categorization of definitions of "globalization"

	Economic dimension	Cultural dimension
Description of "effects"	Internationalization	Universalization
Description of "causes"	Liberalization	Westernization/Americanization

the ideas of westernization or americanization. The attempt to westernize or to americanize the rest of the world can be seen as a description of the causes of universalization.[3] In this sense, the concepts of liberialization and westernization provide more relevant information than the concepts of internationalization and universalization; thus, these are used herein as the definitions of globalization for the economic and the cultural dimensions.

Causes and Historical Development of Globalization

Although this chapter is mainly interested in the ideological causes of globalization—liberalization and westernization—it does not advocate a purely ideological explanation of social change, for the historical development of events and material factors in the sense of technological innovations are just as relevant as the development of ideas. None of these categories of causes can explain globalization alone, as it is insufficient to explain the emergence of a new phenomenon purely historically out of the developments of the previous conditions without adding new ideas and new technology. For example, the French Revolution was not only caused by the financial problems of the old order, but also by the growing influence of the ideas of the Enlightenment. In the same way it is not very convincing to use progress in technology as a standard explanation (cf. Steger 2003, 17). For example, the Chinese admiral Zheng made several expeditions between 1405 and 1433 that extended Chinese influence to Arabia and Africa a century before Columbus's expedition to America. At this time Chinese ships were far superior to European ships, but this did not lead to a Chinese-dominated globalization, as a political decision was made to abandon this program in order to repair and connect the Great Wall (Stearns, Adas, Schwartz and Gilbert 2007, 613–15). Furthermore, the progress of science depends itself on the ideas of tolerance and freedom of speech. Science in the Middle Ages did not develop in Europe as the social environment did not support it. In contrast, the much more tolerant Islamic civilizations "outstripped all others in scientific discoveries" in the same period (Stearns, Adas, Schwartz and Gilbert 2007, 278). Finally, ideas alone cannot create social change. For example, the Nazis thought of Germans as a superior race,[4] but this idea did not automatically lead to world domination, simply because Germany's material resources were insufficient for this endeavor.

Therefore, a meaningful explanation of social change needs to refer to ideas, technology and historical processes.

This approach can now be applied to the explanation of globalization and to the question of whether globalization is an old or a new phenomenon. Concerning the latter question, Scholte (2005) again has provided a useful classification of the answers usually given (19). The first group of researchers interprets globalization as an old phenomenon with a cyclical development. Phases of globalization are interrupted by phases of "fragmentation" (Clark 1997). This point of view is based on the argument that international trade and foreign direct investment (in proportional numbers) as well as migration (in total numbers) were at a similar level in the late nineteenth century to that of recent times (cf. Baker, Epstein and Pollin 1998, 5, 9, 339; Balaam and Veseth 2001, 168; Hirst and Thompson 1999; O'Rourke and Williamson 1999; Scholte 2005, 118; Steger 2003, 32; Wade 1996; Zevin 1992). For example, David Dollar and Aart Kraay (2002) identify three waves of globalization based on merchandized exports, foreign capital stock and immigration to the United States. The first wave started in 1870 and ended with the beginning of World War I, the second wave lasted from 1945 to 1980 and was replaced by the third wave from 1980.[5] Chase-Dunn, Kawano and Brewer (2000) identify different waves by using more detailed statistics of international trade (88). They found a first wave of globalization from 1815 to 1879, a decline in international trade during the heyday of imperialism, a second wave from 1903 to 1924 interrupted by World War I and a very strong decrease of trade from 1925 and 1945, which was finally followed by the more recent third wave of globalization.

A second group of researchers also regards globalization as an old phenomenon, but in contrast to the first group the linearity of the development process is emphasized (Robertson 1992, 58–9). A. G. Hopkins (2002), for example, speaks of a broader historical sequence of proto-globalization (1600–1800), modern globalization (1800–1950) and postcolonial globalization (from 1950) (6–10). Thomas Friedman (2007), on the other hand, makes a distinction between the three phases of globalization 1.0 (1492–1800), globalization 2.0 (1800–2000) and globalization 3.0 (from 2000) by emphasizing how the world has been "shrinking" (248). In contrast to the theorists of the first perspective that emphasize cyclical development, this group insists on the quantitative and qualitative differences between the previous ages and the recent age of globalization (Baldwin and Martin 1999; Bordo, Eichengreen and Irwin 1999; Keohane and Nye 2000). The third group again sees in these quantitative and qualitative differences a justification for regarding globalization as an entirely new phenomenon that breaks with the past. The technological innovations of the microprocessor and the Internet are characterized as the "first global revolution" (King and Schneider 1991) that have led to "new realities" (Drucker 1989) and an age of information (Castells 1996).

Arguably, the position of the third group, namely that globalization is an entirely new phenomenon, is only convincing if history is completely ignored. Of course, life has changed in many aspects as a result of the introduction of new technologies, but humanity did not leap from the Stone Age directly into Castells's information age. The innovations of the microprocessor and the Internet occured because other innovations preceded them. Therefore, it seems reasonable to analyze the causes of globalization from a historical perspective. Furthermore, both approaches of interpreting globalization as an old phenomenon with a cyclical or linear development are useful for different categories of causes. Progress in science and technological innovation can be best described as a linear process commencing in the 1760s with Watt's innovation of the steam-engine—the so-called first industrial revolution. The second industrial revolution began somewhere in the middle of the nineteenth century and is associated with improvements in electricity, steel, chemicals and railways. Further developments finally led to the third industrial revolution at the end of the 1960s. The invention of the Internet and the microprocessor later made possible several path-breaking developments of communication technologies—for example, the World Wide Web (see Table 2). Furthermore, improvements in transportation and communication are closely connected to an increasing integration of local and global markets. These improvements have allowed the outsourcing of production, since the costs of complex networks of production have decreased drastically (Fröbel, Heinrichs and Kreye 2007, 169; cf. Castells 2007, 190).

However, decreasing transportation costs and increasing communication opportunities do not automatically lead to an outsourcing of production in developing countries with cheap labor. Outsourcing is only a cheap alternative to domestic production if goods can be traded cheaply without the interference of trading barriers. This leads to the ideological causes of globalization—liberalization and westernization—which can be better characterized as a cyclical phenomenon in contrast to the linear development of technology. The idea of liberalization of world markets or free trade originates in classical economics, founded with the publication of Adam Smith's (1723–1790) *The Wealth of Nations* (1776). Smith was the first economist to describe trade as beneficial for countries, whether they were buying or selling goods. For example, if an Indian carpet has a value of £10 in India and £20 in England, then every price between £10 and £20 would be beneficial for both sides—the Indian trader would be happy if he receives more than £10, and the English trader would be happy if he pays less than £20. Smith thus concluded that government interventions in international trade are harmful for a country's development. David Ricardo (1772–1823) formulated Smith's intuitive idea later as the law of comparative advantage. On the other hand,

Table 2. The historical development of globalization

Renaissance					Pre-Industrial Era
Absolutism	1614 last meeting of the *états généraux*				
Revolutions and Restorations	1779 Adam Smith's *Wealth of Nations*	liberalization ↓	British sense of mission ↓	1769 James Watt's steam-engine	First Industrial Revolution
Imperialism	1872 Benjamin Disraeli's Crystal Palace speech			1882 Thomas Edison's electricity generating station	Second Industrial Revolution
World Wars and American Isolationism	1914 World War I begins				
Cold War	1945 World War II ends	liberalization ↓	American sense of mission ↓		
US Hegemony	1989 Berlin Wall goes down			1969/71 invention of the Internet and the microprocessor	Third Industrial Revolution

mercantilism—the dominant economic theory in the preceding age of absolutism—regarded international trade as a zero-sum game as what one country gains in a trade another country must lose. Mercantilism was based on the idea that only gold and silver create wealth; and exporting (worthless) goods would imply the acquisition of precious metals. Unfortunately, mercantilist empires were not willing to trade with each other, because none of them wanted to pay in gold or silver in order to receive goods. Therefore, most mercantilist countries tried to acquire colonies, which were forced into unfavorable trading relationships. Also the Physiocratic School (1756–76)—the second important economic theory in the age of absolutism—did not recognize free trade as beneficial for trading countries. For the Physiocrats, only agriculture produced the wealth of a society. International trade was seen as neutral—neither beneficial nor harmful.[6] The idea of the liberalization of global markets and free trade therefore appears for the first time in *The Wealth of Nations*.

With Smith's economic theory rising in popularity, more and more influential politicians—including North, Shelburne, Pitt the Younger and Grenville (Ross 1998, xxii; cf. Rae 1895, 59–60)—also pressed for the application of free trade in Britain. The result was a gradual decline in British trade tariffs until Britain became a strong advocate of free trade worldwide.[7] From the 1810s free trade received a strong boost with the independence declarations of Latin American nations and the breaking of the Spanish monopoly on trade. Free-trade treaties were signed with (or imposed upon) Persia in 1836 and 1857, Turkey in 1838 and 1861, and Japan in 1958 (Gallagher and Robinson 1953, 11). Between 1840 and 1870 anti-imperialistic sentiment in Britain grew so much that there was even discussion of letting the non-white colonies obtain independence (Platt 1973, 87; Schuyler 1945, 45). Such sentiments began to change in the 1870s. At the Crystal Palace in 1872, Benjamin Disraeli attacked the indifference of the liberals towards the colonies. However, in the following years Britain extended its empire. In the late 1890s, Joseph Chamberlain started his campaign to erect high tariff barriers. However, this campaign ultimately failed, as the British Empire did not abandon free trade and international trade declined significantly from 1880, although Britain did not change its liberalization policy. The main reasons were that industrializing Germany, France and the United States all erected trade barriers to protect their infant industries from their British competitors, while the partitioning of the rest of the world into enclosed colonies made trading outside individual empires increasingly difficult (Hopkins 1968, 599; Kautsky 1970; cf. Platt 1968, 306; Platt 1973, 90). For example, only one-sixth of British foreign direct investments between 1815 and 1880 were located in the Empire, but in 1913 this figure had already amounted to nearly one-half (Hancock 1940, 27, as cited by Gallagher and Robinson 1953, 5; Imlah 1952, 237, 239). Thus, although the British Empire pushed for trade liberalization, the age of imperialism experienced economic deglobalization because of unfavorable historical conditions.

Before and after World War I international trade recovered but declined again rapidly during the Great Depression and the later protectionist period until the end of World War II. During the building of the post-war order, the liberalization of world markets again was once again put on the agenda, but this time it was largely due to the efforts of the United States. The Bretton Woods agreement paved the way for a liberal free-trade system with the dollar as the world's reserve currency and led to the establishment of the International Monetary Fund (IMF) and the World Bank Group. The consequence was an integration of the economies of North America, Western Europe and Japan. However, this development did not lead immediately to an integrated global economy, again because historical conditions were not favorable. The division of the world into two opposing camps during the Cold War and the communist bloc's rejection of free trade limited the process of economic integration. The first shift appeared later in the 1980s, when the debt crisis of many developing countries, especially in Latin America and Africa, allowed the IMF and the World Bank to demand structural adjustments to promote the reduction of public spending, privatization of public services, deregulation, legal security for property rights and the liberalization of trade and foreign direct investment

(Glenn 2007, 20; McMichael 2007, 222). As a result, developing countries in the southern hemisphere became more and more integrated into the already-developed northern capitalist economy. The liberalization of global markets received a final boost with the end of the Cold War and the transformation of most centrally planned economies into free-market economies. The historical record therefore shows that liberalization is a necessary but not a sufficient condition for globalization (in the sense of the economic dimension). Although advocated by a hegemon, liberalization policies can fail to lead to an integrated global economy if the historical conditions are unfavorable. Furthermore, liberalization policies themselves are a cyclical phenomenon. The idea of liberalization was introduced by Adam Smith and later applied by the architects of the British Empire. Then it was abandoned during the period of the World Wars and reintroduced by the US following World War II.

The pattern of westernization in the cultural dimension of globalization is in many aspects similar to the pattern of liberalization. Parallel to the agenda of bringing free trade (and British goods) to the rest of the world, British leaders developed a sense of mission in order to make the world more British. For example, the decision of the British judge Lord Mansfield in 1772 that slavery was unlawful in England (although not elsewhere in the British Empire) was immediately interpreted as a declaration that slavery was illegal in the United Kingdom. In 1807, the slave trade became illegal throughout the British Empire, followed by slavery itself in 1833. Britain started to push other countries to abolish the slave trade and slavery as well. Thus, the British fleet seized around 1,600 slave-trading ships and freed 150,000 slaves between 1807 and 1860 (Loosemore 2008). In 1839, The British and Foreign Anti-Slavery Society was established with the aim of abolishing slavery worldwide.

Another aspect of this sense of mission was the export of British team sports not only to the British colonies but to the rest of the world. British traders brought (Association) football (soccer) to Latin America and other parts of the world, and it soon became the most popular sport worldwide. In 1900, three British team sports made their debut at the Olympic Games. Football has been in the program continuously except for 1932. However, rugby lost its Olympic status in 1924, and cricket was never again an Olympic sport after its debut. A third example was the creation of a global standard time, Greenwich Mean Time, at the Royal Observatory in Greenwich, London. This convention was adopted internationally in 1884.

However, the British sense of mission lost impetus after World War II as a result of the decline of Britain's power. America's self-chosen isolationism in the period between the World Wars delayed the development of the American sense of mission as the new world hegemon. This changed again with the end of World War II. The United States exported its ideas of democracy to

Germany and Japan. American team sports replaced British team sports in the Olympic program: volleyball in 1964 and baseball from 1992 to 2008. Furthermore, the success of American companies such as McDonald's and Coca-Cola in foreign markets inspired sociologists to speak of McDonaldization (Ritzer 1993) and coca-colonization (Melnick and Jackson 2002). Thus, the idea of westernization is similar to the idea of liberalization with the first wave beginning in the second half of the eighteenth century under British leadership, and the second wave commencing at the end of World War II under American direction. Second, the combination of idealistic and materialistic causes indeed created a new phenomenon. Liberalization and westernization were able to reach a level never previously achieved because technological progress made this integration possible. However, in order to understand this new phenomenon it is necessary to analyze the causes as part of a long historical process. Moreover, neither the term "americanization" nor the term "westernization" actually describes these waves accurately. The first term seems to be a misnomer because the British are not Americans, and "westernization" seems to be inadequate since the driving forces of the economic and cultural dimension of globalization have their origin in a much smaller area than the West. Therefore, this chapter proposes the term *Calvinization* in order to describe the two globalization waves more accurately. This leads to the question of religious influence on the process of globalization, the subject discussed in the next section.

Calvinization and Trade Liberalization in the Work of Adam Smith

As mentioned before, the idea of free trade and the liberalization of world markets appeared well formulated for the first time in Adam Smith's 1776 *The Wealth of Nations*. In fact, *The Wealth of Nations* was in large part an attack on mercantilism and protectionism. However, what motivated Adam Smith to reject the mainstream economics of his time and to advocate the exact opposite? This is not an odd or irrelevant question considering that Smith did not provide any sound theoretical or empirical argument to support his radical pro-free-trade position. David Ricardo formulated this idea as the law of comparative advantage in 1817 in his book *On the Principles of Political Economy and Taxation*. Forty years before the first reasonable argument, Smith was convinced that free trade was good for Great Britain. How could he be so sure? In order to answer this, it is important to realize that Smith—the founder of modern economics—was not an economist. Smith held the chair of moral philosophy at the University of Glasgow and in this capacity lectured on natural theology, ethics, justice or jurisprudence, and economics (Samuels 1984, 701). One might wonder why Smith was teaching economics as part of his duties. The answer becomes clear after a closer look at the contents of his courses. His course in natural theology concerned the question "Who is God?"; the course in ethics dealt with "How should believers behave in order to please God?"; and the two remaining courses on justice and economics were focused on sinners (or non-believers). The topic of the justice course was "How should sinners, who violate God's rule, be punished?", while economics fulfilled the function of discussing "Which institutions force sinners to behave like believers?" or alternatively "How can sinners be tricked into following God's rules without realizing it?" Therefore the answer to why Smith taught economics, therefore, is that he was not interested in economics as an economist but as a moral philosopher: he saw in economics a tool to convert non-believers into believers.

The dominant role of religion in Adam Smith's work (cf. Anspach 1972, 177; Davis 1994, 90) leads to the question of which interpretation of God he supported. Smith was not a friend of the Catholic Church. He saw in Catholicism "the most formidable combination that ever was formed against the authority and security of civil government, as well as against the liberty, reason, and happiness of mankind, which can flourish only where civil government is able to protect them" (Smith 1976b, 802–3). His attitude towards the Anglican Church was not much better. He feared negative consequences for society from the close connection between church and state (Ditz 1984, 240). Smith was "highly critical of almost every religious order" with one exception (Rosenberg 1960, 568)—he praised the neo-Calvinist churches[8] because they "preached the economic virtues of hard work, enterprise, thrift, frugality, and parsimony" (Ditz 1984, 240). Smith states that nowhere in Europe could be found "a more learned, decent, independent, and respectable set of men, than the greater part of the Presbyterian clergy of Holland, Geneva, Switzerland, and Scotland" (Smith 1976b, 810), continuing:

> the most opulent church in Christendom does not maintain better the uniformity of faith, the fervour of devotion, the spirit of order, regularity, and austere morals in the great body of the people, than this very poorly endowed church of Scotland […] the greater part of the protestant churches of Switzerland, which in general are not better endowed than the Church of Scotland, produce those effects in a still higher degree. (Smith 1976b, 813)

Hugh Blair, Smith's friend and famous preacher, was even compelled to criticize him, arguing that Smith's support of the "little sects" went too far (Blair 1998, 6). Smith was a trained Presbyterian. Although he decided not to enter the ministry, he still lived "a frugal, ascetic, puritanic life" (Ditz

1984, 235). The conclusion is that Adam Smith was a neo-Calvinist in the Presbyterian tradition. His own words are clear proof of this.

The fact that Smith only refers directly to God in rare cases and most of the time used aliases such as "'the great Director of Nature', 'the final cause', 'the Author of Nature', 'the great judge of hearts', 'an invisible hand', 'Providence', 'the divine Being'" (Viner 1927, 202) therefore does not support the interpretation of some economists that Adam Smith was a deist without any affiliation to an organized church (cf. Bittermann 1940, 709; Fleischacker 2004, 71f.; Viner 1984, 114). This is important since this argument is often used to conclude that Smith's science was independent of his religious beliefs (Bittermann 1940, 710, 718, 732; Fleischacker 2004, 44–5). However, Smith's resistance to using direct theological arguments can be better explained by "a Calvinist tradition of theological reticence in non-religious communications. A strong consciousness of minority status is one explanation. Preference for positivistic, empirical affirmations also has Calvinist roots" (Ditz 1984, 235). Therefore, there is no sound reason to believe that Adam Smith constructed classical economic theory independent of neo-Calvinist theology.

The question that then arises is which aspects of neo-Calvinist theology shaped Smith's economic theory and his ideas of free trade. In his course on ethics, later published as *The Theory of Moral Sentiments*, Smith demands that believers should be ascetic and hard-working, and should try to provide some proof for themselves that they were worthy to go to heaven. Smith regards the pursuit of wealth as dangerous, suggesting that it would corrupt the soul (Billet 1983, 209; Ditz 1984, 237; Rosenberg 1960, 557). He rejects utilitarian theories with their emphasis on pleasure as the motive for economic choices (Smith 1976a, 188) and replaces utility as the main motive with virtue (Macfie 1961, 17), social esteem (Smith 1976a, 50) and the approval of the impartial spectator (Smith 1976a, 41). Smith only accepts the accumulation of capital if it resulted "chiefly from [a] regard to the sentiments of mankind" (Smith 1976a, 50) or from "civilization, material and moral progress" (Billet 1983, 210). In other words, the problem is not the possession of money, but that it can be used for consumption. Smith adds that a prudent man should be steady in his profession and willing to sacrifice "the ease and enjoyment of the present moment" for an eternity in heaven (Smith 1976a, 215). The connection to "the Calvinist emphasis upon work and discipline" is obvious (Dwyer 1993, 144). This combination of asceticism and an enduring work ethic in Smith's work was later called "this worldly asceticism" by Max Weber (Ditz 1984, 243). Furthermore, Smith's concept of the impartial spectator fulfills a similar function as the idea of proof in neo-Calvinist theological writings. The impartial spectator can be interpreted as the internalized "individual's social conscience" (Young 1986, 366; cf. Coase 1976, 531–2) or the "superego"

(Heilbroner 1982, 429). An actor can judge whether he or she was able to keep up with the expectations of society by taking the position of the impartial spectator (cf. Fleischacker 2004, 72). In this sense, the impartial spectator can provide some assurance for a successful believer that he or she is chosen.

How can these ideas of asceticism, work ethic and proof be translated into an economic language? Asceticism as the opposite of consumption is called "savings" in economic terms. The classical economist Nassau William Senior (1790–1864) later called the capitalist's act of saving "abstinence," a word with clear religious connotations (1951, 58). Indeed, Smith's central economic thesis was that economic growth depends on the ratio of savings and consumption—savings increase national income, whereas consumption reduces it (Bowley 1975, 371; Smith 1976b, 337). Savings make possible investments in productive labor and determine the extent of the division of labor (Smith 1976b, 277, 295), which again increases the efficiency of an economy. Smith (1976b, 284–5) even goes so far as to claim that someone who "does not employ all the stock which he commands" must be "perfectly crazy." His central thesis is therefore that a national economy with a large number of ascetic actors—who save and do not consume—will grow, whereas other economies will stagnate or even collapse. Karl Marx (1861–1863) and John Maynard Keynes (1935) later show that Adam Smith's thesis had a decisive flaw; namely, that a national economy cannot grow if the ascetic population is not allowed to consume. Without a demand for consumer goods, no one would have an incentive to invest. As a result, Smith's central economic thesis is not very reasonable from an economic point of view, although it makes a lot of sense from a neo-Calvinist perspective.

The second idea of the enduring work ethic finds its expression in Adam Smith's rejection of the attitudes of adventurers. A prudent man who is willing to make sacrifices and to work hard "does not go in quest of new enterprises and adventures, which might endanger, but could not well increase, the secure tranquility which he actually enjoys" (Smith 1976a, 215). He opposes risk-taking, because risks are for him costs that diminish economic growth (Levy 1987, 395; cf. Smith 1976b, 128). However, more important is that risk-taking activities with potentially high profits can make it too easy to become rich—thereby increasing the danger of sloth. Wealth building in this scenario is no longer a challenge and cannot be regarded as a sign of proof of God's favor. Real proof requires that the believer be tested thoroughly. Only if the believer can survive in a hostile environment—in the sense of survival of the fittest (cf. Anderson and Tollison 1982, 1239; Smith 1976b, 163–4)—does it really count.

How then can an institutional system be designed to provide incentives to save and work hard and to punish pleasure-loving and lazy gamblers? The first answer offered by Smith was developed in his course on jurisprudence. He demands, for example, that idleness and beggary be regarded as "public crimes" (Dietz 1984, 238). This first strategy implies a criminalization of actions that do not follow the rules of the neo-Calvinist God. The second more important solution offered by Smith in his course on economics is the introduction of a competitive market.[9] A competitive market has a decisive advantage over other institutional settings. It forces economic actors to work hard in order to make continuous profits, and to invest the profits (investments equal savings) instead of consuming them in order to stay competitive. Only if these rules are followed is survival in the competitive market possible (Smith 1976b, 759, cf. 265). In other words, in a market with economic actors of mixed religious affiliations the neo-Calvinists would create so much pressure on the Catholics, Anglicans, Jews and all the others that they would be forced to adapt a neo-Calvinist attitude to avoid being subsumed. So the competitive market is the perfect tool to convert non-believers and sinners into strict neo-Calvinists believers. The competitive market is God's "invisible hand" that transforms the egoistic interests of all sinners—who had only their own profits in mind—into the best result for all of society (Gray 1976, 157; Macfie 1959, 211–12)—a community of ascetic and hard-working people. Every individual "intends only his own gain, and he is in this, as in many other cases, led by an invisible hand to promote an end which was no part of his intention" (Smith 1976b, 456). Furthermore, the idea that economic actors cannot influence the outcome of their actions because God's invisible hand will finally decide the result is not at all an economic idea. It is "predestinarian Scottish theology" (Gray 1976, 157; cf. Dwyer 1993, 144):

> Smith's impersonal market operates parallel to Calvin's incomprehensible but just deity. In both systems the many were, or thought they were, called as potential saints or profit makers, but only the few are chosen or succeed in making a profit. In both types of selection uncertainty dominates. Both systems must include non-salvation (unredeemable sin) and poverty (economic failure) as necessary components [...] Smith's model requires the richer and the poorer, just as Calvin's model requires the saints and the sinners. (Ditz 1984, 240)

How does the liberalization of world markets or free trade now fit into this picture? Obviously, Smith's agenda was not only to convert British non-believers into neo-Calvinists but every single non-believer in the rest of the world. Free trade simply means establishing a competitive market worldwide and creating enormous pressure on all economic actors through competition with the small minority of neo-Calvinists. It is a mission without the need to pay missionaries (which is thus very efficient). However, this mission project requires that other countries be willing to lower trading tariffs and open up their markets. There are two basic approaches to convince other countries that it is in their best interests to liberalize the home market. The first is (mainstream) economics and the second is the threat of brute force. In contrast to the popular belief that economics was founded by Adam Smith as a social science, it was actually created as a theological application of economic principles in the context of neo-Calvinism.[10] Most economists accept these foundations without ever questioning them. Of course, they have been socialized to *believe* in them. Anyone who studies economics in fact risks being converted into a believer of neo-Calvinist dogma. In some honest moments, modern economists have spoken of Adam Smith as their "prophet" (Sobel 1979, 347) or "patron saint" (Heilbroner 1983, 156) and of *The Wealth of Nations* as their "Bible" (Hutchinson 1976, 484; Meek 1977, 3; cf. Schluchter 1995, 337). With the authority of science it is again easy to convince non-experts that free trade is beneficial for everybody, though whenever "science" has failed to do the job neither Britain nor the United States as free-trade advocates has hesitated to intervene with force. In this sense, the recent American occupations of Iraq and Afghanistan— countries which opposed free trade and foreign direct investment—look much more like a crusade than a reasonable response to 9/11.

Conclusion

The parallel developments of the waves of Calvinization—the periods of the British and American sense of mission—and the liberalization of world markets in the history of globalization are not a coincidence. From the beginning the idea of a competitive global market was used as a tool to convert non-believers into neo-Calvinists. There can be little doubt that in the years after Adam Smith, British and American elites used the idea of free competitive markets in order to make the world more British or more American. Promoting free trade is as much a part of a peaceful mission strategy as the export of human rights (individual human rights in contrast to the needs of the group or society) and team sports. Although it may not at first seem evident, this mission has a neo-Calvinist foundation. The process is essentially driven by a religious sense of mission to bring the right lifestyle to all "sinners." That some religions— not sharing the same values as Neo-Calvinism—are critical of the process of globalization, especially in the form of liberalization and Calvinization, is therefore very easy to understand. Religious people of all backgrounds have a reason to be concerned about the hidden agenda of free-trade advocates. However, religious conflicts should not eliminate the possibility of rational solutions or compromises.

Although calls for freer global trade today cannot be properly understood without reference to Adam Smith's neo-Calvinist beliefs, the choice between a free global market and a controlled national market can be regarded more rationally as a value problem. People who prefer efficiency over equality have good reason to promote free trade, whereas the opposite value choice of equality over efficiency which leads to a rejection of liberalization. In a democratic society, the majority will decide what to do. However, no society should be forced to accept free trade. If the Pashtun people in Afghanistan, for example, wish to live without new technologies and in accord with ancient customs and beliefs, then it is their right to do so. Finally, globalization is not necessarily bad just because it is a neo-Calvinist phenomenon. There are good reasons to accept the neo-Calvinist globalization project as much as there are good reasons to reject it.

Notes and References

1 Although I do not refer to Max Weber's Protestant ethic thesis very often in this paper, it is obvious that my argumentation is compatible with Weber's thesis. For a discussion of the relevance of Adam Smith's work for the Protestant ethic thesis, see Etzrodt (2008).

2 Scholte (2005, 50, 54–9) claims that the four interpretations of globalization as internalization, liberalization, universalization and westernization are redundant and impractical. He advocates instead the concept of respatialization in the sense of "a reconfiguration of social geography with increased transplanetary connections between people" (Scholte 2005, 16; cf. Held, McGrew, Goldblatt and Perraton 1999; Rosenau 2003; Short 2001). I do not, however, follow Scholte's line of reasoning as I am interested in analyzing the connection between the cultural and economic dimensions of globalization, and therefore hesitate to summarize every phenomenon under the same concept. Moreover, Scholte's argument that the four other definitions are redundant and that the concept of respatialization is more useful is not convincing. The current chapter can also demonstrate this.

3 "Hybridization" (Bhabha 1986; Kraidy 2005) and "creolization" (Hannerz 1987, 1992) are not mentioned in this paper as alternatives to westernization because these processes do not lead to a homogeneous global culture and therefore by definition cannot be regarded as phenomena of globalization. Whether westernization, hybridization or creolization is more relevant in reality is an empirical question not discussed herein.

4 Although my stance towards the British and American belief in their cultural superiority and their "sense of mission" is critical for my argument, it is clear that such attitudes could be much worse. At least the British and Americans invented and exported human rights and not an efficient way to commit genocide as the Nazis did in Germany.

5 Dollar and Kraay distinguish the second wave (1945–80) from the third wave (from 1980) because the former period was characterized by an increasing intra-North trade, whereas the latter led to a real global integration that involved the Global South (2002; see Glenn 2007, 103–4).

6 The Physiocrats stated that *only* agriculture creates wealth and that international trade is not harmful. It is therefore a logical conclusion that international trade must be regarded as neutral in such a theory.

7 However, strong advocates of free trade do not always apply these rules to themselves. John Gallagher and Ronald Robinson (1953) point out that the British colony India "in this supposedly laissez-faire period [...] was subjected to intensive development as an economic colony along the best mercantilist lines" (4). They claim that Britain insisted on free trade only in order to break the trade monopolies of other countries or to open closed markets for their traders. Gallagher and Robinson conclude that there is no significant difference between the free trade period until 1870 and the later era of imperialism. They therefore call this policy of liberalization the "imperialism of free trade." This conclusion has been challenged by Platt (1968, 1973), who has argued that there was indeed a significant shift in British foreign policy from non-intervention and laissez-faire in the mid-Victorian era to pre-emptive annexation in the late Victorian era.

8 The term "neo-Calvinism" is used in a manner akin to Max Weber's "ascetic Protestantism," which includes Puritanism, Pietism, Methodism, Baptism, Mennonitism and Quakerism— but excludes Calvinism itself (Etzrodt 2008, 49; cf. Schluchter 2005, 66).

9 Very likely Adam Smith did not think of himself as the innovator of this idea as he spoke of the market as God's beneficent design (Evensky 1987, 449–50). He probably saw himself as God's servant by revealing God's plan for humankind.

10 Salim Rashid (1998; cf. Peil 1989, 54; Price 1893, 239) suggests that Adam Smith was a plagiarist insofar as he did not offer any original economic ideas—for example, the advantages of the division of labor as well as the concept of the invisible hand had been previously published in French—and did not cite his sources. However, Adam Smith was in fact very innovative for his taking of economic ideas out of the Catholic context of the mercantilist and Physiocratic School and application of them in the neo-Calvinist tradition. The ideas themselves were not new, but their synthesis was.

Anderson, G. M. and R. D. Tollison. 1982. "Adam Smith's Analysis of Joint-Stock Companies." *Journal of Political Economy* 90, no. 6: 1237–56.

Anspach, R. 1972. "The Implications of the *Theory of Moral Sentiments* for Adam Smith's Economic Thought." *History of Political Economy* 4, no. 1: 176–206.

Baker, D., G. A. Epstein and R. Pollin, eds. 1998. *Globalization and Progressive Economic Policy.* Cambridge: Cambridge University Press.

Balaam, D. N. and M. V. Veseth. 2001. *Introduction to International Political Economy.* 2nd edn. Upper Saddle River: Prentice-Hall.

Baldwin, R. E. and P. Martin. 1999. "Two Waves of Globalization: Superficial Similarities, Fundamental Differences." In *Globalization and Labor.* Ed. by H. Siebert. Tübingen: Mohr Siebeck, 3–58.

Barber, B. R. 1996. *Jihad vs. McWorld.* New York: Ballantine.

Bhabha, H. K. 1986. "Signs Taken for Wonders: Questions of Ambivalence and Authority Under a Tree Outside Delhi, May 1817." In *"Race," Writing and Difference.* Ed. by H. L. Gates Jr. Chicago: University of Chicago Press, 173–83.

Billet, L. 1983. "The Just Economy: The Moral Basis of the *Wealth of Nations.*" In *Adam Smith: Critical Assessments,* vol. 2. Ed. by J. C. Wood. London: Croom Helm, 205–20.

Bittermann, H. J. 1940. "Adam Smith's Empiricism and the Law of Nature, II." *Journal of Political Economy* 48, no. 5: 703–34.

Blair, H. 1998. "Letter from Hugh Blair: 3 April 1776." In *On the Wealth of Nations: Contemporary Responses to Adam Smith*. Ed. by I. S. Ross. Bristol: Thoemmes Press, 5–8.

Bordo, M. D., B. Eichengreen and D. A. Irwin. 1999. "Is Globalization Today Really Different than Globalization a Hundred Years Ago?" In *Brookings Trade Forum 1999*. Ed. by S. M. Collins and R. Z. Lawrence. Washington: Brookings Institution Press.

Bowley, M. 1975. "Some Aspects of the Treatment of Capital in *The Wealth of Nations*." In *Essays on Adam Smith*. Ed. by A. S. Skinner and T. Wilson. Oxford: Clarendon, 361–76.

Castells, M. 1996. *The Information Age: Economy, Society and Culture*. Oxford: Blackwell.

Castells, M. 2007. "The Informational Mode of Development and the Restructuring of Capitalism." In *The Globalization and Development Reader*. Ed. by J. T. Roberts and A. B. Hite. Malden: Blackwell, 175–94.

Chase-Dunn, C., Y. Kawano and B. D. Brewer. 2000. "Trade Globalization since 1795: Waves of Integration in the World-System." *American Sociological Review* 65, no. 1: 77–95.

Clark, I. 1997. *Globalization and Fragmentation: International Relations in the Twentieth Century*. Oxford: Oxford University Press.

Coase, R. H. 1976. "Adam Smith's View of Man." *Journal of Law and Economics* 19, no. 3: 529–46.

Davis, J. R. 1994. "Adam Smith on the Providential Reconciliation of Individual and Social Interests: Is Man Led by an Invisible Hand or Misled by a Sleight of Hand?" In *Adam Smith: Critical Assessments*, vol. 7. Ed. by J. C. Wood. London: Routledge, 90–101.

Ditz, G. W. 1984. "The Calvinism in Adam Smith." *Tijdschrift voor Economie en Management* 29: 233–54.

Dollar, D. and A. Kraay. 2002. "Growth is good for the Poor." *World Bank Policy Research Department Working Paper No. 2587*.

Drucker, P. F. 1989. *The New Realities*. London: Butterworth.

Dwyer, J. 1993. "Adam Smith in the Scottish Enlightenment." In *Adam Smith: International Perspectives*. Ed. by H. Mizuta and C. Sugiyama. New York: St. Martin's Press, 141–61.

Etzrodt, C. 2008. "Weber's Protestant-Ethic Thesis, the Critics, and Adam Smith." *Max Weber Studies* 8, no. 1: 49–78.

Evensky, J. 1987. "The Two Voices of Adam Smith: Moral Philosopher and Social Critic." *History of Political Economy* 19, no. 3: 447–68.

Fleischacker, S. 2004. *On Adam Smith's Wealth of Nations: A Philosophical Companion*. Princeton: Princeton University Press.

Friedman, T. L. 2007. "It's a Flat World, After All." In *The Globalization and Development Reader*. Ed. by J. T. Roberts and A. B. Hite. Malden: Blackwell, 247–55.

Fröbel, F., J. Heinrichs and O. Kreye. 2007. "The New International Division of Labor in the World Economy." In *The Globalization and Development Reader*. Ed. by J. T. Roberts and A. B. Hite. Malden: Blackwell, 160–74.

Gallagher, J. and R. Robinson. 1953. "The Imperialism of Free Trade." *The Economic History Review* 6, no. 1: 1–15.

Glenn, J. 2007. *Globalization: North–South Perspectives*. London: Routledge.

Gowan, P. 1999. *The Global Gamble: Washington's Faustian Bid for World Dominance*. London: Verso.

Gray, A. 1976. "Adam Smith." *Scottish Journal of Political Economy* 23, no. 2: 153–69.

Hancock, W. K. 1940. *Survey of British Commonwealth Affairs*. London: Oxford University Press.

Hannerz, U. 1992. *Cultural Complexity: Studies in the Social Organization of Meaning*. New York: Columbia University Press.

_____. 1987. "The World in Creolization." *Africa* 57, no. 4: 546–59.

Heilbroner, R. L. 1983. "The Adam Smith Nobody Knows." In *Adam Smith: Critical Assessments*, vol. 2. Ed. by J. C. Wood. London: Croom Helm, 156–9.

_____. 1982. "The Socialization of the Individual in Adam Smith." *History of Political Economy* 14, no. 3: 427–39.

Held, D., A. McGrew, D. Goldblatt and J. Perraton. 1999. *Global Transformations: Politics, Economics and Culture*. Cambridge: Polity.

Hirst, P. and G. Thompson. 1999. *Globalization in Question: The International Economy and the Possibilities of Governance*. 2nd edn. Cambridge: Polity.

_____. 1996. "Globalization: Ten Frequently Asked Questions and Some Surprising Answers." *Soundings* 4 (Autumn): 47–66.

Hopkins, A. G. 2002. "The History of Globalization—and the Globalization of History?" In *Globalization in World History*. Ed. by A. G. Hopkins. New York: Norton, 12–44.

_____. 1968. "Economic Imperialism in West Africa: Lagos, 1880–92." *The Economic History Review* 21, no. 3: 580–606.

Hutchinson, T. W. 1976. "The Bicentenary of Adam Smith." *Economic Journal* 86, no. 343: 481–92.

Imlah, A. H. 1952. "British Balance of Payments and Export of Capital, 1816–1913." *The Economic History Review* 5, no. 2: 237–9.

Kautsky, K. 1970. "Ultra-imperialism." *New Left Review* 59, no. 1: 39–46.

Keohane, R. O. and J. S. Nye. 2000. "Globalization: What's New? What's Not? (And So What?)" *Foreign Policy* 118 (March): 104–19.

King, A. and B. Schneider. 1991. *The First Global Revolution: A Report by the Council of the Club of Rome*. New York: Pantheon.

Kraidy, M. M. 2005. *Hybridity, or the Cultural Logic of Globalization*. Philadelphia: Temple University Press.

Levy, D. 1987. "Adam Smith's Case for Usury Laws." *History of Political Economy* 19, no. 3: 387–400.

Loosemore, J. 2008. *Sailing Against Slavery*. Online: http://www.bbc.co.uk/devon/ content/ articles/2007/03/20/abolition_navy_feature.shtml (accessed January 26, 2010).

Macfie, A. L1961. "Adam Smith's Theory of Moral Sentiments." *Scottish Journal of Political Economy* 8, no. 1: 12–27.

_____. 1959. "Adam Smith's *Moral Sentiments* as Foundation for His *Wealth of Nations*." *Oxford Economic Papers* 11, no. 3: 209–28.

McMichael, P. 2007. "Globalization: Myths and Realities." In *The Globalization and Development Reader*. Ed. by J. T. Roberts and A. B. Hite. Malden: Blackwell, 216–32.

Meek, R. L. 1977. *Smith, Marx, and After*. London: Chapman and Hall.

Melnick, M. J. and S. J. Jackson. 2002. "Globalization American-style and Reference Idol Selection." *International Review for the Sociology of Sport* 37, no. 3–4: 429–48.

O'Rourke, K. H. and J. G. Williamson. 1999. *Globalization and History: The Evolution of a Nineteenth-century Atlantic Economy*. Cambridge, MA: MIT Press.

Peil, J. 1989. "A New Look at Adam Smith." *International Journal of Social Economics* 16, no. 1: 52–72.

Platt, D. C. M. 1973. "Further Objections to an 'Imperialism of Free Trade', 1830–60." *The Economic History Review* 26, no. 1: 77–91.

_____. 1968. "The Imperialism of Free Trade: Some Reservations." *The Economic History Review* 21, no. 2: 296–306.

Price, L. L. 1893. "Adam Smith and His Relations to Recent Economics." *Economic Journal* 3, no. 10: 239–54.

Rae, J. 1895. *Life of Adam Smith*. London: Macmillan.

Rashid, S. 1998. *The Myth of Adam Smith*. Cheltenham: Elgar.

Reiser, O. L. and B. Davies. 1944. *Planetary Democracy: An Introduction to Scientific Humanism*. New York: Creative Age Press.

Ritzer, G. 1993. *The McDonaldization of Society*. Thousand Oaks: Pine Forge Press.

Robertson, R. 1992. *Globalization: Social Theory and Global Culture*. London: Sage.

Rosenau, J. N. 2003. *Distant Proximities: Dynamics beyond Globalization*. Princeton: Princeton University Press.

Rosenberg, N. 1960. "Some Institutional Aspects of the *Wealth of Nations*." *Journal of Political Economy* 68, no. 6: 557–70.

Ross, I. S. 1998. "Introduction." In *On the Wealth of Nations: Contemporary Responses to Adam Smith*. Ed. by I. S. Ross. Bristol: Thoemmes Press, xi–xxxvi.

Samuels, W. J. 1984. "The Political Economy of Adam Smith." In *Adam Smith: Critical Assessments*, vol. 1. Ed. by J. C. Wood. London: Croom Helm, 698–714.

Sander, H. 1996. "Multilateralism, Regionalism and Globalisation: The Challenges to the World Trading System." In *World Trade after the Uruguay Round: Prospects and Policy for the Twenty-first Century*. Ed. by H. Sander and A. Inotai. London: Routledge, 17–36.

Schiller, H. I. 1991. "Not yet the Post-imperialist Era." *Critical Studies in Mass Communication* 8, no. 1: 13–28.

Schluchter, W. 2005. "Wie Ideen in der Geschichte wirken: Exemplarisches in der Studie über den asketischen Protestantismus" [How Ideas Work in History: Examples from the Study of Ascetic Protestantism]. In *Asketischer Protestantismus und der 'Geist' des modernen Kapitalismus*. Ed. by W. Schluchter and F. W. Graf. Tübingen: Mohr Siebeck, 49–73.

_____. 1995. "Ethik und Kapitalismus: Zwei Thesen Max Webers" [Ethics and capitalism: Max Weber's two theses]. *Berliner Journal für Soziologie* 5, no. 3: 335–47.

Scholte, J. A. 2005. *Globalization: A Critical Introduction*. 2nd edn. Houndmills: Palgrave Macmillan.

Schuyler, R. L. 1945. *The Fall of the Old Colonial System*. New York: Oxford University Press.

Short, J. R. 2001. *Global Dimensions: Space, Place and the Contemporary World*. London: Reaktion Books.

Sklair, L. 2007. "Competing Conceptions of Globalization." In *The Globalization and Development Reader*. Ed. by J. T. Roberts and A. B. Hite. Malden: Blackwell, 233–46.

Smith, A. 1976a. *The Theory of Moral Sentiments*. Oxford: Clarendon.

_____. 1976b. *An Inquiry into the Nature and Cause of the Wealth of Nations*. Oxford: Clarendon.

Sobel, I. 1979. "Adam Smith: What Kind of Institutionalist Was He?" *Journal of Economic Issues* 13, no. 2: 347–68.

Stearns, P. N., M. Adas, S. B. Schwartz and M. J. Gilbert. 2007. *World Civilizations: The Global Experience*, 2 vols. 6th edn. Boston: Longman.

Steger, M. B. 2003. *Globalization: A Very Short Introduction*. Oxford: Oxford University Press.

Taylor, P. J. 2000. "Izations of the World: Americanization, Modernization and Globalization." In *Demystifying Globalization*. Ed. by C. Hay and D. Marsh. Basingstoke: Palgrave Macmillan, 49–70.

Viner, J. 1927. 1984. "Adam Smith." In *Adam Smith: Critical Assessments*, vol. 1. Ed. by J. C. Wood. London: Croom Helm, 111–21.

———. "Adam Smith and Laissez-faire." *Journal of Political Economy* 35, no. 2: 198–232.

Wade, R. 1996. "Globalization and Its Limits: Reports of the Death of the National Economy Are greatly Exaggerated." In *National Diversity and Global Capitalism*. Ed. by S. Berger and R. Dore. Ithaca: Cornell University Press, 60–88.

William, N. 1951. *An Outline of the Science of Political Economy*. New York: Kelley.

Young, J. T. 1986. "The Impartial Spectator and Natural Jurisprudence: An Interpretation of Adam Smith's Theory of the Natural Price." *History of Political Economy* 18, no. 3, 365–82.

Zevin, R. 1992. "Are Financial Markets more Open? If So, Why and with What Effects?" In *Financial Openness and National Autonomy: Opportunities and Constraints*. Ed. by T. Banuri and J. B. Schor. Oxford: Clarendon, 43–83.

Chapter 3

DANIEL QUINN ON RELIGION: SAVING THE WORLD THROUGH ANTI-GLOBALISM?

Bei Dawei
Hsuan Chuang University, Taiwan

Introduction

It is easy to celebrate globalization for its promise of an ever-advancing civilization in which barriers of geographic and social distance gradually fall away, and our various cultures recombine and blend together in ways that reflect the highest ideals of humanity. Such rosy projections face two basic types of critique. One is the dystopian prospect that exploitation and inequality will not wither away, but will persist or even accelerate, entrenching themselves in a despotic New World Order impervious to escape or revolt. The other is the threat that globalization will prove unsustainable—whether because of rising oil prices, climatic changes, human overpopulation or some other factor.

The suspicion that at some point humanity has taken a wrong turn resonates with religious tendencies towards conservatism, nostalgia and apocalyptic paranoia (or hope), as well as with environmentalist laments for the disappearance of the natural world. Bron Taylor's *Dark Green Religion* (2010, together with his website, www.brontaylor.com) discusses the spiritual dimensions of environmentalism, which "increasingly [fills] the cultural niches where traditional religious beliefs have come to be seen as less plausible" (Taylor 2010, x). While many religious groups express concern for the environment, few are "dark" green in the sense of regarding nature as sacred in its own right (Taylor 2010, ix, 10). "As environmental alarm has intensified," Taylor writes, "this sort of religion has been rekindled, revitalized, invented, ecologized, localized, and globalized," and as it spreads well beyond the environmentalist milieu, "may even inspire the emergence of a global, civic, earth religion" (Taylor 2010, x, 180).

Although the movement's beliefs are a "bricolage" of numerous sources, Taylor names American ecological and spiritual[1] writer Daniel Quinn (b. 1935) as having "articulated the most prevalent cosmogony found within radical environmental subcultures" (Taylor 2010, 14, 78). Quinn gained public attention in 1991 when he won the (Ted) Turner Tomorrow Fellowship Award, a grant of US$500,000 for fictional works that "create and produce solutions to global problems" (Quinn 1994, 6). (The award was a one-time event.) Quinn's winning entry, a novel called *Ishmael* (1992), centers on a series of philosophical dialogues on the future of humanity and life on earth. The fact that one of the dialogue partners is a professorial, telepathic gorilla turns out to be rather peripheral to the book's substance, which has been forced uncomfortably into the novel form.

Ishmael begins with narrator Alan Lomax answering a newspaper ad that reads, "TEACHER seeks pupil. Must have an earnest desire to save the world" (Quinn 1992, 4). Disillusioned by the youth culture of the 1960s and 1970s, Lomax reacts with incredulity but answers the ad anyway. In this way, he meets Ishmael, a silverback lowland gorilla who uses the Socratic method to argue for various Quinnian principles. Prominent among these is the need to rid ourselves of conceptual biases associated with our species and culture.

The word "culture" is notoriously polyvalent, and Quinn/Ishmael proposes his own definition: a culture is "a people enacting a story" (1992, 41). Most of the world's "civilized" societies, notwithstanding their apparent diversity, turn out to be enacting the same story, namely that "[t]he world was made for man, and man was made to rule it" (1992, 72). Alternative lifestyles exist among the primitive societies, whose prevailing ethos holds that "[m]an belongs to the world" (1992, 239) rather than vice versa; and that "There is no one right way for people to live" (1999, 183). Instead of "civilized" and "primitive" cultures, Quinn speaks of "Takers" and "Leavers" (as in "take it or leave it"), cautioning that "The Leavers are not chapter one of a story in which the Takers are chapter two" (1992, 42).

Taker culture, we learn, originated some 10,000 years ago with the (so-called) Agricultural Revolution. Quinn points out that other styles of agriculture exist, some of them predating the Neolithic, and proposes the term "totalitarian agriculture"[2] to distinguish the Taker practice of subordinating all life-forms to "the relentless, single-minded production of human food" (1996, 247–8). A key consequence of totalitarian agriculture is that it tends to produce food surpluses, which lead to population growth beyond what the surpluses will support, and thence pressure to bring more land under cultivation. Quinn names this vicious cycle the "Food Race" (an analogy with the US/Soviet arms race) and credits the idea to Peter Farb in *Humankind* (Quinn 1992, 109,

133). One important corollary—that increased food production only worsens the problem of hunger—is perhaps Quinn's most controversial insight.

Propelled by totalitarian agriculture, Taker culture has expanded from the Near East to every corner of the globe:

> [The Agricultural Revolution] didn't end. It just spread. It's been spreading since it began back there ten thousand years ago. It spread across this continent during the eighteenth and nineteenth centuries. It's still spreading across parts of New Zealand and Africa and South America today. (Quinn 1992, 153)

Since population growth cannot be sustained indefinitely—there is the carrying capacity of the earth to consider (see Cohen 1995), and the process has already resulted in untold ecological devastation, e.g., in the form of mass extinctions (see Leakey and Lewin 1995; Wilson 2003)—Taker culture is headed for eventual collapse. Quinn states:

> If there are still people here in 200 years, they won't be living the way we do. I can make that prediction with confidence, because if people go on living the way we do, there won't be any people here in 200 years. (Quinn 2002)

Yet our culture shows little awareness of the impending catastrophe. For example, we do not panic at news of mass extinctions, but tend to view such things as speed bumps on the road to the future paradise of *Star Trek*, a show which Quinn criticizes for its promise of limitless expansion and progress (1992, 8, 245). Our task is to undo the "Great Forgetting" (i.e., Taker culture's loss of awareness that we did not always live this way, that there are other ways to live, that we too are subject to natural law) with a "Great Remembering," and find a new guiding vision, "another story to be in" (Quinn 1992, 88). After all, "We don't have to change HUMANKIND in order to survive. We only have to change a single culture" (Quinn 1996, 255).

Quinn elaborates the philosophy of *Ishmael* in two subsequent novels, *The Story of B* (1996) and *My Ishmael: A Sequel* (1998), as well as in his non-fiction essay *Beyond Civilization* (1999), the film *Food Production and Population Growth* (Quinn and Thornhill 1998), and material published on his website (www.ishmael.org). His "Frequently Asked Questions" section is cited extensively below (as "FAQ" followed by the question number). In addition, "B's" lectures (printed at the end of *The Story of B*) read as non-fiction, and are especially helpful. Finally, Quinn's novel *After Dachau* (2001) reworks one of Ishmael's parables (1992, 26–7). Namely, thousands of years after Hitler's victory in

World War II, the exclusively Aryan inhabitants of an alternate-history earth attempt to fathom its former diversity, as well as the extent to which their culture has misled them.

Quinn's Religion

Quinn is a lapsed Catholic. In his autobiography *Providence* (1994), he relates something of his childhood piety, which culminated in his decision to seek holy orders at the age of 20. He became a postulant at the Abbey of Our Lady of Gethsemani, a Trappist monastery in Kentucky, but was soon expelled for immaturity by its novice master (and most famous resident), Thomas Merton. At Gethsemani, Quinn underwent a mystical experience, whose content he retrospectively articulates as follows:

> I am the fire of life that animates the world. I am not to be found in the sky, not to be found in some remote heaven. I live in your midst, and all that lives in the midst of me. I am HERE and never absent. (1994, 140)

While Catholic tradition accepts the possibility of such experiences—Quinn himself volunteers the term "infused contemplation" (1994, 67)—Fr Merton summarily dismissed his claims. In any case, "this was not a Christian vision" (1994, 77).

Nor was it his first such experience. Quinn relates a profound boyhood dream in which a black beetle spoke to him saying, "We need to tell you the secret of our lives" (1994, 15–17). The beetle seemed to be inviting the young Quinn to view himself as part of a magical natural world. (Elements of these two experiences were fictionalized for his 2006 novel, *The Holy*).

Today, Quinn gives his religion as "animism," using an anthropological term self-consciously borrowed from E. B. Tylor's *Primitive Culture* (1871). Besides *Providence*, his most sustained discussion of animism is *The Story of B* (1996, 147–51) and *The Holy* (2006). Recognizing it as an etic, scholarly term rather than a traditional self-ascription and his own interpretation as something of a reformulation (FAQ 183), Quinn nevertheless holds animism to represent the original religion of humanity, and says that it is still universal among Leaver peoples (1996, 148): "Animism has no dogma, no set of universally-accepted beliefs" (FAQ 533). In any case, Quinn has "no religious beliefs to share with others" (FAQ 389). Nor does he belong, or desire to belong, to an animist spiritual community—for him it is simply a worldview (FAQ 151). Indeed, among animists, "religion" is often difficult to distinguish from everyday life (FAQ 658).

The nature of the gods is a thorny point in Quinn's animism. On one hand, he asserts that "the number of the gods cannot be determined by any means" (FAQ 518). This is in contrast to atheists, monotheists and polytheists, who respectively assert the number to be zero, one, or many. "Nor am I an agnostic; I'm not saying I DON'T KNOW whether God exists; I'm saying this knowledge is UNOBTAINABLE" (FAQ 538). Perhaps the gods serve as a kind of metaphor, or reflect an involuntary tendency to personify (see FAQ 518, 601, 618). That said, Quinn's writings often refer to divine entities, and seem to assume they have some basis in reality (which is understandable, considering his personal encounters with them). Having become disenchanted with the image of God as presented in the Abrahamic traditions (FAQ 534), Quinn argues that animistic gods are *less* anthropomorphic (1994, 156), although they behave in human-like ways in his stories (e.g., "Pablo" from *The Holy*). A useful comparison might be with the Yaqui worldview as presented by Carlos Casteneda. (Several of Quinn's fictional works touch on cosmology without, however, seeming to reflect his actual views.)[3]

As for Jesus, Quinn writes that he "has no special importance to me personally, no more than, say, Zoroaster or Diogenes." (The reference to Diogenes is no accident; Quinn admires the Jesus Seminar, several of whose members have interpreted Jesus as a Cynic. See FAQ 475.) Several FAQs (98, 450, 485) reject suggestions to the effect that Jesus might be considered a Leaver; Quinn instead calls him (or his popular image) "the prophet the Takers know they NEED" (FAQ 98), i.e., a sort of super-egoic symbol. Ishmael approvingly quotes Matthew 6: 25–34 ("Consider the lilies of the field […]") as Leaver-like, but notes that these *logoi* are almost universally received as impractical, even by Christians (1992, 228).

Despite his estrangement from Christianity, Quinn's writings constantly resort to biblical themes. Ishmael the gorilla, whose human sponsors are Jewish, owns three translations of the Bible as part of his personal library (1992, 165). Not only is his very name a biblical allusion (cf. Philip Kerr's 1997 novel *Esau*, which features yeti), and is affirmed as such in the text, but his contemplation of it is part of what elevates him to human-like consciousness (Quinn 1992, 16–18).

While primarily grounded in science and secular scholarship, Ishmael's teachings expound upon the Book of Genesis at considerable length, including almost the whole of *Ishmael* Chapter 9. Earlier versions of the book (Quinn had been working on it since 1977) bore titles like *The Genesis Transcript* and *The Book of Nahash* (Hebrew for "serpent") (Quinn 1994, 2). The Genesis theme is repeated in another early Quinn work, *Tales of Adam* (reprinted as Quinn and McCurdy 2007), a series of episodes in which Adam gives animist-themed advice to his son Abel.

Strangely for someone who regards the Abrahamic religions as negative influences, Quinn assumes the Hebrew Bible to contain reliable information about the Taker/Leaver conflict (cf. FAQ 619). Eden represents the cornucopia of earth under Leaver non-management. When Adam eats from the Tree of Knowledge of Good and Evil, this represents Taker man's decision to arrogate to himself (by means of totalitarian agriculture) divine power over life and death (1992, 159). The story of Cain and Abel constitutes a dim cultural memory, preserved by nomadic pastoral Semites, of violence by sedentary agriculturalists (1992, 171). At one point, Quinn considered, but rejected, the notion that the Hebrew prophets were really calling the Israelites back to a Leaver lifestyle (FAQ 50, cf. 1992, 169). Ishmael summarizes: "The story of Genesis must be reversed. First, Cain must stop slaughtering Abel […] And then, of course, you must spit out the fruit of that forbidden tree" (1992, 248).

Quinn's writings often reverse biblical or Christian imagery, suggesting that his former Catholicism remains a living influence on his thought. For example, in *The Holy* (2006), a Jewish private detective accepts a bizarre commission to search for Baal, Ashtaroth, Moloch, and the other "false gods" of the Old Testament. Gradually he learns that divine entities ("creatures at play in the fire of life") (Quinn 2006, 402) walk among us, undetected for the most part; that they are native to this planet; and that their nature is ethically neutral, neither angelic nor demonic. (Ethics is not a category Quinn finds useful; see FAQ 497, 508). At one point, the quest leads to a Satanic couple who invite the detective to join them in ritual sex magic (2006, 88). Quinn depicts the activity non-judgmentally, but elsewhere clarifies that he has no firsthand experience of Satanism (FAQ 630).

The plot of *The Story of B* (Quinn 1996) concerns Jared Osborne, a monk of the fictitious Order of St Lawrence, who is ordered to keep watch on itinerate philosopher Charles Atterley, known for some reason as "B." The Laurentians, we learn, were founded with a "special mandate" to watch for the appearance of the Antichrist. While few of them take their mandate seriously, by the end of the book, B himself embraces this title and is assassinated by a Laurentian agent. Explains Quinn: "Only a fundamentalist Catholic religious order, with strong roots in the Scholastic tradition, would be able to perceive and articulate to itself what a threat B's teachings pose" (FAQ 668). Quinn concedes that neither church nor state have yet shown much interest in his work. In answer to a concerned writer who asks, "Do you fear for your life? Should we?" Quinn acknowledges that "B's persecutor, Fr Lulfre is a far more improbable character than a dozen telepathic apes" (FAQ 375).

Quinn on Religion in General

Quinn views religion as a response to existential concerns. Taker culture, we are told, carries an immense psychological toll. Like a caged tiger at the zoo, we instinctively feel that *something* is fundamentally wrong with our way of life, even if we cannot fathom exactly why we are unhappy (1992, 11). But alienation and depression are predictable, natural reactions to a culture and lifestyle for which we as a species are not well suited. *My Ishmael* tells the story of "Jeffrey," a dropout who drowned himself out of despair over the meaninglessness of life, and the mundane choices available to him (1998, 196–7); *Beyond Civilization* explains that Jeffrey is modeled after Paul Eppinger, whose journal was published posthumously as *Restless Mind Quiet Thoughts* (Quinn 1999, 104).

Taker religions take advantage of our unhappiness, offering "solutions" that cannot possibly work. B tells his audience that

> Anywhere in the world, East or West, you can walk up to a stranger and say, "Let me show you how to be saved," and you'll be understood. You may not be believed or welcomed when you speak these words, but you'll be understood. (Quinn 1996, 241)

This is because Taker culture assumes there to be something wrong with humanity, which explains our present misery in contrast to the obvious rightness of our way of life: "The world was made for Man to conquer and rule, and [...] under Man's rule, the world might have become a paradise except for the fact that he's fundamentally and irredeemably flawed" (Quinn 1999, 183; cf. 1992, 82). Accordingly, our religions produce prophets of various types, whose role presumes that there is only one right way to live, which we do not yet know (but need a prophet to tell us). Quinn informs us that prophets are found only in Taker cultures, or in Leaver cultures reacting to Taker ones (1992, 85).

Needless to say, Leaver cultures do not share these presuppositions. To begin with, there is no one right way to live. (Of course, internal tribal laws inevitably exist, but the Yanomamö of the Amazon do not go around trying to convert others to their way of life.) To be sure, there are also *wrong* ways to live, but these sorts of problems can be expected eventually to sort themselves out (one way or another). Furthermore, members of Leaver cultures, in common with the entire animal kingdom, routinely acquire a sustainable way of life— not from prophets, but while growing up, under the guidance of elders who pass down time-tested tradition and experience. We who find ourselves ill-prepared to adopt such a lifestyle (after all, we cannot just pack up and join the Yanomamö) can at least take the trouble to learn from their examples.

Quinn has little good to say about the world's major religions, the ideas and behaviors of which he portrays as self-serving:

> These cultural siblings would smile on my work if I was willing to introduce animism into their company as a sort of retarded little brother,

but they're certainly going to object strenuously to my identifying it as humanity's ancient, mighty mainstream and relegating them to a very recently-formed (and now stagnant) backwater. (FAQ 77)

At best, they are the symptoms of a diseased culture (FAQ 101). In *Providence*, Quinn reports being asked to speak at an interfaith gathering, whose participants asked how to "reconcile their faiths with what they'd read in *Ishmael*" (1994, 159). Quinn was taken aback by the question, which suggested to him a kind of double-think. (Why should they want to do that, rather than abandon their religions as reason demands?)

As the reader may have detected, Quinn is fond of generalizing about religion, and it is difficult to escape the conclusion that his account is overly reductionist. In particular, it is doubtful whether his categories of Taker religion and Leaver religion (or animism) are adequate or even coherent. Do tribal people lose their status as Leavers when they convert to Christianity? Do Unitarian Universalists and Reform Jews maintain that there is only one right way to live? And what about non-missionary forms of Hinduism, whose adherents mostly take religious and cultural pluralism for granted?

At first glance, Buddhism seems to fit very well with Quinn's expectation that Taker religions perceive something to be wrong with the world and/or with us: *samsara* (the cycle of repeated births and deaths) is characterized by *anitya* (impermanence), *anatman* (lack of self) and *duhkha* (suffering), qualities that Mahayana tradition elaborates into the concept of *sunyata* (emptiness). At the same time, another Mahayana tradition of discourse speaks of "Buddha Nature" (*Buddhadhatu*, cf. *Tathagatagarbha*) or the potential to achieve Buddhahood, as the luminous, hidden essence within all beings. Certain sutras describe the mind as originally pure, though stained by adventitious defilements (*klesas*). A few go so far as to resort to language like "permanent, immutable, eternal" or even "the Self" (*atman*). In East Asian forms of Buddhism, such positive language is often applied to the world as a whole.[4]

Faced with such radical divergences, one might be tempted to doubt the authenticity of certain cycles of Buddhist teaching, or minimize their significance. This is in fact what Quinn does. In one place (FAQ 100), he suspects Buddha Nature of reflecting a westernized Buddhism and seems not to comprehend its venerable Asian pedigree. His comments call to mind the Theravadin bias common in older scholarly works. (Although the relationship between these apophatic and cataphatic strains is much debated, all Mahayana groups accept Buddha Nature in some form.) Elsewhere, in answer to the objection that "The Tibetans are or were a Leaver people at least until the invasion of the Taker Chinese," Quinn responds: "The fact that Tibet has a local variety of Buddhism doesn't change Buddhism any more than the fact that Haiti has a local variety of Christianity changes Christianity" (FAQ 28).

Yet, what form of Buddhism, or Christianity, is not "local"? Scholars of these religions would hesitate to identify certain versions of them as the standards against which the others are to be judged. If pagan elements are found in Haitian Catholicism, much the same is true of Italian Catholicism. Or, if we judge according to sheer numbers, then the world's several million Tibetans and Mongols may pale in significance to the Theravadin population, but these are in turn dwarfed by the Buddhists of East Asia. We might also wonder why traditional Tibet, with its mixed economy (of settled agriculture, pastoral nomadism and trade) and declining population (see Ekvall 1977) would be thought ecologically problematic.

To be sure, Quinn's remarks are not entirely unfounded. One never hears, for example, that thanks to Buddha Nature—because we and the universe are fundamentally pure and luminous—we are perfect just the way we are, spiritual practice is unnecessary and the sentient beings of the ten directions do not stand in need of liberation. While most Buddhists would reject the (supposedly pan-Taker) notions that the world was made for man, or that there is one right way to live, each group does generally assume its own path to be the most sublime. At the same time, Buddhism is generally found co-existing with, or incorporating, folk practices (some of them arguably pre-Buddhist) ranging from the "spirit houses" of Thailand (Tambiah 1970) to the "shamanic" aspect of Tibetan Buddhism (Samuel 1993). Quinn does not consider how to distinguish between Buddhism with animist aspects from an animism with Buddhist trappings, though his biblical examples are suggestive. As a practical matter, any reform which requires the wholesale abandonment of the world's major religions is unlikely to get very far.

Saving the World

Ishmael's ad seeks students with "an earnest desire to save the world." By "saving the world," Quinn means "preserving it as a viable home to life, including human life" (FAQ 702; cf. 1999, 6). In answer to a question about peak oil, he responds that

> maintaining and increasing our population of six billion is not at all equivalent to "saving the world." If the coming oil crisis results in a global famine and the death of billions (which is not unthinkable, though I am personally reluctant to make predictions about the future), then this would not work AGAINST the saving of the world, it would work FOR it. (FAQ 702)

What, then, is to be done? Quinn attempts to address the question are never very satisfactory, and he admits his lack of easy, universal solutions. Quinn wrote *Beyond Civilization* (1999) in answer to the thousands of readers who asked "I understand what you're saying […] but what are we supposed to DO about it?" Quinn at first thought the answer "obvious" (1999, 4), but by the close of the book is left exhorting the reader that "The dynamite ending is for you to write" (1999, 190).

Here it seems appropriate to explain what Quinn does *not* mean. To begin with, he is not urging a return to a lifestyle based on hunting and gathering (1998, 119). This is clearly impossible. Nor is he recommending the abandonment of cities or the economic system (1992, 250), although he often points to ancient cities that were mysteriously abandoned at some point (e.g., 1999, 44–8). The solution will not come from the government: the world will be saved not by "old minds with new programs, but by new minds with no programs at all" (1999, 8). As Ishmael puts it, "You're an inventive people, aren't you? You pride yourself on that, don't you? […] Then invent" (Quinn 1992, 250).

While it is not usually possible to become Leavers, we may at least make modest adjustments to our Taker lifestyle (FAQ 74). Very likely, the next stage will not involve a return to the Leaver way of life, so much as a struggle to find some third possibility that can realistically be sustained. In the end, however, "No paradigm is ever able to imagine the next one" (1999, 20). At one point, Ishmael proposes a "Seven-Point Plan" that is not a plan at all so much as an itemized general description: the revolution will happen incrementally, be led by no one, etc. (1998, 218). We are urged to "teach a hundred," some of whom will teach a hundred more, until the vision is unstoppable (1992, 248).

Unlike certain other anarchist writers, Quinn does not recommend violence against governmental or business institutions, and considers such actions futile and counterproductive (1999, 95). To the various questioners who ask whether they need to change careers, he invariably says no (for example, FAQ 559 is his reply to a sailor in the US Navy), and jobseekers are advised not to limit themselves to supposedly "noble" professions such as environmental activism (FAQ 593). Any revolution that depends on altruism is doomed:

> If the world is going to change, we must […] try to point people in a new direction in which to realize their interests (incrementally). This is what the New Tribal Revolution is about: not expecting people to embrace a poor life but showing them another way to attain a good life—a way that worked for humans for millions of years. (FAQ 481; cf. Quinn 1999, 86)

A key term in the Quinn lexicon is "tribal," and much of *Beyond Civilization* is devoted to explicating it. The term has no fixed anthropological definition, but Quinn uses it to mean "a coalition of people working together as equals to make a living" (1999, 147), preferably with continuity from generation to generation. This way of life, he says, is millions of years old, and as natural to humans as the behavior of various animal species is to those species (1999, 57–62). Accordingly, he speaks of a "New Tribal Revolution" that will gradually return us to these roots, though adjusted to take account of our changed circumstances. To illustrate, he offers the examples of circuses, gypsy bands and *The East Mountain News*, a small newspaper formerly published by himself, his wife and several others in Madrid, New Mexico (1999, 140).

Salvation through changes of worldview and lifestyle being a familiar religious theme, to what extent should fans of Daniel Quinn and *Ishmael* be regarded as a New Religious Movement? As Taylor points out (2010, ch. 1, and expanded on his website), the meaning and scope of the term "religion" is a subject of ongoing scholarly debate and many useful understandings have been proposed, not all of them mutually compatible. Terms like "parareligion," "quasi-religion" or "implicit religion" are available for religion-like phenomena which for whatever reason are thought not to qualify as religious. The category of "audience cult," which Stark and Bainbridge (1985, 169 ff.) recognize in their range of religious phenomena, seems particularly applicable here.

Quinn's New Tribal Revolution bears comparison to the Ron Paul Revolution. Both are decentralized movements whose participants turn to their respective leaders for answers to certain secular, but nevertheless fundamental, questions (a libertarian-style reformation of the US political system, the future of life on earth). Both movements give much attention to the dissemination of propaganda, often with great creativity and initiative. Some participants express a willingness to make great sacrifices for the sake of the ultimate goal. A crucial difference is that whereas few Ron Paul supporters have been moved to follow his example in the area of religion (Dr Paul is a Baptist), Quinn's online guestbook contains a number of posts from readers who indicate that they too have adopted animism as their religion. Note that Quinn disclaims divine authority, and urges readers to study for themselves rather than simply believe what he says (FAQ 616).

Further Criticisms

Although basically sympathetic, I am not quite persuaded by Quinn's arguments. To begin with, I find his Taker/Leaver distinction opaque, insofar as it conflates cultural attitudes (the conviction there is only one right way to live, the world is our dominion, etc.), lifestyle and social practices (e.g., mass agriculture, ownership of food, tribal organization), and the ultimate effect on the ecosystem (e.g., population growth, loss of diversity). It seems that Takers and Leavers cannot be distinguished solely by lifestyle, i.e., in how they obtain food (FAQ 551). According to Quinn, every aboriginal people encourages the regrowth of the foods it prefers, which is all that agriculture really amounts to (FAQ 210). By now, nearly all extant Leaver cultures have adopted sedentary agriculture (FAQ 407, 452). Pastoralism has historically been practiced by both Takers and Leavers (FAQ 123). Quinn clarifies that

> the emergence of our world-dominating culture was not dependent on one factor alone, the development of totalitarian agriculture. What made (and makes) us different are the beliefs that there is one right way for people to live (our way), and that everyone in the world must be made to live that way. (FAQ 623; cf. 123, 563)

I surmise that Takers are defined according to two criteria: a certain absolutist mindset and a lifestyle capable of supporting expansionism and population growth. (FAQ 563 suggests that the Mayan civilization possessed the second qualification, but not the first, and therefore avoids the "Taker" label.) Ecological consequences then follow as a matter of course.

As we have seen with the subject of religion, cultural attitudes are notoriously difficult to ascertain and hazardous to generalize about. Consider the spread of archaic humans across Eurasia and the Americas, which led to population growth and mass extinctions well before the Agricultural Revolution. Quinn sees a qualitative difference in the attitudes of totalitarian agriculturalists, who seek to eradicate pests; and Mesolithic hunters, who would not have desired the eradication of potential food sources had they been able to conceive of the possibility (FAQ 21; cf. 390). On the other hand, socio-biology and game theory encourage a view of both as opportunistic, but responding to different opportunities and threats. Indeed, one likely motivation for the Agricultural Revolution would have been a decline in the viability of hunting in the wake of the megafauna extinctions of the late Pleistocene and early Holocene periods. Quinn objects not to extinctions per se (these being inevitable in the course of evolution), but to the catastrophic loss of biodiversity which threatens to leave "nothing but rice and humans" (1992, 130) or, since this is impossible, system collapse.

In all probability, mass agriculture spread not as a result of missionary outreach by zealous farmers, but because of natural increase on the part of agriculturalists, the importation of brides into agricultural communities and imitation by rival outlying groups. Similarly, European colonialism was motivated not so much by the conviction that there is "one right way" to live, but by practical issues such as territory or trade, and involved competition among rivals with similar lifestyles. Apart from periodic campaigns against nomadism, states and religions have generally recognized the utility of various lifestyles (which can be difficult to distinguish from occupational specialties), concentrating on the promotion of particular identity markers.

And what exactly is "totalitarian agriculture"? Imagine a spectrum in which one extreme represents pure foraging (with a complete lack of input on the part of the forager), while the other extreme is marked by mass agriculture. At what point does a Leaver agriculturalist eat of the forbidden fruit, so to speak, and become a Taker agriculturalist? In answer to this, Quinn formulates what he calls the "law of limited competition," which he summarizes as follows: "You may compete to the full extent of your abilities, but you may not hunt down your competitors or destroy their food or deny them access to food" (FAQ 478; cf. 1992, 120). This last clause should be interpreted as "access to food in general" (Ishmael warns against "waging war" on competitors); otherwise, fenced gardens and guard dogs would constitute violations. Again, Quinn seems to confuse intent, actions and effects; one wonders how to regard cases where these are not perfectly consistent. At the risk of making too much of one remark, his Mayan example suggests that totalitarian agriculture may be practiced even by Leavers. (If them, why not us?)

Quinn disapproves of the human attitude of dominion (an impulse which he associates with the Fall of Man), yet all lifestyles must involve this to some extent. For that matter, Quinn urges us to influence the world in positive ways, e.g., by lowering food production. How can these be reconciled? Takers have arrogated unto themselves the power to decide who shall live and who shall die, yet Quinn approves of birth control (FAQ 670; cf. 1992, 181). I suppose that Quinn means for us to intervene only at the micro level and to refrain from attempting to control the world in general (or doing so indirectly, through incremental population growth). But then why should we sacrifice our immediate interests to save the world? Unless we admit altruism as a motivation (as Quinn seems reluctant to do), we are left with a "Prisoners' Dilemma" situation in which various competing groups must somehow be persuaded to cooperate with one another on ecological issues, when each would benefit from indulgence, and there is little chance of effective enforcement. (Any population group that practices birth control is likely to be swamped by other groups that do not.)

A number of agricultural societies, traditional as well as modern, have experienced zero or negative population growth from birth control, abortion, infant mortality and other factors. It occurs to me that these mimic the effects of food deprivation, with different climactic regions likely to require different levels of human intervention. A rise in consumption (e.g., through a shift of resources to meat or alcohol-based fuels) would also interfere with the simple formula of "more food equals more babies," though it would not address the underlying ecological imbalance. This may be the key to distinguishing, for example, present-day Taiwan (a food importer with a shrinking population) from the Siraya society of the seventeenth century (aboriginal Formosan hunter-agriculturalists who controlled their population through war and abortion; see Shepherd 1995). Although Taiwan's population has been shrinking lately, its ecological imprint is growing thanks to the island's participation in the global industrial economy and the law of comparative advantage. These enable more babies to be born elsewhere; therefore, the Taiwanese are to be numbered among the Takers.

Quinn anticipates that human overpopulation will eventually lead either to large-scale ecological collapse (FAQ 732 warns of "food chains dissolving like soap bubbles"), with humans in the role of the St Matthew Island reindeer;[5] or to the mass abandonment of Taker lifestyles, leaving at most a remnant of our former civilization. Although humans occupy the relatively precarious summit of the food chain, our resourcefulness and adaptability make us less vulnerable (for example, we are dietary generalists), and it is hard to imagine any ecological catastrophe that would not leave bands of survivors. (Could biodiversity really plummet to the extent that the planet's oxygen and food supply become insufficient to support any human life whatsoever?) As for the end of civilization, since societies based on mass agriculture tend to out-compete those based on other lifestyles (by virtue of their greater populations and superior resources), the most likely result of any collapse would not be total abandonment of the "Taker" way of life and its subsequent displacement by rival "Leaver" groups (if any then exist), but mere downscaling. For example, a fall of the world population to nineteenth-century levels would not prevent survivors from practicing mass agriculture or fielding militaries, albeit on a smaller scale. Depending on food supply, their population might even rebound to former levels, perhaps in perpetual cycles of expansion and contraction. In this light, even if the Taker lifestyle turns out to be unsustainable, our ancestors' decision to follow it allowed them to out-compete their Leaver rivals, resulting in a genetic advantage which may well persist even after a collapse or contraction.

Conclusion

Even if Quinn is wrong in expecting a total civilizational collapse (whether from overpopulation and overdevelopment, or from the deliberate abandonment of totalitarian agriculture), such large-scale threats as global warming and mass extinction suggest severe ecological limits to globalization. The prospect that civilization will falter, if not collapse, is viewed in some circles with intense yearning. While *Ishmael* remains obscure outside of certain subcultures, international reactions to the 2009 James Cameron film *Avatar* (which pitted rapacious human colonists against tribal aliens inhabiting a verdant extrasolar moon) point to a widespread, deep-seated sympathy for Ishmaelian ideas.[6]

Might globalist dreams be reformulated to reflect a "dark green" ethos, as Taylor suggests? Rather than an all-or-nothing choice between Taker and Leaver lifestyles, perhaps what is needed is a means of integrating the values (and comparative advantages) of civilization, with an emphasis on ecological repair—parks and preserves, gardens and greenbelts—alongside cultural autonomy and the rights of indigenous peoples. Quinn may have something like this in mind with his remarks in *Beyond Civilization*, when he speaks of the incremental adoption of some third way which we cannot yet imagine, and which offers more in terms of genuine human happiness. (In point of fact, it would be difficult to name any aboriginal group which is entirely separate from the world economy.) In any case, it is easy to see why Quinn's vision would evoke such a profound response, and why so many have come to see their highest aspirations reflected in the face of a gorilla.

Notes and References

1 While Quinn dislikes the term "spiritual" (he is unsure what it means), I am unable to think of a more appropriate label. It may be relevant that I first encountered *Ishmael* on a list of New Age books.

2 Animal husbandry seems basically similar to agriculture, but what are we to make of fishing, which is more akin to hunting or trapping? Since commercial fishermen do not subsist on seafood, or cattlemen on steak, I speculate that Quinn would group them with the Taker agriculturalists, whose diet they largely share thanks to market economics. Nomadic pastoralism ought to be considered analogous to ranching, for most forms turn out to be dependent on trade with settled agriculturalists. (Reindeer herding may be a potential exception; see Vitebsky 2006 and chapter fourteen of Mithen 2003.)

3 The frame story of *After Dachau* (Quinn 2001) is premised upon the reality of reincarnation and alternate timelines. *A Newcomer's Guide to the Afterlife* (Quinn and Whalen 1998) is a whimsical work that vaguely recalls the Spiritualist "Summerland." The graphic novel *The Man Who Grew Young* (Quinn and Elred 2002) imagines that at some point (the Big Crunch?), time will begin to flow backwards and we will relive our lives in reverse before returning to our origin.

4 The two quoted sections are taken from the *Srimaladevisimhanadasutra* and the (Mahayana) *Mahaparanirvanasutra*, respectively. For an introduction to the Buddha Nature/Tathagatagarbha literature, see Chapter 5 of Williams (2008).

5 In 1944, 29 reindeer were introduced to St Matthew Island (Alaska). By 1963, their population had swelled to 6,000. A few years later, nearly all of these died of starvation, having exhausted the island's food supply. Quinn's brief description may be found online: http://www.ishmael.org/Education/Science/carry_capacity.cfm (accessed August

3, 2012). For a more detailed account, see David R. Klein, "The Introduction, Increase, and Crash of Reindeer on St. Matthew Island." Online: http://dieoff.org/page80.htm (accessed August 3, 2012).

6 See Bron Taylor, (n.d.), "Avatar and dark green religion." Online: http://www.brontaylor. com/environmental_books/dgr/avatar_nature_religion.html (accessed August 3, 2012).

Cohen, J. E. 1995. *How Many People can the Earth Support?* New York: W. W. Norton and Co.

Ekvall, R. B. 1977. *Cultural Relations on the Kansu-Tibetan Border*. Chicago: University of Chicago Press. Online: http://www.case.edu/affil/tibet/booksAndPapers/EKVALL. htm?nw_view=1271778526& (accessed May 1, 2012).

Leakey, R. and R. Lewin. 1995. *The Sixth Extinction: Patterns of Life and the Future of Humankind*. New York: Random House.

Mithen, S. J. 2003. *After the Ice: A Global Human History 20,000–5000 BC*. London: Orion Books.

Quinn, D. 2006. *The Holy*. Hanover: Steerforth Press.

_____. 2002. *The New Renaissance*. Address delivered at the University of Texas Health Science Center in Houston. (March). Online: www.ishmael.org/Education/Writings/ The_New_Renaissance.shtml (accessed August 3, 2012).

_____. 2001. *After Dachau*. Hanover: Steerforth Press.

_____. 1999. *Beyond Civilization: Humanity's Next Great Adventure*. New York: Three Rivers Press.

_____. 1998. *My Ishmael: A Sequel*. New York: Bantam Books.

_____. 1996. *The Story of B*. New York: Bantam Books.

_____. 1994. *Providence: The Story of a Fifty-year Vision Quest*. New York: Bantam Books.

_____. 1992. *Ishmael: An Adventure of the Mind and Spirit*. New York: Bantam Books.

Quinn, D. and A. D. Thornhill. 1998. *Food Production and Population Growth*. [Audiotape] Houston.

Quinn, D. and M. McCurdy. 2005. *Tales of Adam*. Hanover: Steerforth Press.

Quinn, D. and T. Elred. 2002. *The Man Who Grew Young*. New York: Context Books.

Quinn, D. and T. Whalen. 1998. *A Newcomer's Guide to the Afterlife: On the Other Side Commonly Known as "The Little Book."* New York: Bantam Books.

Samuel, G. 1993. *Civilized Shamans: Buddhism in Tibetan Societies*. Washington: Smithsonian Books.

Shepherd, J. R. 1995. *Marriage and Mandatory Abortion among the Siraya*. Arlington: American Ethnological Society.

Stark, R. and W. S. Bainbridge. 1985. *The Future of Religion*. Berkeley: University of California Press.

Tambiah, S. J. 1970. *Buddhism and the Spirit Cults in Northeast Thailand*. Cambridge: Cambridge University Press.

Taylor, B. R. 2010. *Dark Green Religion: Nature Spirituality and the Planetary Future*. Berkeley: University of California Press.

Vitebsky, P. 2006. *The Reindeer People: Living with Animals and Spirits in Siberia*. Boston, MA: Houghton Mifflin.

Williams, P. 2008. *Mahayana Buddhism: The Doctrinal Foundations*. 2nd edn. New York: Routledge.

Wilson, E. O. 2003. *The Future of Life*. New York: Random House.

Chapter 4

GLOBALIZED RELIGION: THE VEDIC SACRIFICE (*YAJÑA*) IN TRANSCULTURAL PUBLIC SPHERES

Silke Bechler

University of Heidelberg, Germany

Introduction

In times of flux, such as our current era of globalization, culture and cultural identity can become more meaningful for individuals who may feel alienated or even threatened by forces beyond their control. To make sense of their changing surroundings, people accordingly emphasize their uniqueness and exclusiveness by referring to their group's common ancestry, history, language or religion, as well as to shared customs or values. Identification is made as such with cultures or, as Samuel Huntington (1996) argued in his highly influential book *The Clash of Civilizations and the Remaking of World Order*, with civilizations. Of the many elements helping to define civilization, one of the most important is religion. Of Max Weber's five world religions, four—Christianity, Islam, Hinduism and Confucianism—are associated with major civilizations and are, therefore, as Dawson (1978) suggests, "the foundations on which the great civilizations rest" (128).

While focusing on the "West" as one civilizational entity and Hindu civilization as another representing the so-called "East," the present paper investigates globalization's impact on religious practices through an analysis of *yajña*, an Indian form of worship with ancient Vedic roots characterized by the act of giving oblation to divinities through sacrificial offerings into fire. At first sight, it might seem strange to focus on this traditionally Indian ritual to understand globalization's significance, but this rite currently occurs in both East and West, where it is conducted by people from either civilizational tradition whose ideas and intentions associated with the rite differ accordingly. It is this transnational and transcultural presence of *yajña* that make it a useful subject by which to analyze the effects of globalization on world religions and civilizations.

Beginning by briefly defining *yajña* and its numerous manifestations, the *yajña*'s ritual performance within contemporary Hindu civilization and abroad is first examined. The discussion then turns to how *yajña* has spread from India to evolve within new cultural contexts worldwide. In our current era, when religion as a factor has achieved greater importance in world affairs, people living in Western nations have begun to adopt non-Western religious practices. Often emphasized as a reaction to Western decline, ancient rituals are now being altered and reinterpreted by performers searching for ways to adjust cultural identities to new global obligations.[1] As will be shown, *yajña* has subsequently broken out of its former socially limited context into new transnational and transcultural public spheres, transforming itself in the process into a global phenomenon.

The Vedic Sacrifice (*Yajña*) in its Contemporary Form

Generally understood as a divine act, *yajña* dates back to the Vedic period in South Asian history. Already mentioned in Puruṣasūkta (Ṛgveda X.90.16), where the gods themselves created and worshipped *yajña*, the ritual act's roots lie in the religious practices of India's earliest peoples.[2] Until today, the practice of *yajña* itself has undergone many changes and modifications, most of which cannot be investigated here but which make it necessary to define this rite in terms of its contemporary forms and variations.

Definition

The term *yajña* refers to a traditionally Indian act of worship or devotion, during which various oblations are offered into one or more sacrificial fires (*agni*) and transferred, with the help of the fire-god Agni, to specific gods or goddesses approached by individuals or groups for assistance. It is traditionally practiced for one or more of the four following reasons:

1. to destroy all evil forces (*duṣṭa*);
2. to seek protection of oneself (*rakṣana*) from negative forces;
3. to attain a worldly wish (*sakāma*) (i.e., wealth, prosperity, good health, long life, the removal of obstacles, etc.);
4. to please the divine power in an unselfish way without any desire (*niṣkāma*).

As a central force activating the divine power, specific mantras are recited during the performance to guarantee a positive ritual outcome.

Various forms of yajña

Over time, various forms of *yajña* developed that intermingled and resulted in an elaborate system all subsumed under this common term. In general, five main forms—*homa*, *havana*, *yajña*, *yāga* and *kratu*—can be distinguished, each form linked to specific technical characteristics, ranging from the ordinary to the extraordinary.

According to Monier-Williams (1872), the term *homa* defines "the act of making an oblation to the *devas* or gods by casting clarified butter into the fire" (1178). In contemporary practice, it is not just clarified butter (*ghṛta*) offered into the sacrificial fire, but an assortment of natural oblations (*havirdravya*). As an essential element of domestic (*gṛhya*) rites, *homa* may be performed by a single person, generally the head of a household. A priest is not mandatory.

The term *havana* defines simply "the act of offering an oblation with fire" (Monier-Williams 1872, 1168). According to Ranade (2006), the main offering made in this case is the *śatarudriya* (327), a mixture of various grains. *Havana* is generally performed by a small group of people with strong familial ties. Here, the family priest (*purohita*) may be consulted, but his attendance is not required.

Whereas the term *yajña* on the one hand defines the "act of worship" or in general any "devotional act" (Monier-Williams 1872, 802), it refers at the same time to a specific form of sacrifice. The materials being offered into the sacrificial fire vary in quality as well as quantity. Today, 108 different kinds of natural oblations (*havirdravya*) can be distinguished that serve various specific purposes. Beside these natural materials, cooked oblations (*pākayajña*) are given to the fire as well. For performing the more complicated ritual sequences, priestly support is essential. At least three priests are needed—the *adhvaryu*, the acting priest generally performing all physical ritual actions laid down in the Yajurveda; the *hotṛ*, the priest invoking the gods or goddesses by reciting specific mantras mostly related to the Ṛgveda; and the *udgātṛ*, the priest praising the *devas* by singing the songs of praise (*sāman*) written down in the Sāmaveda. Clearly, great effort is required to perform this form of *yajña*, which is usually conducted for the benefit of a larger community beyond family and kin.

The most sophisticated and grandest form of *yajña* currently performed is *yāga*. Here, copious amounts of oblations are offered, usually into several sacrificial fires. As *yāga* is a costly form of sacrifice, it may only be initiated by worshippers from an affluent sector of society. Generally, it is performed before a very large audience such as for the people of an entire region or even country.

With the lofty aim of fulfilling the wishes of the entire universe, *kratu* was performed in former times. It is not carried out today as it is an exorbitant form of sacrifice. But the intention to become a *śatakratu*—a person who has performed a hundred *yajñas* during his/her life—is still viewed as desirable, indicating that a person associated with *yajña* sacrifice on a large scale is still greatly respected.

The Vedic Sacrifice (*Yajña*) in Contemporary Hindu Civilization

The development of Hindu civilization and its political and religious impact on the Indian subcontinent

In its earliest form, Vedic civilization—today's so-called Hindu civilization—can be traced back to at least 1,500 BCE. Able to construct towns in a systematic way, endow them with a functional water supply system, and use common seals and a shared script, the inhabitants of the Indus Valley at the time were members of a highly advanced ancient civilization.[3]

Regarding religious practices, this early civilization did not possess any temple cults, but erected sacrificial altars (*vedi*) with fireplaces in order to communicate with gods and goddesses. The main aim of their sacrificial practices was the nourishment and strengthening of divine powers to conserve the cosmos. Sacrificial practices as such were viewed as part of a ritual communication system that supported the reciprocal relationship believed to exist between human beings and deities.

The first ideological division associated with religious practices emerged in the fifth century BCE, when a metaphysical worldview developed. Life was regarded as suffering and therefore its thoughts merely concentrated on salvation, which now could be achieved either through sacrifice or through renunciation. When Brahmin priests started to control sacrifice as one path to salvation, several reform movements developed in order to fight against the dominant Brahmanism. Especially ascetic groupings emerged that emphasized the aim of escaping the cycle of rebirth (*saṃsāra*) through renunciation.[4]

With the expansion of the Indian kingdoms of the late Vedic period, dating from 850 to 500 BCE, it became necessary for ruling forces to provide protection to their people as well as to their religion. As a result, in the late Gupta period about 1,000 years later, a symbiotic relationship between politics and religion emerged in which numerous Brahmans linked their duties to royal service. During this time, several priests became advisors to the royal courts, where the kings in turn lavished gifts on them and offered them land. In this manner, some temples rapidly accumulated great wealth.

After the early Muslim invasions of the eleventh century CE and the emergence of the Mogul Empire about three hundred years later, Western civilization was gradually able to expand its influence on the Indian subcontinent. With the establishment of British East India Company rule in 1600, Great Britain gradually became the dominant power in Indian politics. Initially basing their trade on Indian cotton fabrics, the Company established its authority across the subcontinent by both force and persuasion. The first challenge for colonial rule occurred with the Indian rebellion of 1857—the "Sepoy Mutiny"—prompted by religious tensions linked to British attempts to westernize India (Olson 1996, 567). As a result of the uprising, British East India Company rule was abolished in 1858 and India came under the direct authority of the British Crown. In 1876, Queen Victoria assumed the title "Empress of India," which was proclaimed at the Delhi Durbar one year later, and eventually proved to be a milestone in the history of Indian nationalism.

British criticism of indigenous religious practices linked to a desire to spread Christianity and Western values were key factors that generated local religious reform movements in the nineteenth and twentieth centuries. Among many influential Indian leaders of reform, Rām Mohan Roy, who founded the Brāhma Samāj in 1828 to publicize what he saw as the true Vedanta that had been later corrupted by Buddhist and Brahmanical influences, accepted Western critiques of the caste system (*varṇa*) and the ritual of widow burning (*satī*) but emphasized Europeans' overall lack of knowledge regarding Hinduism. In 1875, Dayānanda Sarasvatī established the Ārya Samāj, another highly political organization devoted to restoring a purely Vedic religion. With Svāmī Vivekānandas's foundation of the Rāmakrishna Mission in 1897, a particularly monistic doctrine was introduced based on Śaṃkara's teachings, naming the universal Soul or divine essence (*brahman*) as the highest entity. It is remarkable that all these movements, at least to some extent, inherited aspects of Western criticism but did not adopt Christianity. Rather, according to von Stietencron (2001), a new form of "modern Hinduism" arose (83).

Contemporary practices of yajña *on the Indian subcontinent*

Looking closely at the various forms of *yajña*—*homa*, *havana*, *yajña*, *yāga* and *kratu*—it becomes obvious that these are closely related to the status of the initiator (*yajamāna*) and, accordingly, to his capability. The more he invests on a material as well as on a financial level, the broader the attracted audience will be. Or, briefly speaking, higher investments transfer the *yajña* from the private to the public sphere.

Homa and *havana* are, as outlined above, performed within a merely private context. Generally, the initiator (*yajamāna*) of this form of *yajña* seeks to acquire prosperity; to live a healthy and long life; to remove obstacles or enemies; to gain success, knowledge and wisdom; to gain protection from accidents; or to influence a marriage by identifying an appropriate life partner. In short, the main intentions for performing *homa* and *havana* are based on personal interests and needs, with initiators often trying to overcome individual difficulties in life. *Homa* may easily be performed by a single person; priestly support is not necessarily required. Whereas in former times, the head of the household (*gṛhastha*) generally carried out the whole ritual procedure, today no restrictions regarding the actor are given.[5] *Havana* in contrast is commonly performed by a small group of people, usually related through family ties. Here, the family priest (*purohita*) may be consulted, but his attendance is not obligatory. Today, even the required enclosed space for the consecrated fire, the so-called *agnikuṇḍa*, may be purchased in the form of a ready-made copper container, making the ritual an easy, clean and safe procedure.

In contrast, *yajña* and *yāga* are today mainly performed as major public events. Initiated by religious organizations, wealthy business people or political parties, these forms of *yajña* are practiced with differing intentions. Commonly performed for reasons such as to protect a cultural heritage, benefit the environment, defend oppressed classes, encourage happiness and world peace, or combat disease, *yajña* of this kind are at the same time often used to promote organizers' personal interests, mainly through an increase of social prestige. Merchandized with the help of the media and often accompanied by media coverage, *yajña* and *yāga* attract large audiences at sacrificial venues (*yāgaśāla*). Nowadays, *yajña* and *yāga* as such have evolved into highly stage-managed public spectacles or even festivals.

As the next section discusses, the performance of *yajña* in contemporary India is not simply the continuation of an ancient ritual practice but a means to emphasize practitioners' cultural heritage and identity in times of globalization. In the tradition of nineteenth- and twentieth-century reform movements, supplicants' desire to adhere to a purely Vedic practice highlights how a practice from ancient Hindu civilization can be utilized to define cultural identity through contrast with the traditions and beliefs of "others"– particularly those associated with the Western Judeo-Christian heritage. By integrating and adopting certain Western ideas, organizers react to modern demands and in turn stabilize their own unique community. In gaining support among members through its ritualistic practices, the community more readily represents and defends itself from perceived external threats. Accordingly, a close relationship between politics and religion is maintained to secure and increase adherents' identity positions in their own country as well as in the world at large.

The practice of yajña *in a globalized Hindu civilization*

The Hindu diaspora

Hinduism is not only the dominant religion on the Indian subcontinent, but of many Indians living in the diaspora. Today, according to the *Encyclopedia Britannica Online* (2010), there are about 840 million Hindus in 144 countries, comprising approximately 14 percent of the world's total population (*CIA World Fact Handbook* 2010).

According to Vertovec (2000), the history of large-scale migration of Hindus to other countries can be divided into two periods. The first, involving the mass outward flow of Indian labor, took place in the nineteenth and early twentieth centuries. Under contract labor schemes, many people from the Indian subcontinent migrated to countries such as Mauritius, Guyana, Surinam, Trinidad, Jamaica and other British and French West Indian Islands, South Africa, East Africa, Fiji, Burma and Malaysia.

Following World War II, the second period was characterized by migration movements to industrialized Western nations. Initially dominated by students and businessmen, the main destination at this time was Great Britain, to which large numbers of skilled and semi-skilled laborers flocked in the 1950s and early 1960s. Later, many students and professionals shifted farther afield, to the United States, Canada, Australia and New Zealand. In the 1970s, skilled laborers from South Asia ventured in significant numbers to the Gulf States.

Since the 1980s there has been a rise in the number of "twice migrants"— those moving from one part of the diaspora to another.[6] This spike is largely characterized by East African Asians moving to Britain, Indo-Surinamese to the Netherlands, Indo-Guyanese to Canada and Indo-Fijians to New Zealand.

Religious practices in the Hindu diaspora

In the early twentieth century, especially in Europe, Hinduism was propagated in the diaspora by modern Indian religious movements reinterpreting Hinduism according to Western values or Western Orientalist movements, as for instance the Theosophical Society, which approached Hinduism through an Indian spiritualism (Burghart 1987, 6). This propagation was accentuated through lectures and pamphlets broadcast in private homes and rented halls. During the second migration phase migrants began to establish Hindu religious institutions. With the foundation of numerous cultural associations, several local leaders gained a lofty reputation by organizing religious, cultural and charitable functions to benefit their communities. Throughout the 1960s, many temple trusts were founded to establish devotional centers in the West, with the first temple opening its doors in Leicester, Great Britain in 1969 (Burghart 1987, 9).

Taking a closer look at ritual procedures performed by these diasporic communities, it becomes obvious that many rituals are shortened, refashioned, or eclectically performed. Although local groups prefer that ritual acts be performed according to their regional traditions, such events very often become standardized to attract a larger community. According to Knott (1987), this process has led to the emergence of what might be termed "popular Hinduism" (158); using different terminology, Burghart (1987) labels this phenomenon "trans-ethnic Hinduism" (14).

Contemporary practices of yajña in the Hindu diaspora

At first glance, there seem to be few differences between *yajña* performed on the Indian subcontinent and in the diaspora. Even outside of India, the four variations—*homa*, *havana*, *yajña* and *yāga*—are the dominant ritual forms. The first two are closely related to activities in the private realm, whereas *yajña* and *yāga* are again linked to public events. Upon closer inspection, however, various modifications are associated with *yajña* according to the locality and context in question.

According to Smith (2000), the first public *yāga* outside the Indian subcontinent was performed in 1996 in Roundwood Park, London.[7] Sponsored by several diasporic Hindu communities, the ritual performance was promoted by planners as an authentic Hindu practice. Yet, as was demonstrated in this instance, it would appear that *yajñas* performed outside the Indian subcontinent are usually adjusted to their new environment and local requirements.

One of the most obvious challenges during London's *yajña*—and one of the difficulties nearly every diasporic public *yajña* has to deal with—was the arrangement of the officiating priests (*rtvik*). As the style of the ritual is one of the essential components that already differentiated Vedic ritual practice in India from region to region, the origin of the performing priests is of crucial importance. Stylistic elements vary from reciting techniques to ways to hold sacrificial spoons used for pouring the offerings into the sacrificial fire. As soon as the required priests do not belong to the same traditional background the performance unavoidably has to be based on a compromise (Smith 1996, 254–6).

Further, nowadays formerly prescribed ritual observances—especially for the initiator (*yajamāna*)—are rarely followed (Smith 1996, 256). Just the simple vow that no one should touch the *yajamāna* during the performance is particularly in the Western context unavoidable, as during a public event the shaking of hands is an indispensible social gesture.

Figure 4.1. A devotee preparing to offer clarified butter (*ghṛta*) into the sacrificial fire, Bangalore 2009.

Source: Silke Bechler.

During the first London *yajña* in 1996, the *yajamāna* directed the attention of the audience from the ritual performance towards actions of greater familiarity and popularity. Therefore, he used narrative as well as musical elements between major ritual sequences, in order to explain the performance and to make it more attractive (Smith 1996, 253). Similarly, contemporary *yajña* in general is often reinterpreted in a way to give participants an active role. While the acting priest (*adhvaryu*) alone is said to hold the right to give offerings into the fire according to ancient scriptures, today's offerings are frequently handled by the audience as well (Fig. 4.1).[8] In bestowing the participants with responsibility for offerings, both the importance of the ritual and a feeling of community are stressed.

As can be observed during the participation of various *yajñas* performed in the Hindu diaspora as well as on the Indian subcontinent, these are contemporary occurrences that are usually accompanied by a rich cultural program enhanced by new media and technologies. Broadcast across the sacrificial arena, lectures or music entertain the crowd on the one hand and promote the religion to external viewers on the other. To strengthen promotional efforts, inexpensive booklets, cassettes, CDs and DVDs are also sold. In this way, the ritual becomes a public spectacle, constantly focusing on the enlargement of the community.

Nonetheless, according to Knott (1987) several common ritual elements are shared in all contexts—for instance, homage (*praṇāma*), purification (*śuddhi*), petition (*prārthana*), praise (*bhajana*), offering (*upacāra*) and the sharing of sacred food (*prasāda*)—though their order of appearance might differ slightly (175–6). In particular, the last element, the communal meal, has—as already emphasized by Smith (1886)—an important uniting social function.

Western Civilization and Christendom

Western civilization

According to Kurth (2001), Western civilization was formed through the interactions of three distinct traditions:

1. the classical Greek and Roman tradition;
2. the Christian religion;
3. the Enlightenment tradition of the modern era.

Western civilization is usually understood either as a synthesis of all three threads or as distinct traditions in constant conflict. Carroll Quigley (1961) argues in *Evolution of Civilizations: An Introduction to Historical Analysis* that Western civilization emerged around 500 CE after the collapse of the Western Roman Empire, leaving a place for new ideas that were untenable in classical societies.

Kurth (2003/04) points out that the term "Western civilization" itself first appeared in the nineteenth century in the wake of the European Enlightenment, an event which had served to secularize Europe's intellectual elite. With the rising influence of North America also at this time and then especially after World War II, it increasingly came to be associated with the United States' self-professed values of individualism, democracy and liberty. Yet while the US saw itself as unlike Europe, which it portrayed as a region hopelessly besieged by oppression, class conflict, hierarchy and backwardness, Huntington (1996) rightly observes that it was both American energy and the European cultural legacy that bestowed legitimacy and power upon the concept of Western civilization.

The post-1945 era witnessed a further redefining of "the West" in relation to "the East" and other world regions. The Cold War, which dominated international affairs until the fall of the Berlin Wall in 1989, saw "the West" as linked to "capitalism" and "liberal democracy" and its associated values, while "the East," in the eyes of Americans and their Western European allies, was associated with "socialism," "communism," and "totalitarianism."

Meanwhile, the decolonization process associated with the receding influence of Great Britain and France and the successes of anti-colonial independence movements in Africa and Asia, led to the birth of the "Third World," or in contemporary parlance, "the Global South," leading to further civilizational tensions and divisions as so-called "First World" and "Second World" nations vied for political and economic influence in this region in the postcolonial era from the 1960s and after (Kurth 2003/04).

After the Cold War, at the end of the last century when globalization quickly became a watchword, Western civilization headed towards a crisis. To cope with the rising economic and political status of Asian nations, the West began to redefine itself, but now as a transnational, multicultural entity. By comparison, the "New East" defined itself by referring to its religious heritage—especially in regards to Islamic and Hindu traditions—a crucial factor missing in the West (Huntington 1996).

The impact of religion on Western civilization

As outlined earlier, one of the most important elements defining civilization is religion. Western civilization in this regard has often been viewed as interchangeable with Western Christendom.

During its first century of existence, Christendom conquered gradually the whole Roman Empire, then spread within Persia, Armenia, Georgia, Ethiopia, Sudan, India, Arabia, Asia, Germania and Slavonia. With Islamic expansion commencing in the seventh century CE, however, religious boundaries were redrawn and Islam came to prevail in the Orient, North Africa and Asia.

Even this period was characterized by an array of understandings of the Christian faith, as well as by various attempts to create unity within Christendom. Thus, *ab initio* the necessity existed to demarcate this religion from external influences. This process of restoring identity was not avoidable, but at the same time reduced the Christian movement in its ubiquity, by simply making Christianity unable to incorporate other religious traditions' ideas and practices any longer.

As Kurth (2003/04) posits, Christendom shaped Western civilization in many ways. Even in its early history, Christian theology called for obedience to Christ as the highest authority, higher than any secular ruler. Later emphasized by the papacy of the Roman Catholic Church and its antagonist the local monarchs of the Holy Roman Empire, this idea supported the separation of powers. The religious and political partition was formally laid down in the Treaty of Westphalia in 1648, when the concept of the sovereign nation-state was born. The proceeding secularization process culminated in the Western world in the eighteenth century—in North America in 1776 with the

Declaration of Independence, which constituted the USA as a secular state; and in Europe after the French Revolution in 1789 and the Napoleonic Era, which finally led to a rearrangement of sovereign European nation-states. At the same time, the importance of religion steadily declined, particularly in the political realm.[9]

Although the great political ideologies of the twentieth century, to wit particularly "Marxism," "communism" and "socialism," are all products of Western civilization, the West generated not a single major religion on its own.[10] The world's major religions all have non-Western origins and, in the majority of cases, even precede Western civilization. Especially after the Cold War, when Western ideologies obviously declined, religions have continued to be linked to cultural identity worldwide. The Westphalian separation of religion and politics, a distinctive product of Western civilization, is responsible for the decline of religion on the Western side, yet religion today seems "increasingly to intrude into international affairs" (Mortimer 1991, 7).

Challenges to Western civilization

According to Huntington, when Western expansion ended, "the revolt" of the "New East" "against the West" began (Huntington 1996, 53). Although even after colonial rule the West continued to have a significant impact on other civilizations, international relations were dominated by the reactions of non-Western civilizations, which began to shape their own history and, by implication, the history of the West. At the same time, conflicts among Western states declined in frequency and intensity.

The economic development of Asia—especially of India and China—in the 1990s lead to further integration of the world's leading economies. As economic exchange may bring people into contact but not necessarily into agreement (Huntington 1996, 218), the rise of Asia led to political instability, insofar as it created fear among the Western states and challenged once again the balance of power. Consequently, the economic development of Asia and the rising confidence of Asian societies disrupted international politics. On the one hand, the situation has enabled Asian states to expand their military capabilities, on a technological as well as on a quantitative level, and promote uncertainty as to the future relationships among the Asian counties itself; on the other hand, it has strengthened conflicts between Asian societies and the West and increased the capability of Asia to prevail in those struggles.

Another challenging factor for the West is the current change in its demographic balance. This development is nothing new, as throughout human history political, economic and social tensions have often been linked to population shifts. Massive migration movements, sometimes peaceful, sometimes violent, have been associated with such shifts. During the middle of the last century, mass migrations occurred worldwide as a result of state policies encouraging inward and outward population flows as well as advances in transportation. The result has been what at least one author has called a "global migration crisis."[11] Regarding the demographic issue, migrants coming to the West are associated with higher fertility rates than average Western families and hence account for most population growth. As a result, Westerners increasingly fear, in the words of Weiner (1995), that "they are now being invaded not by armies and tanks but by migrants who speak other languages, worship other gods, belong to other cultures" (2) and who "will take their jobs, occupy their land, live off the welfare system, and threaten their way of life" (2). These fears, often exaggerated but nonetheless grounded in the demographic context just mentioned, Hoffmann (1990) remarks, "are based on genuine cultural clashes and worries about national identity" (30).

More significant than economic change and demographic shifts for Huntington (1996) is the problem of Western cultural decline, a development he believes manifests itself in terms of the following trends:

1. increased frequency of antisocial behaviors;
2. familial breakdown;
3. declining social capital;
4. a weakening "work ethic"; and
5. decreased interest in learning and intellectual activities.[12]

Huntington notes as well that many Westerners perceive Western culture as being challenged by immigrants from non-Western civilizations who do not integrate into their new nations of residence, but prefer to retain and propagate the values, customs and traditions of their home civilizations.

On an individual level, Huntington (1996) further suggests that modernization generates feelings of alienation and anomie as traditional relations and social bonds are broken, leading to crises of identity for which religion may provide answers.

Yajña *in the West*

Whereas *yajña* in the Hindu diaspora seems to be an explainable phenomenon, *yajña* performed in the West for Westerners may seem rather odd at first glance. But such cultural adaptation is in some ways a natural development. Diaspora communities, as Yang and Ebaugh (2001) have shown, generally move from particularism to universalism in their outlooks, especially regarding membership in associations. This shift at least partly occurs because Hinduism in the diaspora must accommodate itself to the diverse indigene traditions of its adherents. Toward this end, religious centers incorporate various customs. From here, it is but a small step to go beyond religious and ethnic boundaries to include Westerners seeking new religious paths.

In the 1960s, various spiritual leaders ventured from India to the West to recruit students from the hippie generation seeking love, peace and harmony in an age of war and conflict. As stated by Carey (1987), the initial plan of these leaders was to change the West from within to save India from rushing into modernity. As a result, various organizations were founded in the West based on traditional Hinduism, including the International Society for Krishna Consciousness (ISKCON) and the Transcendental Meditation (TM) movement. Today, many of these groups conduct *yajñas* on a regular basis to stabilize and expand their community in the West. As these are generally performed as public events, the two forms of *yajña* and *yāga* clearly dominate.

What compels Westerners to attend and participate in these events? Are they simply "exotic" happenings they want to experience or do they seek religious elements they cannot find in their own tradition? Indeed, both factors may be relevant. But as many public *yajñas* are connected to charitable projects, they also provide the opportunity to support people or organizations in need. In such a fashion, people from the West reposition themselves into a dominant position simply by providing financial support and by using an extrinsic religious element while forging a new cultural identity.

Very recently, *yajñas* have even been repackaged in such a way so as to serve a niche market for Western consumers. In 2008, for example, the European non-profit organization Yoga Vidya (2008) organized a 1,008-hour *yajña* in Bad Meinberg, Germany. While the organizer emphasized the spiritual aspects of the event, the participants were offered a rich program focusing on health treatment, wellness and recreation. By appealing to the personal and religious desires of a purely Western-oriented clientele, a new spiritual market was created in which a single religious element was transferred into a new social context, in the process fulfilling the holidaying, personal care and leisure needs of Westerners. The success of this *yajña* resulted in Yoga Vidya's attempt to organize it—even though on a smaller scale—on a monthly basis.

Technologies have long been used by religious organizations to promulgate their aims (Jansen, Tapia and Spink 2010). One of the best early examples is the printing press adopted by religious reformers during the Protestant Reformation in sixteenth-century Europe. Today, religion has gone even more hi-tech with improvements in audiovisual technologies and the advent of the Internet. *Yajña* is no stranger to this trend, having now become part of the virtual world. The Pranashakty Mission, for example, regularly organizes "live" *homas*, which are advertised on their website www.pranashakty.org as "free event(s) […] conducted for the benefit of all who participate," who are promised "special energy activation" (n.d.). After registering online, participants, most of them coming from a Western spiritual background, are emailed instructions about how to join the event. Participants are instructed how to sit during the ceremony in a cross-ledged position or on a chair with the spine straight and are also provided with a time zone converter, essential for knowing at which moment the *homa* is being performed in Penang, Malaysia. Participants also receive a link that allows them to view the performance at home on their computer screens. For further convenience, participants who are not able to view the ceremony at the right time are given a mantra to read at the moment when all participants will receive the promised energy.

In this highly technical form, *yajña* becomes a global event, accessible to anyone anywhere in the world. In its virtual form, this ritual practice has completely left its original domain, adapting and appealing to a new—now Western—public sphere, regardless of its original context.

Conclusion

How may current global shifts in spiritual beliefs and practices be explained? Why has a ritual like *yajña* become important for people living in countries around the world and belonging to different civilizations? Further, how has the ritual of *yajña* itself been reshaped in new global contexts? These are the questions that inevitably arise after one investigates the appearance of *yajña* in different public spheres.

Surely, particular social forces operate everywhere. The most evident and most powerful one, notes Huntington (1996), was paradoxically supposed to bring about the death of religion: namely, the process of "modernization" that captivated the world in the late twentieth century. Yet with the increased geographical mobility and global interactions associated with modernization, individuals have become increasingly estranged from their original cultural roots and identities. As they seek to reconnect to their heritage or find fresh answers to life's questions, they create and interact in new networks with ever larger numbers of people in ever wider geographical zones of influence. Rather than making religion less relevant, modernizing processes have instead prompted new quests for sources of identity, with religion being one such source.

As Hassan al-Turabi (2009) notes, all religions supply "people with a sense of identity and a direction in life" (68). Further, religious groups are small social communities, within which identity can be rediscovered or created. Whatever their goals may be, religions provide people identity simply by distinguishing between believers and non-believers.

In performing a common ritual, participants confirm and consolidate their identities. What occurs during the performance of *yajña* is no exception; an ancient practice is revitalized on the one hand and a common tradition is confirmed on the other. *Yajña* in the process moves from the private to the public sphere, its importance for both individual and community augmented. Promulgated through new media and technologies, the ritual becomes more widely known and spreads to those living beyond communal boundaries.

As *yajña* as a practice spreads to new geographic regions, either physically or virtually, it inevitably is forced to adapt to previously unfamiliar contexts. Whereas in former times the ritual was mainly viewed as a means for individuals to overcome personal difficulties in life, social problems and community needs have come to shape where and why *yajña* is performed in contemporary contexts. In addition to its intrinsic value as a cultural asset, *yajña* in global contexts today is also associated with such issues as the provision of healthcare, education, disaster relief and other forms of social welfare. In a sense, contemporary forms of *yajña* have come to be seen as philanthropic events with both symbolic and practical significance for practitioners' communities and cultures.

The adoption of non-Western religious elements and practices in Western civilization might be seen as a logical response to the resurgence of religion in non-Western settings. As Christendom itself is obviously unable to reestablish its former position in the world, Western civilization either denies religion's importance or selectively borrows religious items from other civilizations and, according to Bozeman (1975), adapts, transforms and assimilates them to strengthen and ensure the survival of its cultural identity.

Notes and References

1 The decline of the West was the focus Oskar Spengler's (1926) acclaimed *The Decline of the West* and Samuel Huntington's (1996) highly influential *The Clash of Civilizations and the Remaking of World Order*.

2 Puruṣasūkta X.90.16 emphasizes, according to Ralph T. H. Griffith (1963), "Gods, sacrificing, sacrificed the victim these were the earliest holy ordinances. The Mighty Ones attained the height of heaven, there where the Sidhyas, gods of old, are dwelling." (Sanskrit: *yajñena yajñamayajanta devāstāni dharmāni prathamānyāsan. te ha nākaṃ mahimānaḥ sacanta yatra pūrve sādhyāḥ santi devāḥ*).

3 The development of Vedic civilization has been analyzed in great detail in Gregory L. Possehl's (1982) *Harappan Civilization: A Contemporary Perspective*.

4 The cultural history of ascetics is discussed in detail by Michaels (2004).

5 V. R. Narasimha Rao (2009) emphasized that "irrespective of the caste of birth, one who is interested in knowledge (especially knowledge of self) and one whose interest in power, money and pleasures is decaying is fit to perform *homam*" (6).

6 The term "twice migrants" was coined by Bhachu (1985).

7 Frederick Smith refers in his article "Indra Goes West: Report on a Vedic Soma Sacrifice in London" to a specific form of *yajña*. As this falls within the classification of *yajña* to the category of *yāga*, it will be named as such in the following text. To go in line with Smith (2000), this *yajña* can be considered as the first ever Vedic sacrifice performed in the West, even though similar forms of sacrifices might have occurred there before, no scholar was able to prove their Vedic origin until now.

8 Śatapathabrāhmaṇa V.13.4.3.1–15.

9 The theory of religious decline was outlined by José Casanova (1994).

10 According to Huntington, the great political ideas of the West include liberalism, socialism, anarchism, corporatism, Marxism, communism, social democracy, conservatism, nationalism, fascism and Christian democracy (Huntington 1996, 53).

11 The term "global migration crisis" is derived from Weiner (1995).

12 The term "social capital" here refers to memberships in voluntary associations and interpersonal trusts.

Al-Turabi, H. 2009. The Islamic Awakening's Second Wave. *New Perspectives Quarterly* 26, no. 4: 66–71.

Bhachu, P. 1985. *Twice Migrants. East African Sikh Settlers in Britain.* London: Tavistock.

Bozeman, A. B. 1975. Civilizations Under Stress. *Virginia Quarterly Review* 51, no. 1: 1–18.

Burghart, R., ed. 1987. *Hinduism in Great Britain. The Perpetuation of Religion in an Alien Cultural Milieu.* London, New York: Tavistock.

Carey, S. 1987. The Indianization of the Hare Krishna movement in Britain. In *Hinduism in Great Britain. The Perpetuation of Religion in an Alien Cultural Milieu.* Ed. by R. Burghart. London, New York: Tavistock, 81–99.

Casanova, J. 1994. *Public Religions in the Modern World.* Chicago, London: University of Chicago Press.

Dawson, C. 1978. *Dynamics of World History.* LaSalle: Sherwood Sugden Co.

Gonda. J. 1960. *Die Religionen Indiens. Der jüngere Hinduismus*, vol. 2 [The Religions of India. The Younger Hinduism]. Stuttgart: Kohlhammer.

————. 1960. *Die Religionen Indiens. Veda und älterer Hinduismus*, vol. 1 [The Religions of India. Veda and Older Hinduism]. Stuttgart: Kohlhammer.

Griffith, R. T. H. 1963. *The Hymns of the Rgveda.* Varanasi: Chowkhamba Sanskrit Series Office.

Gyanshruti, S. and S. Srividyananda. 2006. *Yajna. A Comprehensive Survey.* Munger: Yoga Publications Trust.

"Hinduism." 2010. In *Encyclopaedia Britannica Online.* Online: http://www.britannica.com/EBchecked/topic/266312/Hinduism (accessed February 1, 2010).

Hoffmann, S. 1990/1991. "The Case of Leadership." *Foreign Policy* 81: 20–38.

Huntington, S. 1996. *The Clash of Civilizations and the Remaking of World Order.* New York: Simon and Schuster.

Jansen, B. J., A. Tapia and A. Spink. 2010. "Searching for salvation: An analysis of US religious searching on the World Wide Web." *Religion* 40: 39–52.

Knott, K. 1987. "Hindu temple rituals in Britain: The reinterpretation of tradition." In *Hinduism in Great Britain. The Perpetuation of Religion in an Alien Cultural Milieu.* Ed. by R. Burghart. London, New York: Tavistock, 157–79.

Kurth, J. 2003/04. "Western Civilization, Our Tradition." *The Intercollegiate Review* 39, nos. 1–2: 5–13.

_____. 2001. "America and the West. Global Triumph or Western Twilight?" *Orbis* 45, no. 3: 333–41.

Michaels, A. 2004. *Die Kunst des einfachen Lebens. Eine Kulturgeschichte der Askese.* [The Art of the Simple Life. A Cultural History of Asceticism]. München: C. H. Beck.

_____. 1998. *Der Hinduismus. Geschichte und Gegenwart* [Hinduism. Past and Present]. München: C. H. Beck.

Monier-Williams, M. 1872. "Havana." In *A Sanskrit-English Dictionary. Etymologically and Philologically Arranged with Special Reference to Cognate Indo-European Languages.* Oxford: Clarendon Press, 1168.

_____. 1872. "Homa." In *A Sanskrit-English Dictionary. Etymologically and Philologically Arranged with Special Reference to Cognate Indo-European Languages.* Oxford: Clarendon Press, 1178.

_____. 1872. "Kratu." In *A Sanskrit-English Dictionary. Etymologically and Philologically Arranged with Special Reference to Cognate Indo-European Languages.* Oxford: Clarendon Press, 259.

_____. 1872. "Śatakratu." In *A Sanskrit-English Dictionary. Etymologically and Philologically Arranged with Special Reference to Cognate Indo-European Languages.* Oxford: Clarendon Press, 990.

_____. 1872. "Yāga." In *A Sanskrit-English Dictionary. Etymologically and Philologically Arranged with Special Reference to Cognate Indo-European Languages.* Oxford: Clarendon Press, 814.

_____. 1872. "Yajña." In *A Sanskrit-English Dictionary. Etymologically and Philologically Arranged with Special Reference to Cognate Indo-European Languages.* Oxford: Clarendon Press, 802.

Mortimer, E. 1991. Christianity and Islam. *International Affairs* 67, no. 1: 7–13.

Olson, J. S. 1996. *Historical Dictionary of the British Empire.* Westport: Greenwood Press

Osterhammel, J. and N. P. Peterson. 2007. *Geschichte der Globalisierung: Dimension—Prozesse—Epochen* [History of Globalization: Dimension—Processes—Epochs]. München: C. H. Beck.

Possehl, G. L. 1982. *Harappan Civilization: A Contemporary Perspective.* Warminister: Aris and Phillips.

Pranashakty.org. (n.d.). "Participate in Homa and Watch It Live, through Pranashakty." http://www.pranashakty.org/homalive/ (accessed February 1, 2010).

Quigley, C. 1961. *Evolution of Civilizations: An Introduction to Historical Analysis.* New York: Macmillan.

Ranade, H. G. 2006. *Illustrated Dictionary of Vedic Rituals.* New Delhi: Indira Gandhi National Centre for the Arts.

Rao, N. 2009. *Sri mahaganapathi homam. Laghu paddhati (short procedure).* Online: http://www.vedicastrologer.org/homam/pdf/maha_ganapati_homam_sanskrit.pdf (accessed February 1, 2010).

"Religions." 2010. In *CIA World Fact Book.* Online: https://www.cia.gov/library/publications/the-world-factbook/fields/2122.html?countryName=&countryCode=&regionCode= (accessed February 1, 2010).

Rothermund, D. 2002. *Geschichte Indiens. Vom Mittelalter bis zur Gegenwart.* [History of India. From the Middle Ages to the present]. München: C. H. Beck.

Smith, F. M. 2000. "Indra Goes West: Report on a Vedic Soma Sacrifice in London." *History of Religions* 36, no. 3: 247–67.

Smith, W. R. 1886. "Sacrifice." In *The Encyclopaedia Britannica. A Dictionary of Arts, Sciences, and General Literature. Ninth Edition. Volume XXI.* Edinburgh: Adam and Charles Black, 132–8.

Spengler, O. 1926. *The Decline of the West.* London: Allen and Unwin.

Vertovec, S. 2000. *The Hindu Diaspora. Comparative Patterns.* London, New York: Routledge.

Von Stietencron, H. 2001. *Der Hinduismus*. [Hinduism]. München: C. H. Beck.

Weber, M. 1963. *The Sociology of Religion*. Boston: Beacon Press.

Weiner, M. 1995. *Global Migration Crisis. Challenge to States and to Human Rights*. New York: HarperCollins.

Winkelmann, F. 2007. *Geschichte des frühen Christentums*. [History of Early Christendom]. München: C. H. Beck.

Yang, F. and H. R. Ebaugh. 2001. "Transformations in New Immigrant Religions and Their Global Implications." *American Sociological Review* 66, no. 2: 269–88.

Yoga Vidya Newsletter. 2008. *Abschluss der 1008-Stunden Yajna* [End of the 1,008-hours *yajña*]. Online: http://www.yoga-vidya.de/Newsletter/Newsletter_141.html/#meldung6 (accessed February 1, 2010).

Part Two

COMPARATIVE AND PLURALISTIC APPROACHES

Chapter 5

MARY, ATHENA AND GUANYIN: WHAT THE CHURCH, THE DEMOS AND THE SANGHA CAN TEACH US ABOUT RELIGIOUS PLURALISM AND DOCTRINAL CONFORMITY TO SOCIO-CULTURAL STANDARDS

Evangelos Voulgarakis
Independent Scholar, Taiwan

Introduction

Globalization is a process through which technological advancement, cultural exchange, media networks, trade and educational initiatives lead to awareness of and interaction with different ethnic, religious and social groups (whether domestically or across international borders). However, group-identification and exclusivity continue to prevail in mission-oriented religions (e.g., Christianity, Islam, Buddhism), as well as ethno-religious identity groups (e.g., Judaism). While doctrine is often reinterpreted in conformity with changing social expectations, this process is rarely if ever acknowledged by the religious groups and innovators in question, who more typically lay claim to the rediscovery, reinstitution and reestablishment of *originally intended* truths. This suggests the inevitable influence of exclusivism (soteriological or membership-related), noble origins and group identification. Religious pluralism—in the sense of active engagement with and understanding of otherness without loss of distinctiveness for the purpose of realizing our own multiplicity of origins (Eck 2002)—is incompatible with such approaches, yet consistently "confused" (sometimes sincerely) with mere tolerance and interfaith dialogue for the purpose of projecting a positive public image. For example, the Dalai Lama has stated, on the one hand, that it is better for most people to remain devoted to their own religions than to convert to Buddhism. On the other hand, he has also claimed that there is one, and only one, way to reach enlightenment, namely the Prasangika Madhyamika tenet system. Although there may be many ways of reaching that final stage, from there on it is Prasangika Madhyamika or nothing (Dalai Lama 2001; cf. Revel and Ricard 1998).

This chapter shows how globalization leads some exclusivist religious groups to change their rhetoric (though not their attitudes) in ways that respect pluralist sensitivities. The three "goddesses" of the title are offered as examples of this rhetorical adaptation. Greek Orthodox Christians appeal to the Virgin Mary in order to give their arguments against women's ordination a more "modern"-sounding expression. (A similar rhetorical strategy can be observed in Orthodox approaches to religious pluralism.) Some Western Buddhists view the Bodhisattva Guanyin as evidence that feminism is compatible with a wider international and diachronic Buddhist tradition, a tradition which in reality covers many less modern or feminist-friendly expressions. Finally, Athena can function as a symbol of many different, often mutually exclusive values to both ancient worshippers (obedient daughter, strong and independent female warrior, protector of motherhood, celibate maiden) and modern devotees. Especially in the case of the latter, we may notice that, as a symbol of the Hellenic/Ethnic (Greek neo-pagan) Religion, the worship of Athena and the rest of the ancient Greek deities may point to interpretations and definitions of not only gender relations but also ethnicity and religious exclusivity, all within the context of an often not so agreeable, in terms of principles, European Union. Of course, this line of inquiry might be extended to any number of other female objects of religious adoration; the selection of these three "goddesses" stems from the author's personal acquaintance, and is offered as indication of what might be a larger pattern.

The Virgin Mary and Women's Ordination

Throughout her historical changes, the Virgin Mary has remained a revered symbol of often antithetical groups promoting the mythical notion of Church unity—a unity supposedly compatible with the prevailing morals of each era, including pluralist sensitivities associated with globalization. This flexibility is illustrated by Mary's role as a Christological clarifier at the Council of Ephesus (431 CE), where street demonstrators praised her as the *Theotokos*, or "God-bearer" (as opposed to the lesser Nestorian alternative of *Christotokos*, or "Christ-bearer"), in much the same spirit that their ancestors four centuries earlier had protested a perceived disrespect towards the goddess Diana (Acts 19:23; see Benko 2004). Although Church leaders did not share the crowd's priorities (their focus and object of worship being Jesus and his divine nature rather than Mary and her role), collective memory would depict the Church as unified on the issue of Mary as *Theotokos*. In the same way, Mary is sometimes depicted as passive, and sometimes as actively participating in or directing wars of national sovereignty (Dubisch 1995).

A number of theologians ascribe a salvific role to Mary's consent and obedience to God's plan (Boss 2000, 74). Kyriaki Fitzgerald (1994) suggests that

> the incarnation of our Lord also demanded an active human involvement
> […] [which] has been completely neglected by the main wave of the feminist
> and Protestant theology. We must realize that [Mary] was neither forced [to
> respond affirmatively] nor was she a passive, unthinking subject. (447)

On the one hand, Orthodox tradition maintains Mary's unattainability and uniqueness; on the other hand, it presents her as acting upon the same free will which all human beings possess. In traditional Christian theodicy, which paradoxically demands both accountability for human volition and, at the same time, inherent human inability to meet divine righteousness, it is our free will that simultaneously liberates us and condemns us: it makes *us*, not our Creator, liable for our shortcomings. This device becomes useful to the traditionalists as social change compels the revision of views (including views on gender) that have become obsolete or even unacceptable. Thus, Fitzgerald seeks to retain Mary's volitional independence and, by implication, the independence of her feminine nature from the "male" God. In this way feminist-*sounding* rhetoric is deployed by Eastern Orthodox traditionalists to counter feminist accusations of Christian androcentrism and its limits on feminine volition.

In light of modern Western sensitivities to gender equality, few issues are as polemical or as delicate as women's ordination. Participants at a 1988 Orthodox conference in Rhodes affirmed that, "if the exercise of the sacramental priesthood by women were permitted, then it should have been exercised by the Theotokos" (World Council of Churches 1988, par. 9), a line of thought which "suggested an image for the balance of male and female: that the all-male priesthood showed a correspondence between the priest and Christ, which reflected that between the Virgin Mary Theotokos and the Church" (Matthewes-Green, n.d., par. 32).

Even so, that conference participants felt the need to address the issue at all is remarkable, and demonstrates the influence of globalized feminist-oriented criticism. Demetrios, Archbishop of America, complained that,

> the effort to apply this equality [between man and woman in Christ] to
> […] a leveling even of the *physiological* and *biological* differences […] but
> also to extend such claims into the area of the holy mystery of salvation

and of the Church [...] has no place in Christ's Church[...]. Was the Church misguided, all those centuries, by not allowing the ordination to women? (Demetrios 1994, 25)

Demetrios's fear of violation arises from the transfer of doctrine from the realm of religious devotion to that of rational inquiry. The exotic term *mystery* sanitizes the paradox (that the sexes are equal, yet one is subordinate) and shields it against rational scrutiny in ways that the term *contradiction* never could. The appeal to tradition is also noteworthy.

There exists much Church rhetoric to the effect that women's ordination is a *foreign* issue, *imported* into Orthodox theological discussion (Behr-Sigel 2003; Koukoura 2005). The Greek term *ksenoferti* literally means "brought from outside," i.e., culturally, nationally and geographically foreign. This reflects an attitude of, at best, caution, and, at worst, hostility towards pluralism, since it assumes that only internal group problems need be addressed. Nevertheless, the conference brought a remarkable change: Behr-Sigel (2003) observes

> an obvious split between those for whom the ordination of women was without question an impossibility—having its roots in an immutable Tradition—and those theologians, generally from Western cultures, for whom it represented [...] a pointed question in need of an answer. (Par. 24)

Lymoures (1994) concurs. Demetra Koukoura, professor of theology at Aristotle University of Thessaloniki (and a practicing Orthodox Christian), presented the new, more dialectically oriented approach thus:

> In the intense argumentation of feminist theology [...] the spontaneous initial Orthodox responses of the sort "in our Church, women have no different faith than men" was not sufficient. That was because the immediate question of the fellow participants was as follows: "If this holds true, then why are your women not present to state so themselves?" (Koukoura 2005, 113–14)

An even less traditional approach is noted by Frida Hadad, who invokes Heraclitus on behalf of an almost feminist-*sounding* affirmation of a subordinate role for women: "The masculine instinct of war and death, says Heraclitus, carries within it the possibility of its antithesis [...] the feminine instinct of life, which contributes positively to civilisation" (Hadad 1994, 359). Similarly,

> a World tyrannized by man, a world in which woman is forced to the margin, is a world without God because it is a world deprived of the

virginity of true motherhood and, therefore, the conception of God cannot take place within such a world. (Hadad 1994, 361)

The conclusions of the Rhodes conference display rather egalitarian-sounding language: "[A]ny discrimination against women is completely foreign to the [...] principles of [the Church. Furthermore,] through weakness and human sinfulness, Christian communities have [historically succumbed] to discrimination [and the] sin of sexism" (Behr-Sigel 2003, par. 25). The effect of globalization is demonstrated perfectly (though perhaps neither deliberately nor consciously) by the same author's observation that the Church has entered a "new world *whose language it must speak* if it is to bear *witness* to the Gospel, and all this without losing its deep, spiritual *identity*" (Behr-Sigel 2003, par. 26; emphasis added). In other words, the rhetoric changes so that the traditionally exclusivist soteriology can remain relevant, but without any admission of the tradition's culpability or discontinuity (such blemishes being easily attributed to human weakness). Another Orthodox conference (held October 2002) criticized "misguided" approaches to pluralism for their destructive effect on personhood and individualism, which find their fulfillment only in the Greek Orthodox notion of *koinonia* (communion), conceived as the perfected version of Athenian direct democracy and as a holistically emerging Church unity reflecting that of the Trinity (Yannaras 2002). Thus individuality is conceived not as a personal right that is to be respected axiomatically, but as meaningful only in the context of a particular and exclusive community, namely Orthodoxy. Demetrios, Archbishop of America, defines pluralism as the struggle of an Orthodox Christian

to express, in the microcosm of his own personhood, the full panoply of human diversity [...]. And why does he exhibit this "personal pluralism?" [...] *I do it all for the sake of the Gospel, that I may share in its blessings* [...] (1 Cor. 9:23). (Demetrios, Oct. 2002, par. 15; emphasis original)

Guanyin and Buddhist Feminism

This section follows a brief and rather sketchy path from the Bodhisattva's Eastern (Chinese) settings to her arrival in the hearts of Western converts. The reader will note the wide range of differences between the two and the simultaneous retention of the identifier "Buddhist" by Guanyin's adherents. This mirrors the differences between androcentric and feminist approaches to Buddhism. The latter emerges, predictably, in Western secular environments and proceeds to conform historical analyses to feministic rhetoric.

Guanyin, the Bodhisattva of compassion, is an immensely popular figure in East Asian Buddhism. She protects people from harm on land and sea, grants male children to her petitioners and comforts women through difficult marital issues. She also leads worthy beings, after death, to "the Pure Land of A-mi-t'o Buddha where they are assured of eventual enlightenment" (Reed 1992, 164). However, she neither teaches against the preferential treatment of male offspring nor counsels her worshippers to cease such petitions, despite her insight into the detrimental nature of attachment. She can symbolize filial piety, as in the legend of Princess Miaoshan, and at the same time the rejection of marriage, as in the case of the wife of Mr Ma (Yu 2001).[1]

Like the Christian image of Mary, the Guanyin legends are very much designed to create followers, not rebel heroes. Guanyin's rejection of marriage provides a model for women to cope with their own marital problems through patient submission to their karma. This notion is widespread among Southeast Asian Buddhists, including women (Loy 2007), and is echoed by Master Cheng Yen, founder of the Taiwan-based international Buddhist charity organization Tzu Chi, whose members view themselves as the thousand arms and thousand eyes of Guanyin (Li 2005, 245). To a female victim of marital infidelity, Cheng Yen says that "[s]ince you love your husband, you should love the one your husband loves." In another story, Cheng Yen points out that "both you and [your husband's mistress] are women, yet, she has to hide her life in the dark and is unable to see the sunlight. Isn't her life more miserable?" (Madsen 2007, 25–6). In this way Tzu Chi, despite its predominantly female membership and leadership, promotes a conservative (albeit modernized) Chinese morality based on a Confucian emphasis on marriage and the family over considerations of individual fairness and gender equality.

In the rather different social reality of Western Buddhists, Guanyin is interpreted through a cultural preference for personal meditation, indifference to superstition and a tendency toward psychological approaches to religion. Philip Kapleau taught that "[r]ather than a supernatural being, Kannon [the Japanese name of Guanyin] is the embodiment of your own compassionate heart […] a vague 'energy' of compassion" (Wilson 2008, 288). Wilson suggests that a major element of her popularity in the United States is gender: "for women who have left Catholicism she is a warm reminder of the Virgin Mary yet without the negative implications for sexuality" (Wilson 2008, 290). Interestingly,

[t]he chapter of the Lotus Sutra that most embodies [compassion] considers the Bodhisattva to be a male. The willingness of the Bodhisattva to help others in any situation was a trait before he was transformed into a female in China […] but American Buddhists consistently derive her compassionate mutability from the fact that she is female. (Wilson 2008, 290)

Wilson detects a similar phenomenon at work in connection with a statue of the "Water and Moon" Guanyin (from the collection of the Nelson-Atkins Museum in Kansas City, Missouri), a "somewhat androgynous male figure" which "Americans have persistently mistaken […] for female" (Wilson 2008, 290–91).

The Western reception of Guanyin is closely tied to attempts to present Buddhism as a gender-egalitarian religion. Faced with such problematic lore as the legend of Mahaprajapati (Shakyamuni Buddha's aunt, who overcame his reluctance to ordain nuns), feminists struggle to explain such details as a result of society's, not the Buddha's, misogyny (Tsomo 2004). Gross (1993) suggests that Buddhism has traditionally respected women in every phase of its history and geography: "Buddhism *is* feminism: when Buddhism *is true to itself*, it manifests the same vision as does feminism" (116; emphasis added). The implication is that, for Gross, there exists a *real* Buddhism inherent in the original sources of the religious system. Instances of misogyny or androcentrism are always to be attributed to a corruption of these primary sources. For example, women must be respected because wisdom is in the feminine: "One should not denigrate women *because they are of the nature of wisdom and show both wisdom and shunyata*" [Sanskrit for "emptiness," the lack of inherent, independent nature] [emphasis original] (Gross 1993, 101). Of course, the selective emphasis on egalitarian doctrines for the purpose of presenting Buddhism as egalitarian, thereby culling "corrupt" and "unfortunate" offshoots of that tradition, is as erroneous and inaccurate as the androcentric method of neglecting pro-feminine Buddhist discourse. Jose Ignacio Cabezon points out that female subservience is still intrinsic to the traditions to which Gross refers, since (feminine gendered) wisdom is of a lower rank than the (male gendered) method (Cabezon 1992, 198, 35n). Anne C. Klein notes the failure of Buddhist teachings to address power differentials in male–female relationships, and asks how the doctrine of emptiness would help (for example) a woman living with an abusive man (Klein 2004, 28).

Another well-known theme in Buddhist feminism, and a product of globalization's intercultural contact, is a Western individualistic approach to an originally very Asian set of traditions. It has been suggested that many women come to Buddhism as an expression of their own deliberate and informed choice rather than through obedience to the Asian equivalent of a "patriarchal" Christianity which has disillusioned them and curtailed their volition: "[W]omen don't have to 'accept' anything. American women, having broken with [the] patriarchal path, are creating their [own] direction, incorporating wisdom wherever they may find it" (Wurst 2000, 98). By contrast, Zen and Tibetan Buddhism boast long traditions of enquiry and dialectic (albeit with non-Western methodological approaches). Distancing herself from hierarchical and teacher-oriented Buddhist structures, Maurine Stuart, an American Zen teacher, stated during an interview that "Dogen Zenji said, 'If you cannot find a true teacher, it is better not to practice.' […]. [B]ut what I feel at this moment is that our practice, whatever it is, is our teacher. *Life* is our practice" (Friedman 1987, 71). Her interviewer describes the delicately carved Guanyin statue in the hall, and reports Stuart's "down to earth" attitude: "This is not some occult, faraway, Eastern […] mystical thing. This is an essential matter for every human being, wherever you live […]. You don't have to think in terms of some other country or place" (as cited in Friedman 1987, 78).

The question, then, emerges: Why the robes? Why the Japanese language? Why Guanyin? Tsultrim Allione's experiences only serve to emphasize the question. One of the first American women to be ordained as a Tibetan nun, and the founder of Tara Mandala retreat center in southern Colorado, Allione writes: "To me, the point of robes was to simplify one's external appearance so that one could concentrate on one's inner development. The novelty of the Tibetan robes in America seemed to have the opposite effect" (Allione 2005, 330). It is instructive to observe instances when these forms are downplayed yet kept; instances when they are *emphasized* and kept but with Western style explanations, as in Pema Chodron's view of forms as teaching tools toward the respect for hierarchy (Friedman 1987, 115); and instances when they are altogether dismissed (Friedman 1987, 115). In all of these diverse attitudes, the common denominator is not the search for temporal and transcendental answers, but the search for such answers within a diverse yet commonplace *and* westernized category known as *Buddhism*. Jan Willis, a professor at Wesleyan University, Connecticut, and a student of prominent Tibetan teacher Thubten Yeshe, was asked by a group of female audience members about the possibility of attaining enlightenment in a female form. She replied: "Oh, come on, now. Just look at Lama Yeshe; look at your own experience. Have you ever experienced that?" A few days later, Lama Yeshe grabbed Willis's arm during a lecture and exclaimed to the audience, "Look, all of you! Look! Look! You want to see women's liberation? *This* is [pointing at her and patting her on her shoulders] this *is* women's liberation" (Willis 2005, 309; emphasis original).

Athena and Greek Neo-paganism

Athena is a remarkable study of contradictions considering the status of women in ancient Athens. She is a warrior goddess but also patroness of the crafts—that is, emphasizing, though not confined to, the traditional household crafts assigned to females. Though forever virgin and constantly clad in armor, she is also Athena Meter (Mother) of the Elis cult, an epithet identifying her as

Goddess of Motherhood in the truest sense (Kerenyi 1978). She is the patroness of wisdom, who offers wise counsel to the epic hero Achilles against his uncontrollable anger, but who, as a result of an offense against her father, gives into her own anger and transforms Arachne into the insect bearing her name. When she defeats Poseidon and assists Erectheus (the autochthonous demi-god who founded the city), she teaches citizens the meaning of autochthony and, by implication, racial chauvinism (Loraux 1986).

Athena is used here as a symbol of the Greek neo-pagan movement[2] because the diverse and often contradictory perceptions of her in antiquity mirror the contradiction between the neo-pagans' claims and their actual practices—particularly in the areas of women's rights and ethnic and religious pluralism—as the movement combines efforts to reinstitute ancient religious practices with attempts to make them relevant to modernity. Greek neo-pagans have conducted rituals to Athena in the form of praise (Societas Hellenica Antiquariorum, n.d.b) as well as petition (Elginism, May 2006). The latter context has included individual blog entries by Greek neo-pagans calling for "Re-Hellenization [*epanellinisi*]" (Anaxagoras, April 2012) and prominent groups such as ELLINAIS whose followers assembled at the Acropolis, "praying to Athena to stop the removal of sculptures and pieces of the temples to museums […] [and] to protect the 2,500-year-old site and spare the city from harm" (The Associated Press, par. 1, 5).

Greek neo-paganism first emerged in the 1980s, although some adherents trace its origins to the revival of the Delphic Games at the beginning of the twentieth century, to the medieval neo-Platonist Plython Gemistos, or even to Julian "the Apostate." The first public neo-pagan ritual was performed in 1987 by Vlasis Rassias, at the altar of Dionysus/Apollo at the Dionysos of Attica (Naoum 2006). He claims unbroken continuity with the ancient Greek religion, which apparently survived underground since its suppression by the Byzantine Empire. Rassias is the founder and Secretary General of the largest Greek neo-pagan group, an umbrella organization called the Supreme Council of Ethnic Hellenes (Ypato Symvoulio Ellinon Ethnikon, hereafter YSEE) which has branches in the USA, Canada, Australia and Germany. It is known for its (generally futile) political activism, ethno-national chauvinism and promotion of conspiracy theories. Vlasis Rassias postulates the invocation of Athena as coupled with that of Hermes and/or Hephaistos, in keeping with what he views as the practice of petitioning Hellenic deities in pairs of opposite gender according to the function they supervise. As usual, he comments on what he regards as the negative aspects of monotheism by noting that gender designations within the Pantheon "have nothing to do with the sexism and dualism dwelling in the minds of narrow-minded followers of *alien* cultures" (Rassias 1995, par.11, 12; emphasis added). Due to the decentralized and diverse nature of Greek neo-paganism, it would be misleading to ascribe such views to the movement as a whole; nevertheless, it is YSEE which presents the main neo-pagan challenge to Greek Orthodox claims to represent Hellenicity. For example, YSEE calls for the recognition of Hellenic religion as the national religion of Greece and demands the return of ancient Greek archaeological sites to them for their exclusive use, graciously waiving their implied claim to full ownership (YSEE, n.d.b).

Neo-pagan groups can be broadly divided into *eclectic* and *reconstructionist* categories (Adler 1979; Campbell 2000; Linzie 2004). Briefly,

> while most neo-pagans draw on different traditions to create a very eclectic and individualistic spirituality, European movements, among them the Greek one, are more concerned with issues of identity, social justice and creating a new human being with values deeply rooted in ancestral tradition. (Fotiou, n.d., par. 6)

Like most Greek neo-pagan groups, YSEE belongs to the reconstructionist category, insofar as it purports to promote a historically genuine version of ethnic identity in contrast to eclectic movements, such as Wicca (Hellenistai, Aug. 2009; Hellenismos US, Dec. 2009). At the same time, this approach must not be misunderstood (as it has been misunderstood by Greek Orthodox critics of neo-paganism—see Tsouros 2008) as the mere imitation of ancient practice; rather, the movement purportedly applies the lessons, methodologies, attitudes and values of its progenitors in diachronic and humanistically orientated ways (Rassias 2007). This is not to say that the Greek neo-pagan movement (especially overseas, where adherents of non-Greek ethnic origin are more common) lacks for debate over what to modify and to what degree. For example, despite their opposition to "superstition" (by which they usually mean Christian belief), Greek neo-pagans are cautious in their rejection of magic (Beliefnet, n.d.; *The Couldron*, July 2011; Elaion, Sept. 2004; Rassias, April 2010), an element (defined in a variety of ways) common in other forms of neo-paganism (Harvey 2007, 84).

Responses to Feminism

The YSEE website carries with approval an article on ancient traditions of the goddess, in contrast with the patriarchal, and supposedly brutal, social and religious system which succeeded them (Haugen, n.d.). Furthermore, the organization stresses—in an obviously implicit comparison to the Church—the active participation of women in priestly duties: "Women aren't just involved in ceremony, but the gods themselves have decreed their participation" (YSEE, n.d.b). Rassias predictably associates the fear of sexuality with the Christian religion:

> Sexuality is essentially suppressed as transcendence by a fear-oriented culture that hates every earthly transcendence. Monotheism seeks transcendence only in the untouchable and incomprehensible, thus, in the currently and even permanently non-existent. Hatred toward sexuality comes essentially from hatred toward existence. (Rassias 2006, par. 3)

Diïpetes, a YSEE journal, provides many examples of rather romantic Greek neo-pagan views on the position of women in ancient Greece and predictably negative coverage of the attitude of Christianity (the entire religion, throughout the ages and all of its variations) toward women (*Diïpetes*, n.d.). Similarly, Charikleia Mene denies that the ancients exhibited the type of misogyny that modern commentators detect in them. Her comment is revealing:

> Many of the things that we are taught are totally one-sided since we are looking at antiquity through the eyes of men—the enormous treasure of writings/documents left to us by our female ancestors [*progonnises mas*] was destroyed by the Christian fanatics with the result that only a very few fragments survive today. (Mene 2000, 317)

Mene seeks to disprove historical views to the effect that the education of women in antiquity was extremely limited, by mentioning exceptions, in the single-digits, followed by the unqualified phrase "and countless others" (Mene 2000, 317).

Concerning the position of women in ancient Greece,[3] one quickly realizes that modernity and antiquity did not converge on this particular issue. Simon Goldhill observes that,

> [t]o the Athenian of the classical period, the view that a woman, who did not speak the language of the polis, did not worship its gods, and had political links to another area, had to become automatically a citizen with voting privileges would mean the most comical or most tragic flight of fancy [...]. Aristotle is absolutely willing to consider slaves and women as beings inherently and naturally incompetent. (Goldhill 2006, 261)

In ancient Greece, the woman was, on the one hand, a symbol of hypersensitivity and hysteria (literally, *wombiness*), which the Hippocratic doctors treated not as a physical or mental ailment but as a source of social disorder (Cartledge

1993); on the other hand, she was also a symbol of the wild, natural forces outside the limits of ordered society. Mythological examples include Anchises and Aphrodite; Paris and the three goddesses, "in most [versions] of which, the meeting ends with the destruction of the man" (Goldhill 2006, 142); Hesiod's tale of Pandora as *dolos* (deception) (see Gould 2001, 155); and Sophocles' Antigone, with her etymological allusion to opposition to procreation (childbirth being the normative role of females in Greek society, in contrast to involvement in—let alone opposition to—male political authority) (Cartledge 1993). Referring to reason, Aristotle says, "the deliberative faculty is not present at all in the slave, in the female it is inoperative […] [and] as regards male and female, this relationship of superior and inferior is permanent" (Murray 1986, 254). Such beliefs did not prevent a high respect for mythological women. For example, Praxithea was celebrated for championing the autochthony of the Athenians, even to the extent of sacrificing her daughters to save the polis (Sissa and Detienne 2000). As her name implies, she acted under the authority of a goddess—namely Athena, the guardian of Athens and the personification of wisdom. Nevertheless, Praxithea was honored not for her active participation in the city's management, but for her supreme sacrifice.

The reality of female participation within the Greek neo-pagan community has become something of an issue. Mene writes:

> In [Greek neo-pagan] religious circles [both genders] participate in equal numbers […] [;] however, the role of the female participants is usually marginal […]. [I]n the symposium entitled *The Ancient Greek Tradition in the Third Century* (Athens 1999) the cultural movement was represented by M. Verettas, A. Keramydas, P. Marinis, and V. Rassias. Similarly, in a series of nine interviews published by *Avaton* (issue 3, 1999) […] only one (!) woman [participated]. [Most of the literature of the movement, written by men] does not consider Greek women's issues. (Mene 2000, 315)

According to Mene, Marinis's *Helliniki Kosmotheasis* (Hellenic Worldview) devotes no more than a few paragraphs to the subject of women and when women are mentioned the discussion is either patronizing or self-contradictory. Such accusations are apparently known to neo-pagan leadership, and have occasionally been challenged. During a high-profile gathering of all major neo-pagan organizations held on January 16, 2010, in which various leaders were recognized for their contributions, Evangelos Beksis (owner of the archeolatric magazine *IHOR*) commented:

> So that people won't say that the Hellenic movement has only men […].
> It has also women, many women. However, the point is that they should

be able to come forward [...]. Come forward, do not be afraid. The Hellenic movement has two works: that of Vasilios Mysirinies, and the other of Takis Kyriakopoulos, which essentially debunk a myth. It is about the very important role that you [women] had in antiquity. Thus, it is a very great pleasure for us that a woman will close the third part of this presentation. (Schizas 2010)

The woman was Rea Karayanni of the Gaia Theatrical Schema (Theatriko Schema Gaia). The only other woman who spoke at the gathering was Maria Dzani, an Athens University professor and director of a university workshop, "Nevrofysiko Perivalon, Neoepistimes kai Mathisi" (Neurophysical Environment, Neo-sciences and Learning). Shortly thereafter, Iason Schizas, a blogger of the neo-pagan movement, commented, "Ask women in Kabul [...] when were they living better, during the 50s when Greek learning was at its zenith? Or now when the textbooks are from the USA?" (Schizas 2010). Not present was Doretta Peppa, the former president of ELLINAIS. ELLINAIS is the only Greek neo-pagan organization to be granted (limited) recognition by the state—over the protests of many other neo-pagan groups, most vocal among them the YSEE (Naoum 2006, 29–30). Similarly, among a large number of prominent neo-pagan leaders, only Urania Dzani appears as a female representative and speaker in feature-length film on the Prometheia festival which appears on neo-pagan blogs and which seems to be an attempt at making known the movement's beliefs and grievances. (Pileus 2011, Jan. 6) This is not to say that local organizational initiatives have not been observed by female adherents. One example is Marina Tontis, a computer programmer and co-founder of the Apollonian Society, a philosophical club in Thessaloniki, Greece. (Miller, n.d., par. 10) However, as far as the movement's prominent leadership is concerned, the absence of women in positions of authority is notable.

The attitude towards gay issues may also be relevant. While there is no consensus within the neo-pagan movement (*The Couldron*, August 2009), Societas Hellenica Antiquariorum and YSEE are against homosexuality. Although Societas considers the possibility that religions which exclude women from priesthood should be made illegal (Societas Hellenica Antiquariorum, n.d.a, par. 9), it nevertheless states that homosexuality does not "sit well" with their religion because,

the concession by the state of various privileges to married couples is justified, as we see it, by the fact that it represents the only legal form of reproduction. Otherwise, there opens a Pandora's box of irrational demands [...]. People could perform marriages just for the economic benefits, one could pass on his pension to his porter if he wanted to!

The social status of marriage becomes a farce [...]. Secondly [...] our religion considers that the marriage of post-reproductive age people demeans the institution and does not bless such marriages [and likewise with homosexual couples]. (Par. 18, 19)

YSEE follows a less discriminatory approach, emphasizing procreation as the *ancient* basis for marriage, and thus prohibiting homosexual marriage as far as *ritual* is concerned:

YSEE respects all kinds of diversity, and is a member of the Greek chapter of the EU Committee for the Elimination of Discrimination [...]. [W]e do not object any kind of civil contract between two individuals of any sex, aimed at providing them with legal rights [...]. On the ritualistic level, though, since marriage symbolizes the sacred union of two opposite elements (male–female, Zeus–Hera) for further *demeourgia* (creation, birth), we perform marriage rituals only between people of the opposite sex [...]. YSEE respects homosexuals, it does not deny them membership, or even the priesthood [...]. Our stand for only heterosexual "religious" marriages is only ritualistic [...]. If we change even once our ritualistic Tradition then there will be no Tradition (ritualistic, I repeat!) at all, because then we'll also have to perform marriage rituals for a polygamist with five brides, a nudist couple that may want to be blessed in the nude, or a BDSM couple that may want one partner collared, and so on. (Hellenismos US 2009, Aug. 6)

Given that Hellenic reconstructionism presents itself not as an exact reproduction of ancient traditions but as an adaptation of them to modern circumstances, it would be fair to ask why ritual cannot be modified as well (as has already been done with the unofficial abolition of blood sacrifice; see YSEE, n.d.b). The answer can only be speculated upon, and its direction may lead to either incrimination (Greek neo-pagan ritual views women primarily as mothers, as in ancient times, not as individuals) or cautious indifference (the issue is not important—YSEE is doing its best; it is never easy to adapt ancient practices to modern concerns). In either case, however, the discrepancy between orthopraxis and modern morality remains, and is made all the more visible by the explanatory language of Rassias, as examined above.

Responses to Pluralism

If gender egalitarianism and religious pluralism are parallel values, then it is useful to note that although YSEE advocates freedom of religion, it constantly expresses hostility towards the Greek Orthodox Church, which YSEE views as a theocratic occupation force. Indeed, even a casual perusal of YSEE websites reveals a relentless verbal war against monotheism in general, and Orthodox Christianity in particular. (As we shall see, the hostility and confrontational rhetoric is reciprocated.) Specifically, YSEE protests the degree and scope of the national church's political authority, and argues for a return to what it views as the only authentically Greek (that is, pre-Christian) values. Its rhetoric invokes, on the one hand, nationalistic chauvinism and religious superiority over standards originating with modern globalization; and, on the other, a realization of neo-paganism's total dependence on that globalized, international context—wavering between praise for classical times and appeals to modern European standards. Thanks to "the Church-controlled mass media,"

> a foreign dogma has not only succeeded in imposing itself as the 'dominant' religion, but also in monopolizing Hellenicity [...] [Ellinikotita, Greekness], even though the foreign dogma [i.e., Orthodox Christianity] always co-operated with the foreign conquerors of this land (Christianized Romans of Constantinople and Ottomans) for the total annihilation of our ethnic consciousness. (YSEE, n.d.b)

On the other hand, the same website states that "We, ETHNIC HELLENES, view as respected, despite their foreign origins, all the other religions that one can encounter today on Greek soil, including the Orthodox Christian, and we do not view ourselves as enemies or rivals of those religions" (YSEE, n.d.b). The combination of purported tolerance and dismissal of the religion of over 90 percent of the population as foreign and dictatorial is intriguing. Equally interesting is YSEE's attempt to trace this false Greekness to a Jewish schizophrenia: "We stand for the reinstitution of the True Hellenic Identity, rejecting the sick, schizophrenic Judaic-begotten worldview of Christianity [...]. Hellenism and Christianity are two diametrically antithetical concepts, impossible to either mix or compromise on the foundations of common logic" (YSEE USA, n.d.). Thus YSEE rhetoric proceeds from the eccentric, historically inaccurate and romantic straight into the anti-Semitic.

In the event that political authority is granted to the YSEE, the only requirement it would impose on other religions would be that their "sermons not offend our ethnic tradition" (YSEE, n.d.c). From that starting, or limiting, point, anything may be regarded as offensive by virtue of its failure to accord with neo-pagan preferences. Note that the privileges which YSEE is seeking are exactly the same ones enjoyed by Orthodoxy: Article 3 of the Greek Constitution establishes the Orthodox Church as the state religion, while Article 199 of the Penal Code specifies that "Whoever publicly and with hostile intent verbally offends in whatever manner the Eastern Orthodox Church of Christ, or another religion *tolerated* by Greece, is punishable by a jail sentence of up to two years" (Krippas 2004, 344; emphasis added).

EAR (Elliniko Ananeotiko Revma; Hellenic Renewal Movement/ Current)—an unsuccessful avowedly secular, but predominantly neo-pagan political party whose ideology borrowed heavily from YSEE—has stated its disdain for other religious systems as "foreign imports" (a mildly derogatory designation: *ksenoferti*). Stephanos Mytileneos, Communications Secretary of EAR and a member of YSEE, has expressed through the use of by-now-familiar terminology his grievance against the government's unwillingness to recognize neo-paganism as a religion: "It is unacceptable for Greeks to be prohibited from honoring their ancestral gods within their own country when foreign (*ksenofertes*) religions, even harmful superstitious sects, operate undisturbed" (Kleitor 2007). The same epithet, interestingly enough, is used by the majority of Greek neo-pagans to describe Eastern Orthodox marriage rituals (Pileaus, Jan. 2011). EAR is itself an interesting case of an absolutist ideology with an oscillating rhetoric in the face of an egalitarian European context. It pushes for "the re-Hellenization [*tin epanellinisi*] and logical management of public [...] life in accordance with the principles of the Ancient Greek Enlightenment and the European Enlightenment" (EAR 2005). Despite a very YSEE-informed aspiration to "re-Hellenize" over 90 percent of the country's population, EAR announced itself as unaffiliated with any religious groups (as one would expect from a movement claiming to derive its founding principles from the Enlightenment): "EAR is neither a religious nor a polytheistic movement but a political movement of [by and for] Hellenes in morals and customs" (EAR 2005). The very typical Greek neo-pagan phrase, "Hellenes in morals and customs" (*Ellines sto ithos kai sto ethos*), is suggestive.

By now EAR has all but collapsed. In 2008, Rassias quit after internal disputes over leadership, according to former YSEE affiliates. Mytilenaios followed in 2009, the same year the website of the political party went down permanently. Later the same year, EAR was renamed the World Society of Knowledge and Virtue, or WSKV (its Greek name, PELA: Politeia Eleftherias kai Aretis), although EAR maintains a separate formal legal existence due to procedural problems regarding its financial records.

An interesting event occurred in 2010, when EAR participated in demonstrations against government-sponsored plans to offer citizenship to immigrants. At the popular level, the debate revolved around two rather simplistic slogans: the opponents of the government initiative proclaimed that "A Greek is something you are born as, not something you can become" (*Ellinas genniesai, the ginesai*), while supporters countered with "A Greek is something you become, not something you are born as" (*Ellinas ginesai, the genniesai*). EAR took the side of the opponents. Schizas, a known archeolatric blogger and friend of Rassias, was one of the participants in an IHOR-sponsored event which gathered representatives of all the archeolatric and neo-pagan communities in an awards ceremony. He, along with Rassias and most of the prominent neo-pagan figures, was also honored with an award for his contributions to the cause (Schizas 2010). In his blog, Schizas comments favorably on EAR's participation in the demonstration. Although EAR co-founders Rassias and Mytilenaios are no longer members of the organization, their ties are still strong enough to dissuade them from morally and ideologically opposing the positions of EAR and Schizas.

By now the YSEE's ethnic chauvinism will have become familiar. During a radio show in Cyprus, Rassias noted that "our faith is a complete systematic worldview, encompassing everything. No need for others, although we celebrate variety" (Pittas 2006). Again, on a TV show in the same country, Rassias referred to the recognition of ethnic faiths by other countries, and asked rhetorically how much more imperative it is for the Greek state to recognize the Hellenic ethnic religion, which is far superior in terms of evolution and sophistication to other faith systems: "May it be like this for all nations which have a glorious past—and if so, how much more glorious, then, the ancient Greek one!" (Ioannides 2006). On the same show, he referred to modernity and post-Enlightenment societies as "the impersonal melting pot of the European Union" (*Aprosopo kazani tis Evropaikis Enosis*) (Ioannides 2006). For Rassias, globalization is by definition disastrous: "The only true and final globalization occurred with the Christianization and Islamization of the nations of the Earth. These two words are equally appalling and essentially describe the exact same crime" (Rassias 2005).

At the same time, YSEE recognizes the usefulness of the European Union, and Enlightenment values in general, in the struggle against the Orthodox Church: "Under pressure from the European Union, theocratic Greece was forced, under law 2462/1997, to recognize […] the right to religious convictions and free worship" (YSEE, May 2005), albeit as only an individual right. Furthermore, the neo-pagan organization's homepage has links to the European Commission's initiatives against religious and racial discrimination, initiatives in which YSEE took part (YSEE 2005). Rassias claims his initial interest in polytheism began with "the religion's focus on humanity, ecology, cosmic connections and reverence for the past" (Smith 2007, par. 2), all very admirable pursuits according to modern Western public opinion. The supposedly ecological orientation of ancient Greece is a myth followed relentlessly by Greek neo-pagans, as any time spent on YSEE's home page will make clear. Unfortunately, historical research seems to suggest a rather different picture of Rassias's ethnic ancestors than that of the nature-respecting, harmoniously coexisting society imagined by neo-pagans (Hughes 1994). Nevertheless, the author of a *Guardian* article on Greek neo-paganism could not possibly have described the effects of globalization on the fringe movement more concisely or successfully than when she commented that "Greece's pagans will need every ally they can get in their battle with the immensely powerful Orthodox establishment" (Smith 2007, par. 14). Rassias reveals who this ally will have to be: "If the intolerance continues we'll go to the European Court of Human Rights" (Smith 2007, par. 14). Greek (Orthodox or neo-pagan) scorn of the European context and Western norms may stem from a commonly felt, though differently interpreted, sense of nationalist chauvinism, but it is that Western context that features prominently in the foreigner-directed rhetoric of both camps. In the case of the neo-pagans, "outbound" rhetoric places Western modernity and European expectations at the top of the ethical hierarchy. As a member of YSEE put it, "Greece is not like other *modern European democracies*—it is semi-theocratic" (Smith 2007, par. 12; emphasis added).

When the Greek government commissioned award-winning director Kostas Gavras to film a video to be shown to tourists at the Parthenon depicting the history of that site, the Orthodox Church pressed for the elimination of scenes of Christians destroying pagan statues. YSEE responded with protests. At one, YSEE members held up signs that read: "Yes, they did smash our statues" and "Stop Theocracy" (YSEE, July 2009). The fact that protesters took the trouble to translate their protest banners into English demonstrates the cultural momentum globalization has gathered. Yet the resulting propaganda seems rather pointless: unlike (say) Serbian propaganda during the 1998 Kosovo War, the topic is neither known nor relevant to the international community, which in any case has no jurisdiction in Greek affairs. Zissis Papadimitriou, a sociologist at the University of Thessaloniki, observes the effects of globalization on the need of a population perceived as largely ethnically homogeneous to maintain an unchallenged sense of identity: "Because of globalization, because of the European Union, the Greek people are in a period of transformation [...] so they are seeking a new identity—a Greek identity" (Miller, n.d., par. 10).

Orthodox Reactions

Greek Orthodox representatives gathered in 2003 and 2005 to discuss the issue of neo-paganism. The 2003 conference, titled "The Phenomenon of Idolatry," was conceived as an *academic* answer to Greek neo-pagan claims to Greekness and, predictably, included only anti-pagan Orthodox voices. It opened with an Orthodox ritual blessing (*efcheleo*) and Byzantine choral music, and featured priests who spoke from a decidedly emic perspective and who defended their points with reference to the authority of the Bible, the Church Fathers and Orthodox councils.

One of the speakers, hieromonk Arsenios Vliagoftes, is a member of the Greek Ecclesiastical Committee Against Heresies and an outspoken opponent of ecumenicalism, neo-paganism and pluralism; he had recently been involved in the sentencing of Greek academic Takis Alexiou, president of the Greek Rumi Committee and of the Panhellenic Historical and Philosophical Society (Amnesty International 2005). Vliagoftes views interfaith dialogue as a form of "dogmatic pluralism," emphasizing the "dogmatic" part of the characterization in order to distinguish it from pluralism in general: His grievance is that "pluralism is elevated to the status of dogma. Whoever questions the validity of this dogma is labeled a fanatic and is rejected" (Vliagoftes 2006; 12–13). Making use of anti-New Age pamphlets which are in abundant supply from Orthodox publishing houses, Vlagioftis set out to demonstrate that Greek neo-paganism is part of the New Age Movement and therefore Satanic (such accusations are often heard in Greece), a source of "poison" to our "collective ethnic consciousness" (Vlagioftis 2005, 380). Neo-paganism, we are told, is a "Supermarket Religion" (*Yperagora Threskeia*), which proselytizes deceitfully and displays an "extremely hostile attitude toward whoever applies criticism against them" (Vlagioftis 2005, 376–7). (The double standard is amusing.) Pluralism is thus seen by him as a futile commercialization of religion which perpetuates a spiritual vacuum.

Fr Georgios Metallinos, Dean of the School of Theology in the University of Athens, Greece, is another powerful anti-pagan voice. To Metallinos, "the holy Fathers [of the Orthodox Church are] the most genuine exponents of the natural continuation of Greekness" (Metallinos 2003, 26). Only the philosophers (Xenophanes, Socrates, etc.)—although not all of them—came near the truth, but they are categorized as Christians who lived before the advent of Christ (Metallinos 2003, 28). Metallinos rejects the ecological and feminist movements in Greece as dangerously permeated by neo-paganism. He speaks of

the attack against the *continuity* and cohesiveness of our civilization/ culture [*politismos*] […] [so that] our collective consciousness is poisoned […]. [We] open[ed] ourselves to *Western invasions-intrusions* (New Age, neo-paganism, neo-apocryphism) […] [until] our national/ethnic immunity system [became] weakened. (Metallinos 2003, 47; emphasis added)

Contrasting the civilization of "Hellenorthodoxy" with the purportedly alienating values of Carolingian Europe, Metallinos specifies that,

[h]istorically, the Hellene is the Orthodox Hellene, who saves the entire diachronic Hellenism in him. A Hellene, according to the law, may be

any [man or woman] who fulfills the pertinent legal criteria. Spiritually, however, only one who is Patristically Orthodox can be a Hellene. The westernized or Frankicized Hellene cannot authentically represent Hellenism, except partially. (Metallinos 2003, 44)

The echo of Rassias's exclusivism-disguised-as-inclusivism is unmistakable. Like Greek neo-pagan leaders, Metallinos defines Greekness in exclusivist terms. The attempt (however inept) of both camps to use cautious phraseology is noteworthy and points to their awareness of a Western European and American humanistic context. For example, Metallinos complains of anti-Semitism among the neo-pagans (Metallinos 2003, 31) on the thought-provoking grounds that "this way, they provide the greatest service to International Zionism and to the Jews, the latter basing their efforts (to appeal to international sympathy) on [anti-Jewish] 'persecutions' (real or artificial)" (Metallinos 2003, 21).

Another interesting Orthodox voice against neo-paganism was that of the late Archbishop of Athens and Greece, Christodoulos (Paraskevaides) (1939–2008). The late archbishop stated that "only from the prevalence of Christianity onward can we perceive religion as a unified and fundamentally self-consistent system, as a fundamentally unified teaching" (Paraskevaides 2005, 69), a rather convenient approach for a constitutionally established dominant religious organization which does not regard non-monotheistic systems as bona fide religions meriting analogous recognition by the state (Krippas 2004, 344).

Further official Orthodox ecclesiastical reaction to Greek neo-paganism appears in the form of an undated entry on the article section of the YSEE website regarding a memorandum sent by Metropolitan Agathonikos of Ekaterini-Platamon to the churches under his jurisdiction, concerning the celebration of the Prometheia, a Greek neo-pagan festival that took place in that same area. In the memorandum, Promethia organizer Tryphon Kostoloulos's (a.k.a. Tryphon Olympios) choice to follow a different religious belief than Orthodox Christianity is described as "provocative." Agathonikos writes,

[i]t is about a utopian and irrational attempt to revive events and myths which were extinguished two and a half thousand years ago, and which have nothing to add to our ethnic tradition and heritage [...]. The non-existent gods of the ancient idolatrous religion were murdering, committing adultery, envying and hating. That was a religion whose spirituality regarded pederasty as initiation into higher spiritual knowledge [...]. Our Greece is the country of the first Christian Saints and Martyrs [*sic*] (YSEE, n.d.a).

As we have seen with the issue of women's ordination, the Orthodox Church conceals an exclusivist stance behind pluralist-sounding rhetoric. The Orthodox accusation that "the modern neo-pagan movement is a foreign import" (*ksenoferto*) (Apostoliki Diakonia 2003, 25)—and general suspicion of the foreign, exogenous, imported or westernized (*ksenoferto, eksoggennes, eisagomeno, ekdytikevmeno*)—curiously mirrors the neo-pagan characterization of Orthodoxy as a foreign/imported (*ksenoferti*), "Hebraic" religion (Vlagioftis 2006, 52). Meanwhile, Orthodoxy continues to send representatives to ecumenical religious meetings, organizes conferences on pluralism and moves masterfully through the grey areas of European and Greek anti-cult legislation (Krippas 2004, 344)—even as Greece is regularly condemned by the European Court of Human Rights, as well as groups like Amnesty International, for violations of religious freedom.

Conclusion

Diana Eck very correctly states that "diversity is not only the characteristic of the worlds we study but of our own identities, our multiply situated selves" (Eck 2007, 1–34). Predictably, religious organizations find it hard to admit this multiplicity of influences and adaptations to changing circumstances, but cling to dubious claims of continuity and purity of tradition. Nevertheless, like the empires of the past, globalization forces at least some groups to feign compatibility with the new order, while competing for primacy and exclusivity within it. This explains the discrepancy between exclusivist and pluralist rhetoric that we have seen, as symbolized by the three "goddesses."

Religion's relevance—especially in post-industrial, globalized societies where the issue of pluralism obviously emerges—entails competition that, parallel to group identification, makes pluralism appear at best inconvenient and at worst dangerous. Thus, a secular legal framework is needed to provide the arena in which exclusivist groups can compete, and prevent the domination of any one group. The vast majority of such groups (i.e., all except the traditionally dominant and privileged ones) stand a better chance of prospering under a secular, pluralist regime. This would not prevent intense competition among religious groups—on the contrary, analogous to sports teams, it is the existence of a reliable referee which allows meaningful competition to occur.

Notes and References

1 In the story of the wife of Mr Ma, a young maiden promises to marry whoever masters the Buddhist scriptures. When Mr Ma accomplishes this task, she disappears from the earthly realm, having enlightened him by subterfuge. Princess Miaoshan rejected marriage

in favor of the religious life, and thus suffered at the hands of her unsupportive father. Later in life, he fell ill and was saved by Miaoshan herself, now a Bodhisattva. Further examples of Guanyin-inspired rejections of marriage include early nineteenth- to early twentieth-century accounts of women living in rural Guangdong, who took vows in front of Guanyin images to never marry or live as married women (Yu 2001). Yu also reports that pilgrims at Hangzou's Upper Tianzhu Monastery, who were mostly middle-aged or elderly wives, sang songs of admiration for the Bodhisattva's freedom from marriage (Yu 1995, 142–3).

2 Neo-paganism emerged in various Western countries during the nineteenth and twentieth centuries, often in the context of Romantic nationalist folk revival. As yet there is no good global survey of these movements. Most academic literature on neo-paganism focuses on the English-speaking world, with a few exceptions (e.g., Strmiska 2005). For more information on Greek neo-paganism, see Naoum (2006) and Tsouros (2008). The latter, although sponsored by and admitting partiality to the Greek Orthodox Church (Tsouros 2008, 21), and although ultimately failing to maintain an academically detached approach, nevertheless offers a complete resource of groups, categories, journals and websites associated with Greek neo-paganism. The reader will find in its 696 pages currently most, if not all, sources, lists of organizations, subtopics and views within the phenomenon.

3 The literature on the issue of women's status in ancient Greece is obviously vast. In addition to the works cited in this paper, a brief but representative list consists of the following works: Cartledge (2003, 2007), Dean-Jones (2003), Farrar (2007), Keuls (1985), King (2002), Patterson (1994), Pomeroy (1995), Raftlaub (1988), Rehm (2003), Scafuro (1994) and Tyrell (1984).

Adler, M. 1979. *Drawing Down the Moon: Witches, Druids, Goddess-Worshippers, and Other Pagans in America Today*. Boston: Beacon Press.

Allione, T. 2005. "In Search of Women's Wisdom." In *Adventures with the Buddha: A Buddhist Reader*. Ed. by J. Paine. New York: W. W. Norton, 217–316.

Amnesty International. 2005. "Greece: Trial against Professor Takis Alexiou." *News Service* no. 329 (December 5), AI Index Eur.

Anaxagoras. 2012. "Thea Athena: I alithini Thea ton Ellinon" [Goddess Athena: The True Goddess of the Hellenes]. (April 26). Online: http://www.youtube.com/watch?v=3Gdo1HEfDfA (accessed May 12, 2012).

Apostoliki Diakonia 2003. *Neo-paganism, a Threat from the Past: The Essence, Origins and Intentions of the Neo-pagan Movement*. Athens: Apostoliki Diakonia.

Beliefnet (n.d.). "Neopagans vs. the Recons." Online: http://www.beliefnet.com/Faiths/Pagan-and-Earth-Based/2002/02/Neopagans-Vs-The-Recons.aspx (accessed February 10, 2011).

Benko, S. 2004. *The Virgin Goddess: Studies in the Pagan and Christian Roots of Mariology*. New York: Brill Academic Publishers.

Behr-Sigel, E. 2003. "The Ordination of Women: A Point of Contention in Ecumenical Cialogue." Paper presented at the Orthodox Theological Society of America, Crestwood, NY (May).

Boss, S. J. 2000. *Empress and Handmaid: On Nature and Gender in the Cult of the Virgin Mary*. London: Cassell.

Buddhanet. (n.d.). *Buddhism and Women: Position of Women at the Time of the Buddha*. Online: http://www.buddhanet.net/e-learning/history/position.htm (accessed August 12, 2008).

Cabezon, J. I. 1992. "Mother Wisdom, Father Love: Gender-based Imagery in Mahayana Buddhist Thought." In *Buddhism, Sexuality and Gender*. Ed. by J. I. Cabezon. New York: State University of New York Press, 37–61.

Campbell, D. 2000. *Old Stones, New Temples*. Bloomington: Xlibris.

Cartledge, P. 2007. "Origins of Democracy: Contribution to a Debate." In *Origins of Democracy in Ancient Greece*. Ed. by K. A. Raaflaub, J. Ober, and R. W. Wallace. Berkeley: University of California Press, 155–69.

_____. 2003. *The Spartans*. New York: The Overlook Press.

_____. 1993. *The Greeks: A Portrait of Self and Others*. Oxford: Oxford University Press.

Dalai Lama 2001. *Answers: Discussions with Western Buddhists*. New York: Snow Lion Publications.

Dean-Jones, L. 2003. "The Cultural Construct of the Female Body in Classical Greek Science." In *Sex and Difference in Ancient Greece and Rome*. Ed. by M. Golden and P. Toohey. Edinburgh: Edinburgh University Press, 183–201.

Demetrios, Archbishop of America. 2002. "The Orthodox Churches in a Pluralistic World: An Ecumenical Conversation." Keynote speech at The Orthodox Churches in a Pluralistic World: A Conference, Boston, October 3–5, 2002. Holy Cross Greek Orthodox School of Theology, in cooperation with the World Council of Churches, Boston Theological Institute and the Initiatives in Religion and Public Life Harvard Divinity School. Online: http://www.goarch.org/special/pluralistic2002/presentations/demetrios (accessed November 10, 2009).

_____. 1994. Keynote speech at The Status of Woman in the Orthodox Church and on the Ordination of Women. Inter-Orthodox theological seminary, Rhodes, October 30–November 7, 1988. Ecumenical Patriarchate. Katerini: Tertios Publications, 21–5.

Diipetes (n.d.). "Index." Online: http://diipetes.tripod.com/newpage1.htm (accessed January 5, 2010).

Dover, K. J. 2003. "Classical Greek Attitudes to Sexual Behaviour." In *Sex and Difference in Classical Greece and Rome*. Ed. by M. Golden and P. Toohey. Edinburgh: Edinburgh University Press, 114–38.

Dubisch, J. 1995. *In a Different Place: Pilgrimage, Gender, and Politics at a Greek Island Shrine*. Princeton: Princeton University Press.

EAR. 2005. *Elliniko Ananeotiko Revma* [Hellenic Renewal Movement/Current]. Online: http://www.ear.gr (accessed February 1, 2005).

Eck, D. L. 2002. "The Christian Churches and the Plurality of Religious Communities." Paper presented at The Orthodox Churches in a Pluralistic World: A Conference, Boston (October 3–5, 2002). Holy Cross Greek Orthodox School of Theology. Online: http://www.goarch.org/special/pluralistic2002/presentations/eck (accessed November 10, 2009).

Eck, D. L. 2007. "Prospects for Pluralism: Voice and Vision in the Study of Religion." Pluralism Project at the University of Harvard. Online: http://jaar.oxfordjournals.org/cgi/content/abstract/lfm061v1?ijkey=hwfP56s1RLBhmWt&keytype=ref (accessed November 10, 2009).

Elaion. 2004. "Magic and Mysticism: Why I Don't Believe in Them." (September) Online: http://www.elaion.org/mm.htm (accessed January 5, 2009).

Elginism. 2006. "Athena's Worshipers Want to Use the Acropolis." *Elginism* (May 5). Online: http://www.elginism.com/20060505/athenas-worshipers-want-to-use-the-acropolis/ (accessed May 1, 2012).

Farrar, C. 2007. "Power to the People." In *Origins of Democracy in Ancient Greece*. Ed. by K. A. Raaflaub, J. Ober and R. W. Wallace. Berkeley: University of California Press, 170–96.

Fitzgerald. K. 1994. "Orthodox Evaluation of Feminist Theology." In The Status of Woman in the Orthodox Church and on the Ordination of Women. Inter-Orthodox theological seminary, Rhodes, October 30–November 7, 1988. Ecumenical Patriarchate. Katerini: Tertios Publications, 423–56.

Fotiou, E. (n.d.). "Research." Online: http://www.madanthro.com/1_2_Curriculum-Vitae.html (accessed August 5, 2010).

Friedman, L. 2000. *Meetings with Remarkable Women: Buddhist Teachers in America*. Boulder: Shambhala Publications.

Goldhill, S. 2004. *Love, Sex and Tragedy*. London: John Murray.

Gould, J. 2001. *Myth, Ritual, Memory and Exchange: Essays in Greek Literature and Culture*. Oxford: Oxford University Press.

Gross, R. M. 1993. *Buddhism after patriarchy: A feminist history, analysis, and reconstruction of Buddhism*. Delhi: Sri Satguru Publications.

Hadad, F. 1994. "The Woman in Secular Society." In The Status of Woman in the Orthodox Church and on the Ordination of Women. Inter-Orthodox theological seminary, Rhodes, October 30–November 7, 1988. Ecumenical Patriarchate. Katerini: Tertios Publications, 138–67.

Harvey, G. 2007. *Listening People, Speaking Earth: Contemporary Paganism*. 2nd edn. London: Hurst and Company.

Haugen, A. M. (n.d.). "Women in Ancient Religions and the Rise of Patriarchal Tradition." *YSEE*. Online: http://www.ysee.gr/index.php?type=article&f=gynaika (accessed November 10, 2009).

Hellenismos US. 2009. "On Same-sex Marriage." *Hellenismos US* (August 6). Online: http://hellenismos.us/b/2009/08/homophobia-and-hellenismos/ (accessed June 2, 2010).

_____. 2009. "You May Be a Fluffy Bunny Hellenic Polytheist If…" *Hellenismos US* (December 20). Online: http://hellenismos.us/b/2009/12/you-may-be-a-fluffy-bunny-hellenic-polytheist-if/ (accessed June 2, 2010)..

Hellenistai. 2009. "Question about Hellenic Wicca." *Hellenistai Project Forum* (August 7). Online: http://forum.hellenistai.com/viewtopic.php?f=32&t=77 (accessed April 2, 2010).

Hughes, J. D. 1994. *Pan's Travail: Environmental Problems of the Ancient Greeks and Romans*. Baltimore: The Johns Hopkins University Press.

Ioannides, K. (Host). 2006. *Tolmo* (television show) (February 17). Nicosia: Sigma Channel.

Kerenyi, K. 1978. *Athena: Virgin and Mother in Greek Religion*. Woodstock: Spring Publications.

Keuls, E. C. 1985. *The Reign of the Phallus: Sexual Politics in Ancient Athens*. Berkeley: University of California Press.

King, H. 2002. "Bound to Bleed: Artemis and Greek Women." In *Sexuality and Gender in the Classical World: Readings and Sources*. Ed. by L. McLure. London: Blackwell Publishers, 109–27.

Klein, A. C. 2004. "Buddhist Understanding of Subjectivity." In *Buddhist Women and Social Justice: Ideals, Challenges, and Achievements*. Ed. by K. L. Tsomo. New York: State University of New York Press, 23–34.

Kleitor. 2007. Blog post (September 21, 2006): http://kleitor.blogspot.com/2006/09/blog-post_21.html (accessed January 12, 2008).

Koukoura, D. A. 2005. *I thesi tis gynaikas stin Orthothoksi Ekklisia* [Woman's Position in the Orthodox Church]. Athens: Kornelia Sfakianaki Publications.

Krippas, G. 2004. "The Legal Measures against Neo-idolatry." In the Phenomenon of Neo-idolatry: Dodekatheism, Devaluation of the Old Testament, and the Olympic Games;

Records of the academic conference, Thessaloniki, May 25–27, 2003; Association for Orthodox Studies; Theodromia Publications.

Li, Y.-C. 2005. "Guanyin and the Buddhist Scholar-Nuns: The Changing Meaning of Nunhood." *Journal of Women in Culture and Society* 1: 4–25. Online: http://www.rci.rutgers. edu/religion/SSCR/li_miaoshan.pdf (accessed January 10, 2009).

Linzie, B. 2004. "Uncovering the Effects of Cultural Background on the Reconstruction of Ancient Worldviews." Online: http://www.angelfire.com/nm/seidhman/cultural_ bkgd.pdf (accessed February 21, 2007).

Loraux, N. 1986. *The Invention of Athens: The Funeral Oration in the Classical City*. Trans. A. Sheridan. Cambridge, MA: Harvard University Press.

Loy, D. R. 2007. "Karma and women." *Kyoto Journal*. Online: http://www.kyotojournal. org/gender/karma_women.shtml (accessed November 30, 2009)

Lymoures, G. 1994. "The Orthodox Position toward the Heterodox Opinions in Favor of Women's Ordination." In The Status of Woman in the Orthodox Church and on the Ordination of Women. Inter-Orthodox theological seminary, Rhodes, October 30–November 7, 1988. Ecumenical Patriarchate. Katerini: Tertios Publications. 395–423.

Marinis, P. 1996. *[Helliniki Threskeia-To Dodekatheon] Hellenic Religion – The Dodecatheon*. Athens: Eleftheri Skepsis Editions.

Madsen, R. 2007. *Democracy's Dharma: Religious Renaissance and Political Development in Taiwan*. Berkeley: University of California Press.

Matthewes-Green, F. 2007. "Women's Ordination. The Self-Ruled Antiochian Orthodox Christian Archdiocese of North America." *Beliefnet* (January 10). Online: http://www. antiochian.org/node/17953 (accessed January 10, 2011).

Mene, C. 2000. *Neopaganism: The Renaissance of the Ancient Religion*. Athens: Archetypo.

Metallinos, G. 2003. *Paganistic Hellenism or Hellenorthodoxy? A Response to the Neo-pagan Provocation*. Athens: Armos.

Miller, J. (n.d.). "The Return of the Hellenes. Worlds of Difference: Local Culture in a Global Age." Radio documentary. Homeland Productions. Online: http://homelands. org/worlds/hellenes.html (accessed February 2, 2011).

Murray, O. 1986. "Life and Society in Classical Greece." In *The Oxford History of Greece and the Hellenistic World*. Ed. by J. Bordman, J. Griffin and O. Murray. Oxford: Oxford University Press, 52–74.

Naoum, M. 2006. "Elliniki thriskeia: Anagnorisi, diafores, erithes" [Hellenic Religion: Recognition, Differences, Grievances]. *Aneksigito* 212 (July–August): 5–9.

Paraskevaides, C. 2005. *Hellenism Proselytized: The Transition of Hellenism from Antiquity to Christianity*. Athens: Holy Synod of the Church of Greece.

Patterson, C. 1994. "The Case against Neaira and the Public Ideology of the Athenian Family." In *Athenian Identity and Civic Ideology*. Ed. by A. L. Boeghold, and A. C. Scafuro. Baltimore: The Johns Hopkins University Press, 199–216.

Paul, D. Y. 1985. *Women in Buddhism: Images of the Feminine in the Mahayana Tradition*. 2nd edn. Berkeley: University of California Press.

PELA. 2009. *Politeia Eleftherias ki' Aretis* [World Society of Knowledge and Virtue]. Online: http://www.pela-polites.org/index.php?option=com_content&view=article&id=80&It emid=161 (accessed May 5, 2010).

Pilaeus. 2011. "Olympus: The Gods Never Left—Full Movie." (January 6). Online: http:// www.youtube.com/watch?v=2P4TeC6BA9A (accessed January 1, 2012).

Pittas, G. (Host). 2006. *Sta monopatia tou galaxia*. Radio broadcast, July 5. Nicosia: Astra 92.8 FM.

Pomeroy, S. 1995. *Goddesses, Whores, Wives and Slaves*. New York: Shocken Books.

Raaftlaub, K. 1988. "The Transformations of Athens in the Fifth Century." In *Democracy, Empire and the Arts in Fifth-century Athens*. Ed. by D. Boedeker and K. Raaflaub. Cambridge, MA: Harvard University Press, 275–96.

Rassias, V. 2010. "Aposafeniseis gia tin eimarmene kai mantiki" [Clarifications Regarding Fate and Divination]. *Philosophikon Athenaion Ekatevolos* (April). Online: http://www.youtube.com/watch?v=2CwFzGAj4To (accessed February 10, 2011).

———. 2007. "The Relevance of the Ancient Greek Spirit: A Necessity for Our Modern World." Online: http://ysee.gr/index.php?type=article&f=epikerotitaap (accessed April 3, 2011).

———. 2007. "Politiki thesi gia tin paideia" [Political Position on Education]. Speech delivered at the meeting of EAR at EAR Main Offices, Athens (February). Online: http://www.rassias.gr/1069.html (accessed August 1, 2007).

———. 2006. "Thoughts on Human Sexuality." *Philosophikon Athenaion Ekatevolos* (May). Online: http://ekatevolos.ysee.gr/html/06_05_31.html (accessed November 10, 2009).

———. 2005. "Church and State: Will Their Traditionally Parallel Journeys Hold Together in the New Environment of Globalization?" Paper presented at a YSEE meeting in the Aithousa Logou kai Technis, Athens (March). Online: http://www.rassias.gr/1038.html (accessed June 21, 2010).

———. 1995. "Hellenism: What We Believe, What We Stand For." *Vlasis G. Rassias*. Online: http://www.rassias.gr/9025.html (accessed October 2, 2010).

Reed, B. E. 1992. "The Gender Symbolism of Guanyin Bodhisattva." In *Buddhism, Sexuality and Gender*. Ed. by J. I. Cabezon. New York: State University of New York Press, 159–80.

Rehm, R. 2003. *Radical Theater: Greek Tragedy and the Modern World*. London: Gerald Duckworth and Co. Ltd.

Revel, J. and M. Richard. 1998. *The Monk and the Philosopher: A Father and Son Discuss the Meaning of Life*. New York: Schocken Books.

Scafuro, A. 1994. "Witnessing and False Witnessing: Proving Citizenship and Kin Identity in Fourth-century Athens." In *Athenian Identity and Civic Ideology*. Ed. by A. L. Boeghold and A. C. Scafuro. Baltimore: The Johns Hopkins University Press, 156–98.

Schizas, I. 2010. "IHOR: I Megalyteri Ekdilosi Ton Telefteon Hronon" [IHOR: The Greatest Festivity In Recent Years]. Online: http://www.schizas.com/site3/el/ihor-i-megalyteri-ekdilosi-ton-teleytaion-hronon.html (accessed January 18, 2010).

Societas Hellenica Antiquariorum (n.d.a). "Official Theses of the Greek Religion: Concerning Important Social Issues." Societas Hellenica Antiquariorum; Committee of the Greek (Hellenic) Religion of Dodecatheon. Online: http://homepage.mac.com/dodecatheon/24HRT (accessed February 12, 2012).

Societas Hellenica Antiquariorum (n.d.b). "The Orphic Hymns: To Pallas Athena. Societas Hellenica Antiquariorum." Online: http://homepage.mac.com/dodecatheon/24OR4 (accessed February 12, 2012).

Sissa, G. and M. Detienne. 2000. *The Daily Life of the Greek Gods*. Stanford: Stanford University Press.

Smith, H. 2007. "By Zeus!" *Guardian* (February 1). Online: http://www.guardian.co.uk/world/2007/feb/01/religion.uk (accessed January 30, 2010).

Strmiska, M. F. 2005. *Modern Paganism in World Cultures: Comparative Perspectives*. Santa Barbara: ABC-CLIO.

The Cauldron. 2011. "Modern human needs and Hellenic religion." (July 5). Online: http://www.ecauldron.com/forum/showthread.php?188-Modern-Human-Needs-and-Hellenic-Religion (accessed April 20, 2012).

————. 2009. "Hellenic marriage." (October 22). Online: http://www.ecauldron.net/forum/index.php?topic=10463.0 (accessed May 1, 2010).

Tsomo, K. L. 2004. "Is the Bhiksuni Vinaya Sexist?" In *Buddhist Women and Social Justice: Ideals, Challenges, and Achievements*. Ed. by K. L. Tsomo. New York: State University of New York Press, 45–72.

Tsouros, K. 2008. *O neopaganismos tis Neas Epohis* [The Neo-paganism of the New Age]. Athens: Panellinia Enosi Goneon gia tin Prostasia tou Ellinorthodoxou Politismou, tis Oikogeneias, kai toy Atomou [Panhellenic Union of Parents for the Protection of the Greek-Orthodox Culture, the Family and the Individual].

Tyrell, W. B. 1984. *Amazons: A Study in Athenian Mythmaking*. Baltimore: Johns Hopkins University Press.

Vliagoftes, A. 2004. "Neo-idolatry and the New Age." In The Phenomenon of Neo-idolatry: Dodekatheism, Devaluation of the Old Testament, and the Olympic Games. Records of the academic conference, Thessaloniki, May 25–27, 2003. Thessaloniki: Association for Orthodox Studies, Theodromia Publications.

Vliagoftes, A. 2006. *Ecumenism, Neo-idolatry, and the New Age*. Athens: Parakatathiki.

Willis, J. 2005. "An African-American Woman's Journey into Buddhism." In *Adventures with the Buddha: A Buddhist Reader*. Ed. by J. Paine. New York: W. W. Norton, 317–46.

Wilson, J. 2008. "Deeply Female and Universally Human: The Rise of Guanyin Worship." *Journal of Contemporary Religion* 23, no. 3: 285–306.

World Council of Churches. 1998. "Faith and Order Discussions on the Ordination of Women." Conference at New Skete Monastery, Cambridge, NY, May 26–June 1, 1998 (June 1). Online: http://www.oikoumene.org/en/resources/documents/wcc-programmes/ecumenical-movement-in-the-21st-century/member-churches/special-commission-on-participation-of-orthodox-churches/sub-committee-ii-style-ethos-of-our-life-together/faith-and-order-on-womens-ordination.html (accessed January 5, 2011).

Wurst, R. 2000. "Sakhyadhita in Western Europe: A Personal Perspective." In *Women's Buddhism, Buddhism's Women: Tradition, Revision, Renewal*. Ed. by E. B. Findly. Somerville: Wisdom Publications, 97–102.

Yannaras, C. 2002. "Human Rights and the Orthodox Church." Paper presented at The Orthodox Churches in a Pluralistic World: A Conference, Boston, MA, October 3–5, 2002. Holy Cross Greek Orthodox School of Theology, in cooperation with the World Council of Churches, Boston Theological Institute and the Initiatives in Religion and Public Life Harvard Divinity School (October 4). Online: http://www.goarch.org/special/pluralistic2002/presentations/yannaras (accessed November 10, 2009).

YSEE. 2009. *Ypato Symvoulio Ellinon Ethnikon* [The Supreme Council of Ethnic Hellenes]. Press release (July). Online: http://www.ysee.gr/index.php?type=d&f=antitheocracy (accessed November 30, 2009).

————. 2005. "What is Discrimination?" From the information leaflet by the Ethnic Coordinating Commission on Discrimination and the New European Legislation. *Ypato Symvoulio Ellinon Ethnikon* [The Supreme Council of Ethnic Hellenes] (May). Online: http://www.ysee.gr/index.php?type=d&f=stopdiscrimination (accessed November 30, 2009).

————. (n.d.a) "About YSEE." *Ypato Symvoulio Ellinon Ethnikon* [The Supreme Council of Ethnic Hellenes]. Online: http://www.ysee.gr/index-eng.php?type=english&f=about (accessed February 4, 2010).

_____. (n.d.b). "FAQ." *Ypato Symvoulio Ellinon Ethnikon* [The Supreme Council of Ethnic Hellenes]. http://www.ysee.gr/index-eng.php?type=english&f=faq (accessed June 1, 2007).

_____. (n.d.c). "Theseis pano stin aneksithriskia" [Position on Freedom of Religion]. *Ypato Symvoulio Ellinon Ethnikon* [The Supreme Council of Ethnic Hellenes]. Online: http://www.ysee.gr/index.php?type=article&f=anexithriskeia (accessed November 10, 2008).

YSEE USA. (n.d.). *Ypato Symvoulio Ellinon Ethnikon Amerikis* [The Supreme Council of Ethnic Hellenes of the USA]. Online: http://www.ysee.us (accessed January 23, 2009).

Yu, C.-F. 2001. *Guanyin: The Chinese Transformation of Avalokitesvara*. New York: Columbia University Press.

_____. 1995. "Chinese Women Pilgrims' Songs Glorifying Guanyin." In *Buddhism in Practice*. Ed. by D. S. Lopez Jr. Princeton and Oxford: Princeton University Press, 139–43.

Chapter 6

THE GLOBALIZATION OF THE NEW SPIRITUALITY AND ITS EXPRESSION IN JAPAN: THE CASE OF MT IKOMA[1]

Girardo Rodriguez Plasencia
Ritsumeikan Asia Pacific University, Japan

Introduction

The development of New Spirituality, also called New Age or alternative spiritualities, is closely associated with globalization, a process that mobilizes a wide range of religious referents and practices. However, globalization does not imply merely a local, passive appropriation of external religious beliefs and practices, for it involves interactions with local contexts that in turn provide symbols and ideologies leading to cultural hybridity. In this regard, New Spirituality has found fertile soil in Japan, a nation that has long cultivated a religious culture that is vibrant and dynamic in its own right, yet is receptive to foreign influences that suit local purposes.

The present work is part of an ongoing research project and is partly based on the data collected during fieldwork in the summer of 2009 around Mt Ikoma, a mountain range in the Kinki area of Japan where the religious culture has been shaped by Buddhist schools of thought, folk religion, Korean shamanism and New Religions. Due to the paucity of information on new spirituality in Ikoma and limited empirical data collected through fieldwork to date, this research is still in its infancy and as such this chapter only aspires to: 1) provide an overview of the emergence of New Spirituality in Mt Ikoma; and 2) explore the neo-syncretism or interaction of New Spirituality with Ikoma's traditional religious culture as one way in which New Spirituality and the process of globalization are closely related.

After a brief overview of the development of New Spirituality in Japan, the chapter analyzes the globalization of New Spirituality through Inoue Nobutaka's (2001) concept of neo-syncretism and Shimazono Susumu's (1999, 2004) arguments regarding the hybridization of New Spirituality with Japan's religious culture. The specific geographical focus of this chapter is Mt Ikoma, where neo-syncretism or interaction of New Spirituality with local religious culture is expressed through the sacralization of nature and the self.

New Spirituality in Japan

Since the 1970s, Japan has witnessed a growing interest in religion and spiritualism in the form of a fascination with products and services related to psychic powers, spiritual healing, contact with other realms of existence, near-death experiences, channeling, UFO beliefs, energy crystals, out-of-body experiences, chakras, transpersonal psychology, New Age charms, spiritual counseling, Tarot, divination, horoscopes and the like. Particularly in urban areas, numerous bookstores have opened special sections labeled "spiritual world," selling books on these topics. Likewise, many New Age shops have appeared throughout the country supplying a variety of spiritual items. Many of these spiritual themes have also been popularized through mass media and diverse forms of entertainment such as manga (comics) and anime (animation), and in cyberspace. But the interest in spiritual matters is not limited to passive consumption and the commercialization of the sacred. In fact, quite a few individuals are engaged in activities by which they can put such ideas into practice, through meditation, yoga, breathing techniques, bodywork, esoteric practices, *qigong*, healing methods, self-development seminars and so on (Haga and Kisala 1995; Itō 2002; Kisala 2002; Mullins 1992; Reader 1991; Shimazono 1999, 2002, 2004; Yumiyama 1995).

"The Japanese New Age scene is booming," writes Inken Prohl (2007, 359), referring to the rising interest that the Japanese show towards Western New Age publications by authors such as Shirley MacLaine, Fritjof Capra, Gurdjieff, Carlos Castaneda, Ram Dass and Rudolf Steiner, among others. But publications are not limited to Western authors; there are also growing numbers of Japanese writers covering topics pertaining to New Spirituality (Haga and Kisala 1995; Prohl 2007). Ecology, the environment and agriculture are other areas where New Spirituality is manifested in Japan, with Japanese authors suggesting alternative approaches that diverge from modern rationalism and science. Shimazono (1996) has proposed the term "alternative knowledge movements" (AKM) to refer to this trend based on the interaction of Japanese folk traditions of community life, traditional religions, and modern science and technology.

The popularization of things spiritual in Japan has been influenced by several social factors arising at critical stages in Japanese history. The oil shocks of 1973, which interrupted the nation's rapid post-World War II economic progress, spawned different attitudes among the Japanese, leading many to question their faith in consumerism and modern technology. A second major psychological shift occurred during the economic recession of the 1990s which encouraged the cultivation and development of Japanese individuality on spiritual and other matters, thus creating an opportunity for Japanese to challenge their culture's emphasis on social conformity (Berthon and Kashio 2000; Kisala 2002; Mullins 1992; Yumiyama 1995).

During the 1990s, New Spirituality in Japan was linked to a "healing boom" (*iyashi būmu*) and concern with individual destiny (*unmei*). Both healing and destiny are subjects that are discussed with a view to improving personal lifestyles and spiritual development. Those interested in these subjects often mix an eclectic array of methods, beliefs and techniques from sources such as modern science, Western New Age beliefs and practices, Eastern religions, alternative medicine, and Japanese popular and consumer culture. Many Japanese are only interested in the quest for wellbeing, while others wish to go further and attain mystical experiences. In any case, the central notion is the possibility of connecting with the "original," "inner" or "higher" self to realize self-improvement (Ozawa-de Silva 2006, 160–62; Prohl 2007; Yumiyama 1995).

The Japanese interest in the "spiritual world" reached its peak in the late 1990s, which witnessed a marked psychologization of religion and healing methods. The term "spiritual world," however, has been increasingly replaced by the concepts "spirituality" and "spiritual" (*supirichuariti* and *supirichuaru*, respectively), which have been borrowed directly from English. Although some Japanese words (*reisei* and *seishin*) had been previously used to refer to "spirituality," the English loan words are preferred at both the popular and academic level because of the associations with the realm of the deceased that the Japanese terms carry, as well as the diffuse and vague meaning of the English words, which allow for the accommodation of a plurality of practices and beliefs under a single hard-to-define phenomenon (Itō, Kashio and Yumiyama 2004; Prohl 2007; Shimazono 2004).

As part of a general tendency among contemporary Japanese to refuse any association with "religion," particularly religious institutions, Buddhism is commonly seen as a funerary and often corrupt religion, Shinto is still remembered for its strong connections with imperialism and the New Religions (*shinshūkyō*) are thought to be profit-making organizations that threaten social stability. Negative images attached to religion must also be seen in the anti-cult context that developed after the "New-New Religion" Aum Shinrikyō perpetrated the Sarin gas attacks in the Tokyo subway in 1995, strengthening the common view of religion as "a social problem" (Dorman 2007; Inoue 2001, 2003; Kisala 2002, 2006; Lifton 1999; Tsujimura 2008). If the occult and the acquisition of psychic powers were common themes in the "spiritual world," after the Aum incident and with the increasing use of the term "spirituality," the emphasis has shifted to a culture of wellbeing. "The spiritual," though undefined, is associated with positive things, avoiding any dark connotations (Tsujimura 2008). Related to this point, Prohl (2007) notes that the most significant trend in contemporary Japanese healing is its focus on body aesthetics (*esute de iyasu*).

New Spirituality as a Global Phenomenon

Concerns with "spirituality" and the "spiritual world" in Japan are viewed by some scholars as a regional manifestation of New Age Religion (Mullins 1992; Prohl 2007). For Shimazono (1999, 2004), however, "New Age" refers to the specific expression of a religious phenomenon common to industrialized societies in Europe and the US. In Japan, although an equivalent term exists (*niu eiji*), interest in "New Age"-like spiritual matters is associated with the terms "spiritual world" (*seishinsekai*) and "spirituality" (see also Itō 2003).

Shimazono (2004) feels that the use of the expression "New Age" to designate a worldwide phenomenon is misleading mainly because the socio-cultural context in which related religious movements arise varies from place to place, creating unique belief systems that differ from European and American New Age thinking. Hence, Shimazono proposes the expression "new spirituality movements and cultures" (*shinreisei undō bunka*) to encompass both the Western New Age phenomenon and the Japanese emphasis on the "spiritual world," and which can be applied to similar phenomena elsewhere in the contemporary world. Different degrees of participation can be observed in new spirituality movements and cultures, which vary, as seen above, from a passive attitude of spiritual goods consumption to a deeper engagement in spiritual practices and associations. An important point here is the fact that, regardless of the degree of participation, New Spirituality is part of contemporary Japanese popular culture, which means it can appear in places such as Japanese animation, the writings of "spiritual intellectuals" or in the way people express their identities (Itō 2002; Prohl 2007; Shimazono 2004).

There is some relation also between New Spirituality and those New Religious Movements (NRMs) that stress the role of the individual or emphasize a more open communitarian regime, such as the Rajneesh movement, or the Japanese New Religions, especially the so-called "New-New Religions" (*shinshinshūkyō*)

(Shimazono 1999, 2004). However, most Japanese New Religions—particularly those that developed before the religious boom of the 1970s—show remarkable differences with the NSMC regarding their organizational structure, teachings on salvation, the role of the founder and the place of the individual (Shimazono 1999, 2004).

As it happens in Europe and North America, where many individuals engaged in these contemporary spiritual practices refuse to identify their worldviews or values as "New Age" (Sutcliffe 2003), in Japan too some dislike the label "spiritual world," hence making it difficult to identify such individuals. Notwithstanding *emic* preferences, it is possible to find common traits among people engaged in new forms of spirituality. Under the expression "new spirituality movements and cultures," Shimazono (2004, 276) sees a "wide range of individualistic spiritual quests developing in many parts of the world, especially in advanced industrial societies […] representing one new global religious culture." Despite their diverse beliefs, most such movements, according to Shimazono (2004), share similar features, such as an emphasis on the transformation of consciousness, a belief in a spiritual existence or supra-consciousness, a belief in the inner possibilities of the individual to achieve self-development and an attempt to reconcile religion and science (see also Haga and Kisala 2005; Itō, Kashio and Yumiyama 2004; Kisala 2002).

Although some authors have suggested that New Spirituality is predominantly a Western phenomenon (Lynch 2007; Sutcliffe 2003), research done not only in Japan but also in South Korea (Woo 2008), Southeast Asia (Ackerman 2005; Howell 2005), Taiwan (Chen 2008), Latin America (Carozzi 2007; Maldonado 2009) and, to some extent, in Africa (Hackett 1992; Oosthuizen 1992; Steyn 1994) and Eastern Europe (Doktór 1999) reports its appearance in other latitudes. Thus, Peter Beyer (2007) notes that even if much research takes the nation as its unit of analysis, scholars are increasingly approaching New Spirituality from a global perspective (Beyer 2007; see also Rohstein 2001). By reviewing the literature on religion, spirituality and globalization, and by clarifying the relation between these notions, Kale (2004) identifies the following key trends that characterize contemporary spirituality in the context of globalization: reterritorialization through spirituality, which provides new identities in an increasingly globalized world; the integration of spirituality in everyday life; the individualization of spirituality; the active use of cyberspace; and syncretism. The present discussion focuses on syncretism, or more accurately "neo-syncretism," as Inoue Nobutaka labels it (Inoue 2001), to explore the way in which New Spirituality (the global) interacts with Japan's religious culture (the local), particularly at Mt Ikoma.

Neo-syncretism: Interaction between New Spirituality and Japan's Religious Culture

Several authors have pointed out that New Spirituality in Japan maintains a remarkable continuity with Japanese religious culture, unlike New Age ideologies in the West and their tendency to clash with the dominant Judeo-Christian tradition (Berthon and Kashio 2000; Itō 2002; Kashio 2002; Mullins 1992; Shimazono 2004). In fact, sections on the "spiritual world" in Japanese bookstores also include publications on Shintoism, Japanese Buddhism and famous Japanese religious figures, while sections with New Age publications in Europe and the United States do not typically include books on mainstream Christianity (Chryssides 2007). New Spirituality has thus contributed to a renewed interest in Japanese religious traditions, an example of which is the popularity of books on Dōgen Kigen (1200–1253), an important figure in Japanese Zen Buddhism from the Kamakura period (1185–333) (Itō 2002; Prohl 2007; Shimazono 2004).

Japanese traditional religions are also an important source upon which Japanese New Spirituality draws its discourse on overcoming modern dualist science. This is particularly the case with the re-appropriation of ancient Shintoism (*koshintō*) as an alternative ideology to cope with environmental degradation. Such a perspective bases its claims on the notion that the animism of ancient Shinto spirituality—as distinguished from militarist state Shintoism and modern-day sectarian Shintoism—is the essence of Japanese religiosity and teaches humankind how to live harmoniously with nature, making Shinto animism ideal for guiding life in a postmodern society. These claims are tinted with a certain degree of nationalism, as revealed in the writings of "spiritual intellectuals": mainstream Japanese writers articulating a religious discourse on Japaneseness (Prohl 2004; Shimazono 2004).

Buddhism also provides a source of continuity between New Spirituality and Japanese religious culture. Although participants of new spirituality may be disappointed with traditional Japanese Buddhist sects and institutionalized religion, they do sympathize with the teachings and practices of "original" Buddhism, referring not only to Indian Buddhism but also to the teachings of Japanese founders of Buddhist schools such as Kōbō Daishi (a.k.a., Kūkai) (774–835), Dōgen (1200–1253) and Saichō (767–822), respectively the founders of the esoteric Shingon, Sōtō and Tendai schools. New spirituality practitioners usually join meditation groups (*zazenkai*) mostly managed by Buddhist organizations but to which they do not belong, participate in pilgrimages to Buddhist sacred places or borrow Buddhist practices for bodywork (Hoshino 2001, as cited in Reader 2003; Reader 1991, 103, 104; Shimazono 2004).

This interaction within Japan's religious culture is not limited to traditional religions, for a common ground also often exists within Japanese New Religious Movements. Indeed, many members of Japanese New Religions have first been attracted to religious themes through books on the "spiritual world" and more amorphous spiritual practices. This is particularly the case with Aum Shinrikyō, a Japanese "New" New Religion that started simply as a small yoga group and was nurtured by New Spirituality interests in psychology and the attainment of supernatural and psychic powers (*chōnōryoku*). Members of Japanese New Religions will often consume goods and services of the New Spirituality, even while they maintain official affiliations with their original religious organizations (Reader 2000; Shimazono 2004).

The idea of continuity between New Spirituality and Japan's religious culture can be complemented with the notion of neo-syncretism, proposed by Inoue Nobutaka as one of the trends in the globalization of religion (Inoue 2001). Although syncretism is a phenomenon that is evident in societies with diverse religious traditions, in an information society neo-syncretism is a contemporary variant by which elements of diverse religions are merged "intentionally and aggressively, merely on the basis of available information, and without the necessity of any actual contact between the religious groups involved" (Inoue 2001). The following sections attempts to explore some aspects of the neo-syncretism in Ikoma.

Exploring the New Spirituality in Ikoma

The study area

Mt Ikoma is located along the border of Osaka and Nara prefectures, in the Kinki region of Japan. Located in Kongo-Ikoma Quasi-National Park, Ikoma has popular hiking courses and other recreational facilities, such as the Skyland Ikoma amusement park. Although it is not so high (642 m), Mt Ikoma has served as an important sacred place in the region since ancient times, hosting a variety of religious traditions and influences and accommodating a mixture of both asceticism and folk practices related to attaining worldly benefits. Shintoism is well represented at Mt Ikoma with the popular Ishikiri Shrine, believed by some to have special healing powers. Ikoma is also associated with popular religious figures such as En-no-Gyōja, a legendary ascetic of the seventh century believed to be the founder of the Shugendō school,[2] and Kōbō Daishi (Kūkai), the founder of the Shingon school of esoteric Buddhism. The mountain hosts famous Buddhist centers of the area. Hōzanji temple, affiliated with the Shingon-Ritsu sect and commonly known as Ikoma's Shōten-san, owns important cultural properties of Japanese Buddhist art, and is especially popular as a pilgrimage site for believers to pray for business success, good health and a long life. Shigisan (Chōgosonshi-ji), a Buddhist temple of the Shingon school, also possesses important cultural assets and pilgrims visit it to attain worldly benefits (Ikoma City Official Website, n.d.; Shūkyō Shakaigaku-no-Kai 1985).

In modern times, too, Mt Ikoma has functioned as an important place for folk religion, with mediums, diviners and Shugendō priests there engaging in ascetic practices, notably waterfall austerities (a ritual in which practitioners endure immersion under a waterfall or other steady stream of water for protracted periods), and providing religious services to the population of the Osaka Metropolitan Area.[3] Several Japanese New Religions have also established their missions and facilities in Ikoma. Moreover, Ikoma possesses the largest concentration of so-called "Korean temples" in Japan, offering religious services mainly to the Korean community of the region while blending elements of Korean Buddhism, Korean shamanism, Shugendō and Japanese mountain worship (Iida 1988; Shūkyō Shakaigaku-no-Kai 1985).

In examining Mt Ikoma to discuss examples of the New Spirituality, several instances exhibiting the features of this phenomenon were identified. The discussion below now turns to the fasting training centers and the Kundalini Yoga Center in the region.[4]

Fasting training centers

In a study carried out by the Kinki-based Association for the Sociology of Religion in the 1980s (Shūkyō Shakaigaku-no-Kai 1985), a section on contemporary Ikoma was found to be devoted to folk medicine, referring to healing practices that are marginal to mainstream modern medical science. As examples of new forms of these folk medical practices, two fasting training centers were identified.

Ikoma's fasting training centers appeared prior to the emergence of the Japanese "spiritual world" phenomenon, and the study mentioned above did not explicitly categorize them as "New Age" or "New Spirituality," but aspects of their discourses, practices and organizational structures suggest they deserve further consideration as such, displaying as they do the basic tenets of the New Spirituality outlined by Shimazono (2004).

Beliefs and practices

As establishments operating in our present age, the two training centers offer health services that combine modern science and alternative therapies, the intention being to overcome the shortcomings of standard contemporary medicine.

In naming religious centers, the term *dojo*, which has a long history in Japan, is applied to places devoted to the training of the mind and body through martial arts, Japanese traditional arts (tea ceremony, flower arranging, etc.) and *zazen* (meditation). The fasting centers as such are given the *dojo* designation. They focus on fasting combined with other practices such as meditation and *sutra* chanting to achieve spiritual balance. In line with their holistic approach to healing, they also make use of the natural environment of Mt Ikoma, treating it as a space to escape and recuperate from the stresses of urban life, return to nature and find the original self.

However, each of these centers struggles to differentiate its identity, as evidenced in their individual interpretations of the religious or non-religious nature of their practices. Thus, the fasting training center in the Shigisan area in south Ikoma stresses the religious character of the institution and even encourages participants to visit neighboring temples. On the other hand, the fasting center located in the Houzanji area in north Ikoma denies any connection with religion, articulating a discourse that places health of body and mind as their only purpose, in spite of the religious associations implied by practices such as meditation and *sutra* chanting.

Structure and demographics

The organizational structure of the fasting *dojo* revolves around the instructor, supported by an administrative staff. Commonly, participants do not attend on a regular basis, but rather might join the program only once as patients and/or clients.

Despite its religious influences, the fasting *dojo* in south Ikoma does not seem to qualify as a New Religious Movement, mainly because it lacks the requisite organizational structure. Since its participants are rather irregularly involved on a client basis, it might better be classified as a client cult, along the lines posited in Possamaï's (2007) revision of the network paradigm and the cultic milieu. Recently, this fasting *dojo* has incorporated practices such as yoga and macrobiotics in an effort to accommodate itself to contemporary Japanese society, and also as a result of the influence of globalization. In so adapting, it has diversified its services to attract a wider clientele. The worldviews of clients are bound to be affected in the process, but more empirical data needs to be collected to reach any firm conclusions on the consciousness effects of Ikoma's fasting *dojos*.

Kundalini Yoga Center

Also known as Ikoma Yoga Dojo, this is the headquarters of the 3HO (Healthy, Happy, Holy Organization), a global movement founded in the USA in the

1970s by an Indian master, Yogi Bhajan, to promote Kundalini yoga while keeping a close association with its religious arm, the Sikh Dharma of the Western Hemisphere. The instructor, an American converted to Sikh Dharma, was sent in the late 1980s by Yogi Bhajan to establish the 3HO in Japan.

The 3HO derives its practices and beliefs from Kundalini yoga, Tantric yoga and Sikhism. There are also strong Western elements, such as the belief in the coming of the Aquarian Age and other New Age influences that proliferated in the countercultural North American context in which they emerged. The center stresses that through the practice of Kundalini yoga it is possible to achieve awareness of the unity of mind, body and spirit and to discover "God within." Bodywork, mantras[5] and Sikh prayers are combined to awaken the inner energy that leads to the transformation of individual consciousness and an eventual age of spiritual liberation (Jakobsh 2008; Tobey 1976).

Because of the ambivalence of the 3HO as an organization promoting both yoga and Sikhism, students and practitioners exhibit diverse motivations and commitments. Most Japanese students come from Osaka and Kobe and are interested only in yoga on a client basis, while a small Sikh community sometimes gathers in Ikoma for retreats and specific practices.

The main activities focus on teaching Kundalini yoga at various levels and holding seminars, workshops and teacher training courses. According to the instructor, their main goals are to build a 3HO community in Japan, to reactivate the spiritual energy of Mt Ikoma, and to foster an international ambience in the region.

Accordingly, the center functions also as a sort of window through which global influences enter Ikoma, attracting foreign practitioners who temporarily join Japanese students. An example of the globalizing role of this New Spirituality movement was the hosting of a seminar in 2009 called "Inner Journey to the Self," conducted by a Taiwanese master who learned Kundalini yoga in the US and teaches the subject in Thailand, Singapore and Malaysia (3HO Japan homepage, n.d.). Although the Kundalini Yoga Center appeared late in the history of Ikoma, a local magazine devoted to the promotion of Ikoma's cultural sites included it and its Sikh instructor in its list of attractions (*IN/SECTS*, May 2009). New Spirituality as manifested by this group is thus contributing to the globalization process in Ikoma, where diverse ethnic and cultural influences from India, North America and other parts of Asia are meeting and intermingling.

Neo-syncretism in Ikoma

My preliminary research in Ikoma appears to suggest that neo-syncretism as one of the main traits of contemporary globalized spirituality is establishing itself in the region, mainly through the articulation of practices and worldviews based on the sacralization of nature and the self.

"Overcoming modernity": The sacralization of nature and the self

In explaining the process by which New Spirituality is attempting to generate a new universalistic identity, Shimazono (2002) shows how previous cultural sources of universalistic identities, i.e., religion (particularly salvation religions) and secular humanism (based on modern science), have failed to establish lasting and harmonious relations between humankind and nature in our modern globalizing world. New Spirituality thus claims to be a third cultural source aimed at generating a universalistic identity for the postmodern era, one which overcomes mind/body dualism while preserving harmony between man and nature, the individual and society, the global and the local.

In the search for alternatives to "overcome modernity" (to echo the title of a 2008 book by Yasuo Yuasa, a prominent Japanese expert on Oriental spirituality), bodywork and *qi* energy reflect the emerging view of the New Spirituality (Shimazono 2004) while pre-modern wisdom and traditions enjoy widespread acceptance in New Spirituality contexts. In explaining the epistemic significance that the ideology of New Spirituality confers to pre-modern and primal cultures, Partridge (2007) states that the turn from modern to pre-modern perspectives is not regressive as it is modernity itself that is regressive in its scientific and technological reductionism. With such a perspective in mind, it becomes easier to understand the romanticized views many adherents hold of pre-modern cultures in which man is believed to have lived in harmony with himself, nature and others.

The sacralization of nature

Nature was once revered as sacred in many cultures and societies that held pantheistic and animistic worldviews. With the process of modernization, however, scientific worldviews, rationalist reductionism and the secularization of society have contributed to rising disenchantment in the world. Desacralized by modernization, nature became the object of human domination and industrial exploitation that favored economic growth and technological progress. In addition, modern urbanization gradually separated people living in big cities from direct interaction with their natural environment, leading to a sense of alienation and otherness of nature (Hanegraaff 2007; Lynch 2007; York 2001).

New Spirituality ideology claims to overcome alienation from nature and nature/man dualism by proposing a view in which the world is re-enchanted and thus nature becomes an object of reverence and celebration. Awakening to the unity within nature is valued in itself as a spiritual experience conducive to the feeling of interconnectedness, a core notion of New Spirituality (Bowman 2007; Lynch 2007; Tacey 2004; York 2001).

The quest for unity with nature entails the active search for natural surroundings that can provide reflective spaces for spiritual practice, especially for those who usually reside in urban areas. Natural sites are thought to provide environments that enable individuals to reconnect to their inner selves and recover what humanity has lost through modernization and urbanization. These beliefs help explain the trend of establishing facilities and gathering points at natural spots outside urban areas (Ozawa-de Silva 2006; Tacey 2004).

Opinions on the degree to which nature can be sacralized vary among practitioners of New Spirituality. The strongest sacralizing perspective considers nature as holy, the manifestation of and/or the dwelling of the divine spirit(s), and therefore worthy of worship (Lynch 2007). The philosophy of the Fasting Training Center in south Ikoma exhibits elements that clearly sacralize nature, such as a belief in the healing powers of nature granted by the gods and buddhas. In discussing the environment, the Kundalini Yoga Center supports certain Shinto practices, such as inviting a Shinto priest to opening ceremonies for new facilities and for the ritual pruning of trees surrounding the center, or the association of a rock at the center's entrance with Amaterasu Omikami, the sun goddess of Shinto mythology. A participant in the Kundalini Yoga Center talked about experiencing similar spiritual feelings at Ikoma as when visiting a revered Shinto shrine, referring to the surroundings of the yoga center as a "spiritual location."

Weaker sacralizing perspectives separate the divine from nature, but they nevertheless depict nature as a catalyzing realm for spiritual development, an escape from the artificial world of contaminated modern human culture (Lynch 2007). The role of Mt Ikoma for promoting spiritual reconnection through its natural surroundings as such has been discussed in a study mentioned above ("Shūkyō Shakaigaku no Kai" 1985). The mountain's convenient location between Osaka and Nara prefectures and the large urban populations nearby serve to reinforce notions of Mt Ikoma's environmental benefits. To attract people to the area, advertisements for the fasting *dojos* and the Kundalini Yoga Center stress the healing properties of the surrounding environment. By promising "authentic" experiences in lush natural surroundings, the center thus contrasts its spiritual or holistic activities with those in urban settlements. As York (2001) suggests, nature in such a way is transformed into a commodity within the spiritual marketplace.

As Ian Reader has frequently noted in his studies on pilgrimages in contemporary Japan, there is a sort of irony in this nostalgic search for natural spaces located far away from modernity, for it is modern technological development, particularly modern means of transportation, that allow contemporary residents of urban settlements to easily reach nature spots and calmly return to their comfortable modern lives (Reader 1987, 2001, 2005). This can be seen with participants in the Kundalini Yoga Center, who most often come to Ikoma to connect with nature not by climbing the mountain as in past times, but by using the cable car of the Kintetsu railway company that connects Ikoma city with the mountaintop.

The sacralization of the self

The self is considered to be the "most powerful metanarrative" in the ideology of New Spirituality (Partridge 2007), conceived as a manifestation of the divine essence of the universe and a source of truth or energy. Interconnectedness, as in the sacralization of nature, constitutes a central notion within this view of the self, the "original," "true" nature of which is believed to be the union of mind, body and spirit. Once again, modern rationalism and materialism are blamed for contributing to an artificial and mechanical disintegration of the self, by separating mind and matter, body and consciousness. In its holistic view of the self, the ideology of New Spirituality emphasizes personal experience as the source of authority to approach the sacred. This is especially evident in the value accorded to embodied experience, which encourages bodywork and practices oriented towards self-awareness through physical exercises. Practices such as yoga, *qigong*, martial arts, ascetic techniques, meditation, therapies and ritualized breathing all enjoy popularity in New Spirituality circles for the importance they place on the body as the prime means for acquiring self-knowledge and attaining self-actualization (Bowman 2007; Heelas 1996; Heelas and Woodhead 2005; Lynch 2007; Shimazono 2004).

Since the self is seen as an indissoluble unity of mind/body/spirit, bodywork leads or constitutes in itself consciousness development and spiritual awakening. Human consciousness is often seen as deriving from a larger or greater supra-consciousness, which is conceived in many different ways by people who are interested in New Spirituality but represented with images of a divine source, a universal energy or an authentic higher self. Thus, the degree to which the self can be sacralized in New Spirituality varies in intensity, with weak to strong interpretations. In any case, it is the goal of bodywork and other spiritual practices to achieve attunement or connectedness between the individual self and this divine consciousness or universal energy.

Embodied experience becomes therefore similar to the revelation of divine truth (Heelas 1996; Lynch 2007; Shimazono 2004).

Ikoma has long been a place chosen by ascetics and believers to perform religious practices that involve bodywork. Waterfall austerities, very often associated with the Buddhist divinity Fudō Myō, are a common practice not only among priests of Buddhist temples of the area but also adherents of Shugendō and Japanese New Religions, worshippers at Korean temples, and mediums and diviners who bring their urban clients to Ikoma. Some members of these groups combine waterfall austerities with other practices such as meditation (*zazen*), pilgrimages and *goma* fire rituals.[6]

The emphasis on bodywork is also central in the fasting *dojos* and in the Kundalini Yoga Center. In fact, in interviews conducted with the instructor of the yoga center, a recurrent theme in the instructor's statements was an argument that Kundalini yoga does not differ from Japanese spiritual traditions. While stressing that Kundalini yoga is a *shugyō* (ascetic practice), the instructor pointed out similarities with other practices found in Ikoma, such as waterfall austerities, pilgrimages, meditation, fasting, *goma* fire rituals and mantra chanting. By engaging in such practices, individuals are expected to attain unity of mind, body and spirit, and to find "God within the self."

The fasting *dojos* display different views toward the sacralization of the self. As already mentioned, the *dojo* in the Hōzanji area in north Ikoma denies any association with religion yet shares a discourse on the unity of mind/body/spirit common to traditional asceticism in Ikoma, not to mention its practice of *sutra* chanting and meditation as part of a fasting program. The fasting *dojo* in the Shigisan area in south Ikoma explicitly emphasizes notions concerning sacralization of the self, linking the same practices of the northern *dojo* with beliefs by which bodywork connects the individual with the sacred. Fasting itself is believed to be a natural and divine self-healing method that allows us to reconnect with the energy of the universe.

Conclusions

In an increasingly globalized world, New Spirituality is introducing novel influences and elements into Japan's religious culture. At Mt Ikoma, we have noted the example of the introduction of foreign cultural and religious elements at the Kundalini Yoga Center, which in addition to yoga also promotes aspects of Sikhism and other non-Japanese influences.

The introduction of global cultural elements, however, is not the only side to the globalization of New Spirituality, as one of the key trends of contemporary globalized spirituality is neo-syncretism (Inoue 2001; Kale 2004). New Spirituality not only adds another layer to Mt Ikoma's diverse religious history, it also interacts with the already rich religious resources available in the region. In this negotiation between the global and the local, the neo-syncretism that emerges from the interaction between New Spirituality and Ikoma's religious culture finds common ground in the sacralization of nature and the self. Again, this is illustrated with the example of the Kundalini Yoga Center, which explicitly emphasizes its commonalities with Japanese religious traditions, particularly those practices involving bodywork and nature reverence.

There is no question that the preliminary reflections presented in this chapter require further investigation and fieldwork. For example, the sustainability of the syncretism described above remains to be seen, given the apathy that contemporary Japanese express towards "religion," especially after the 1995 sarin gas attacks of the Aum Shinrikyō cult (Ama 2005; Covell 2005; Dorman 2007; Inoue 2003; Kaplan 1996; Kisala 2002, 2006; Reader 1996, 2000; Shimazono 2004; Tsujimura 2008).

Notes and References

1 I wish to express my gratitude to the Kinki-based Association for the Sociology of Religion (Shūkyō Shakaigaku no Kai) and its members for kindly giving me the opportunity to join them on a fieldwork trip in Ikoma in the summer of 2009 and for their support in introducing me to Ikoma's religious world. Special thanks also go to Professor Katsurajima Nobuhiro of Ritsumeikan University and his colleagues Professors Yumiyama Tatsuya (Taisho University) and Sakurai Yoshihide (Hokkaido University) who first introduced me to this group. I also wish to thank Professor Joseph Progler from Ritsumeikan Asia Pacific University for his invaluable comments on my field report, upon which this chapter is partially based.

2 A syncretic traditional ascetic religion of mountain worship, blending several religious sources, notably esoteric Buddhist teachings and rituals with Shinto beliefs and practices.

3 Mediums and diviners can be considered as participating in a phenomenon of folk religion. Their activities do not necessarily take place in the frame of religious institutions. Many of them have their own divination spaces in cities and come to Ikoma to worship or to perform waterfall austerities with their clients. But this can be found also in religious organizations in Ikoma, especially the Shugendō priests who offer this kind of services in their own temples. In any case, the people who come seeking these services often do not belong to these particular temples. These religious specialists, whether affiliated or not, are sought because they are popularly credited with special powers or capacities for solving clients' problems (Shūkyō Shakaigaku-no-Kai 1985).

4 Information about the fasting *dojos* and the Kundalini Yoga Center are drawn from their websites, pamphlets, personal observations and/or interviews conducted during fieldwork.

5 Mantra: a Sanskrit term referring to the chanting of syllables, words or phrases whose vibration is believed to have special effects in spiritual transformation.

6 *Goma*: the Japanese transliteration of the Sanskrit word *homa*, a fire ritual performed in Hinduism and Vajrayana Buddhist traditions, such as esoteric Buddhism in Japan.

Ackerman, S. 2005. "Falun Dafa and the New Age Movement in Malaysia: Signs of Health, Symbols of Salvation." *Social Compass* 52: 495–511.

Ama, T. 2005. *Why Are the Japanese Non-religious? Japanese Spirituality: Being Non-religious in a Religious Culture*. Lanham: University Press of America.

Berthon, J. P. and N. Kashio 2000. "Les nouvelles voies spirituelles au Japon: État des lieux et mutations de la religiosité" [The New Spiritual Ways in Japan: Present Conditions and Changes in Religiosity]. *Archives de sciences sociales des religions* 109. Online: http://assr.revues.org/index20176.html (accessed January 6, 2009).

Beyer, P. 2007. "Globalization and Glocalization." In *The Sage Handbook of the Sociology of Religion*. Ed. by J. A. Beckford and N. J. Demerath III. Los Angeles: Sage, 98–118.

Bowman, M. 2007. "Ancient Avalon, New Jerusalem, Heart Chakra of Planet Earth: The Local and the Global in Glastonbury." In *Handbook of New Age*. Ed. by D. Kemp and J. R. Lewis. Leiden: Brill, 291–314.

Carozzi, M. J. 2007. "A Latin American New Age?" In *Handbook of New Age*. Ed. by D. Kemp and J. R. Lewis. Leiden: Brill, 341–58.

Chen, S. C. 2008. *Contemporary New Age Transformation in Taiwan: A Study of the New Age Movement in Taiwan*. Ampeter: Edwin Mellen Press.

Chryssides, G. D. 2007. "Defining the New Age." In *Handbook of New Age*. Ed. by D. Kemp and J. R. Lewis. Leiden: Brill, 5–24.

Covell, S. G. 2005. *Japanese Temple Buddhism: Worldliness in a Religion of Renunciation*. Honolulu: University of Hawai'i Press.

Doktór, T. 1999. "The 'New Age' Worldview of Polish Students." *Social Compass* 46, no. 2: 217–24.

Dorman, B. 2007. "Representing Ancestor Worship as 'Non-religious': Hosoki Kazuko's Divination in the Post-Aum Era." *Nova Religio* 10 no. 3: 32–53.

Hackett, R. 1992. "New Age Trends in Nigeria: Ancestral and/or Alien Religion." In *Perspectives on the New Age*. Ed. by J. R. Lewis and J. G. Melton. Albany: State University of New York Press. 215–31.

Haga, M. and R. Kisala 1995. "Editor's Introduction: The New Age in Japan." *Japanese Journal of Religious Studies* 22 no. 3–4: 235–247.

Hanegraaff, W. J. 2007. "The New Age Movement and Western Esotericism." In *Handbook of New Age*. Ed. by D. Kemp and J. R. Lewis. Leiden: Brill, 25–50.

Heelas, P. 1996. *The New Age Movement: The Celebration of the Self and the Sacralization of Modernity*. Oxford: Blackwell.

Heelas, P. and L. Woodhead 2005. *The Spiritual Revolution: Why Religion Is Giving Way to Spirituality*. Oxford: Blackwell.

Hoshino, E. 2001. *Shikoku henro no shukyogakuteki kenkyu: Sono hozo to kingendai no tenkai* [Research for the Study of Religions through a Pilgrimage to the Shikoku Area: Preservation and the Present Situation]. Kyoto: Hōzōkan.

Howell, J. 2005. "Muslims, the New Age and Marginal Religions in Indonesia: Changing Meanings of Religious Pluralism." *Social Compass* 52: 473–92.

Iida, T. 1988. "Folk Religion among the Koreans in Japan—The Shamanism of the 'Korean Temples.'" *Japanese Journal of Religious Studies* 15: 12–13.

Inoue, N. 2003. *Japanese College Students' Attitudes towards Religion: An Analysis of Questionnaire Surveys from 1992 to 2001*. Tokyo: Kokugakuin University.

———. 1997. "The Information Age and the Globalization of Religion." In *Globalization and Indigenous Culture*. Ed. by N. Inoue. Tokyo: Institute for Japanese Culture and Classics, Kokugakuin University. Online: http://www2.kokugakuin.ac.jp/ijcc/wp/global/06inoue2.html (accessed November 3, 2009).

Quishe. 2009. "Seigensha." *IN/SECTS* 34 (May).

Itō, M. 2003. *Gendai shakai to supirichuariti. Gendaijin no shūkyō no shakaigakuteki tankyū* [The Modern World and Spirituality. A Sociological Search for the Religion of Modern People]. Hiroshima: Keisuisha.

———. 2002. "The New Spirituality in Contemporary Societies: A Comparative View on Japanese 'Spiritual World.'" In *Zen, Reiki, Karate: Japanische Religiosität in Europa*. Ed. by I. Prohl and H. Zinser. Münster: Lit Verlag, 91–108.

Itō, M., N. Kashio and T. Yumiyama, eds. 2004. *Supirichuariti no shakaigaku. Gendai sekai no shūkyō no tankyū* [The Sociology of Spirituality. The Search for Religion in the Modern World]. Kyoto: Sekaishisōsha.

Jakobsh, D. 2008. "3HO/Sikh Dharma of the Western Hemisphere: The 'Forgotten' New Religious Movement?" *Religion Compass* 2, no. 3: 385–408.

Kale, S. 2004. "Spirituality, Religion, and Globalization." *Journal of Macromarketing* 24, no. 2: 92–107.

Kaplan, D. and A. Marshall 1997. *The Cult at the End of the World: The Incredible Story of Aum*. London: Arrow.

Kashio, N., ed. 2002. *Supirichuariti wo ikiru. Atarashii kizuna wo motomote* [Live in Spirituality. Seek New Bonds]. Tokyo: Serika Shobō.

Kisala, R. 2006. "Japanese Religions." In *Nanzan Guide to Japanese Religions*. Ed. by P. Swanson and C. Chilson. Honolulu: University of Hawai'i Press, 3–13.

———. 2002. "Japanese religions." In *Religions in the Modern World: Traditions and Transformations*. Ed. by L. Woodhead, P. Fletcher, H. Kawanami and D. Smith. London: Routledge, 125–47.

Lifton, R. J. 1999. *Destroying the World to Save It: Aum Shinrikyō, Apocalyptic Violence and the New Global Terrorism*. New York: Henry Holt.

Lynch, G. 2007. *The New Spirituality: An Introduction to Progressive Belief in the Twenty-first Century*. London: I. B. Tauris.

Maldonado, A. 2009. "'Una Nueva Forma de Vida': Seeking 'New Spiritualities' in Urban Mexico. A Note on Research in Progress." *Journal of Alternative Spiritualities and New Age Studies* 5. Online: http://www.asanas.org.uk/files/005Maldonado.pdf (accessed October 3, 2009).

Mullins, R. M. 1992. "Japan's New Age and Neo-New Religions: Sociological Interpretations." In *Perspectives on the New Age*. Ed. by J. R. Lewis and J. G. Melton. Albany: State University of New York Press, 232–46.

Oosthuizen, G. C. 1992. "The 'Newness' of the New Age in South Africa and Reactions to It." In *Perspectives on the New Age*. Ed. by J. R. Lewis and J. G. Melton. Albany: State University of New York Press, 247–70.

Ozawa-de Silva, C. 2006. *Psychotherapy and Religion in Japan: The Japanese Introspection Practice of Naikan*. London: Routledge.

Partridge, C. 2007. "Truth, Authority and Epistemological Individualism in New Age Thought." In *Handbook of New Age*. D. Kemp and J. R. Lewis. Leiden: Brill, 231–54.

Possamaï, A. 2007. "Producing and Consuming New Age spirituality: The Cultic Milieu and the Network Paradigm." In *Handbook of New Age*. Ed. by D. Kemp and J. R. Lewis. Leiden: Brill, 151–66.

Prohl, I. 2007. "The Spiritual World: Aspects of New Age in Japan." In *Handbook of New Age*. Ed. by D. Kemp and J. R. Lewis. Leiden: Brill, 359–78.

———. 2004. "Religion and National Identity in Contemporary Japan." In *Civil Society, Religion, and the Nation: Modernization in Intercultural Context: Russia, Japan, Turkey*. Ed. by G. Steunebrink and E. van der Zweerde. Amsterdam: Rodopi, 135–52.

Reader, I. 2005. *Making Pilgrimages: Meaning and Practice in Shikoku.* Honolulu: University of Hawai'i Press.

_____. 2003. "Local Histories, Anthropological Interpretations and the Study of a Japanese Pilgrimage." *Japanese Journal of Religious Studies* 30, no. 1–2: 119–32.

_____. 2001. "Interior Travels: Pilgrimage, Nostalgia, Identity and Quest." In *Return to Japan: From "Pilgrimage" to the West.* Ed. by Y. Nagashima. Aarhus: Aarhus University Press, 13–32.

_____. 2000. *Religious Violence in Contemporary Japan: The Case of Aum Shinrikyō.* Nordic Institute of Asian Studies Monograph Series. Richmond: Curzon.

_____. 1996. *A Poisonous Cocktail? Aum Shinrikyo's Path to Violence.* Copenhagen: Nordic Institute of Asian Studies Publications.

_____. 1991. *Religion in Contemporary Japan.* Honolulu: University of Hawai'i Press.

_____. 1987. "Back to the Future: Images of Nostalgia and Renewal in a Japanese Religious Context." *Japanese Journal of Religious Studies* 14, no. 4: 287–303.

Rothstein, M., ed. 2001. *New Age Religion and Globalization.* Aarhus: Aarhus University Press.

Tacey, D. 2004. *The Spirituality Revolution: The Emergence of Contemporary Spirituality.* Sydney: HarperCollins.

Tobey, A. 1976. "The Summer Solstice of the Healthy-Happy-Holy Organization." In *The New Religious Consciousness.* Ed. by R. Bellah and C. Glock. Berkeley: University of California Press, 5–30.

Shimazono, S. 2004. *From Salvation to Spirituality: Popular Religious Movements in Modern Japan.* Melbourne: Trans Pacific Press.

_____. 2002. "New Spirituality Culture and Religious Tradition." In *Traditional Religion and Culture in a New Era.* Ed. by R. Bachika. New Brunswick, NJ: Transaction, 155–70.

_____. 1999. "'New Age Movement' or 'New Spirituality Movements and Culture'?" *Social Compass* 46: 121–33.

_____. 1996. "Alternative Knowledge Movements as Religion: An Alternative Farming Movement in Japan." *Social Compass* 43: 47–63.

Shūkyō Shakaigaku-no-Kai, ed. 1985. *Ikoma no kamigami: Gendai toshi no minzoku shūkyō* [Ikoma Gods: A Modern City Folk Religion]. Osaka: Sōgensha.

Steyn, C. 1994. *Worldviews in Transition: An Investigation of the New Age Movement in South Africa.* Pretoria: University of South Africa.

Sutcliffe, S. J. 2003. *Children of the New Age: A History of Spiritual Practices.* London: Routledge.

Yuasa, Y. 2008. *Overcoming Modernity: Synchronicity and Image-Thinking.* Trans. Shigenori Nagatomo and John W. M. Krummel. Albany: State University of New York Press.

Tsujimura, S. 2008. "Religious Issues in Japan 2007. Religion in a Consumer Society: In the Shadow of Spirituality." *Bulletin of the Nanzan Institute for Religion and Culture* 32: 40–54.

Woo, H. 2008. "New Age in South Korea." *Journal of Alternative Spirituality and New Age Studies* 5: 1–32.

York, M. 2001. *Selling Nature in the Spiritual Supermarket.* Paper presented at The Spiritual Supermarket: Religious Pluralism in the 21st Century, International Conference. London: INFORM and CESNUR. Online: http://www.cesnur.org/2001/london2001/york.htm (accessed September 4, 2009).

Yumiyama, T. 1995. "Varieties of Healing in Present-day Japan." *Japanese Journal of Religious Studies* 2, nos. 3–4: 267–82.

Primary Sources on Ikoma

Ikoma City Official Website: http://www.city.ikoma.lg.jp/en/

Shigisan Danjiki Dōjō Website [Fasting Training Center in South Ikoma]: http://www.danjiki.or.jp/index.htm

Shigisan Danjiki Dōjō. (n.d.). *Shūkyō houjin dai uchū kyō. Shigisan danjiki dōjō annai* [The Religious Foundations of Macrocosmo Sutra. Showing the Fasting Dojo] [brochure]. Nara.

Seiyōin Ryōyōjo Website [Fasting Training Center in North Ikoma]: http://www.danjiki.jp/index.html

3HO Japan Website: http://3ho.kundalini-yoga.jp/

Chapter 7

GLOBALIZATION AND RELIGIOUS RESURGENCE: A COMPARATIVE STUDY OF BAHRAIN AND POLAND

Magdalena Karolak
Prince Mohammad bin Fahd University, Saudi Arabia

Nikodem Karolak
Adam Mickiewicz University, Poland

Religious Revival: Primary Considerations

The role of religion in state politics has grown more significant in modern times, and religious revival (considered as a single phenomenon) has arguably become the most important characteristic of the post-Cold War era. This worldwide increase in religiosity has been studied and documented by a number of scholars, including Martin Riesebrodt (1990), Mark Juergensmayer (1993) and Lester Kurtz (1995), among others. A combination of factors, such as the rejection of modernity and secularism, as well as concerns with safeguarding local culture and identity, underlie religious resurgence. All of the factors mentioned above are closely linked to the concept of globalization, a process which should not be oversimplified. Globalization threatens religious traditions yet has simultaneously contributed to religious revival thanks to the spread of information and communication technologies (ICT). It is also important to assess religious resurgence from geographic and demographic perspectives. The phenomenon of religious revival has been observed not only in developing nations but also in the USA (Bacevich and Prodromu 2004) and to a lesser extent in Europe (excluding Muslim immigrant communities). However, the success of Polish populist religious parties is unique. Poland, a member of the European Union, is unusual even among other Central European post-communist countries (Grün 2008) insofar as no other EU member country has had fundamentalist religious parties gain such influence in politics.

This comparative chapter analyzes the Islamic revival in the Middle East, specifically Bahrain, and the Catholic revival in Poland. These examples offer an interesting parallel since both reveal a close relationship between religion and politics. Moreover, they both bear witness to the phenomenon of religious revival. The present analysis focuses on the following characteristics: economics, fundamentalist ideology, and the growth of religious parties and their influence in politics.

Socio-economic factors

Religious revival in a variety of contexts has been linked to rapidly changing socio-economic conditions (Norris and Inglehart 2004). Bahrain and Poland vary considerably in size and population as well as in economic structure, yet the Human Development Index reveals striking similarities, with Poland ranking 41st and Bahrain 39th in 2009 (UN 2010). Both countries have undergone economic transformations in the second half of the twentieth century. Although the histories of Poland and Bahrain have not followed identical trajectories, worsening social inequality has been evident in both countries.

In 1989, Poland adopted the Balcerowicz Plan for rapid transition from a centrally planned to a free-market economy. The plan called for, *inter alia*, the privatization of state-owned companies, incentives for foreign investment and price liberalization. The results of these reforms were income distribution disparities and a rise in unemployment. Rising social inequality comes as no surprise, considering the fact that the earlier communist government artificially suppressed labor-income gaps (Keane and Prasad 1998). Consequently, the Gini coefficient shows an overall increase of social inequality after 1989. In 1989, the Gini coefficient stood at 20.7 while in the years 1989–2009 it rose to 34.9 (*Index Gini*).

Another significant problem was an increase in unemployment. Before the transformation, joblessness was virtually non-existent, since the communist government guaranteed job security to everyone. Economic reforms led to the bankruptcy of many state-owned companies, and even though preventive measures were taken (Keane and Prasad 1998), unemployment sky-rocketed from 0.3 percent to 20.6 percent during 1990 to 2004, remaining high through 2006. A gradual decrease to 8.8 percent (October 2008) was observed due to economic migration within the EU. Since then, unemployment has fluctuated between 10 percent and 12 percent (GUS 2010). It is important, however, to understand that inequality has affected certain socio-economic groups more than others. Highly skilled workers have found it easier to adapt to the new labor market, while low educational attainment is often a direct cause of long-term joblessness (Rutkowski 1998). The reforms produced "winners" as well as "losers." A study conducted in 1993 discovered that the precarious economic conditions most affected 1) households headed by pensioners, single parents, young workers or persons with low educational attainment; 2) households located in small towns of less than 20,000 inhabitants; and 3) large families of more than 5 members (Ebrill et al. 1994). These socio-economic determinants of poverty remain roughly unchanged today (Tarkowska 2007).

It is also important to note as well that inequalities follow a geographical distribution. Since Polish independence in 1918, differences have existed between "Poland A" (the industrialized and developed areas west of the Vistula river) and "Poland B" (agricultural areas with little infrastructure east of the Vistula river) (Borkowska 2010). Although economic progress has been made, Eastern voivodeships (administrational regions) still lag behind in industrialization, infrastructure and standard of living. In 2010, the Subcarpathian, Lublin and Świętokrzyskie voivodeships were the poorest in the country (Maciejewicz and Kokot 2010). These divisions are not absolute, since there are distinctive patterns of development within each voivodeship. Even though Poland is situated near the EU average in terms of the number of citizens affected by poverty, Polish society overall is considered one of the poorest among Organisation for Economic Co-operation and Development (OECD) members in terms of buying power (Hałabuz 2010). In certain areas, disparities between socio-economic groups have been growing. The salaries of specialists, CEOs and skilled workers have risen in comparison to the wages of low-skilled workers. However, income disparity should not be confused with the causes of poverty (Kurowska 2008), since better skills attract higher remuneration. Thus the main cause of poverty in Poland remains unemployment due to lack of skills and education, as well as low productivity.

Bahrain's economic conditions differ considerably from Poland's. Bahrain's economy, like the economies of other Gulf Cooperation Council (GCC) members, relies heavily on oil revenues. As oil resources provide an "economic rent," these countries are known as "rentier states" (Luciani and Beblawi 1987). Thanks to the flow of oil income, rentier states have been able to establish extensive welfare programs—providing their citizens with free healthcare, free education, as well as subsidies on daily commodities—without taxing their population. As such, the discovery of oil in Bahrain has transformed Bahraini society. Oil revenues have accelerated the rapid development of the country with the creation of modern industries and a vast range of services that exacerbate the demand for labor. In the 1930s, Bahraini society hardly had enough labor to warrant the need for growth. Foreigners filled various occupations, from manual labor to highly qualified professional jobs. The foreign population grew steadily, reaching half of the total number of Bahrain's inhabitants in 2008 (Bowman 2008). Further, during the capitalist era of the 1970s, oil wealth promoted consumerism and a lifestyle geared towards acquiring imported goods (Robbins 1994). This era significantly widened the gap between rich and poor, and made more obvious the prosperity of those who could afford residence-type homes, cars and shopping at Western franchises (Moghadam 2003).

The economic transformation of Bahrain was not a change from one economic system to another, as in Poland, but was linked to oil production and price fluctuations on international markets. Although oil brought prosperity in the 1970s, in the 1980s the GCC economies suffered from falling oil prices, as well as growing financial strain due to the Iraqi invasion of Kuwait and rising expenditures on arms, security and defense (Luciani and Beblawi 1987). Subsequently, high demographic growth, rising unemployment and inflation have combined with a growing consciousness of a decline in oil supplies to put further strain on the GCC economies. Having grown accustomed to extensive social welfare measures, these societies entertained high expectations of their governments. Longrigg (1966) observes that before the discovery of oil, states such as Bahrain "had been satisfied with a low standard of living and government" (105). Despite centrally directed redistribution policies, Bahrain's pattern of socio-economic disparity is similar to Poland after it commenced its economic transformation in the 1990s. In 1997 an estimated 15 to 30 percent of Bahraini households were needy (Wilkenson and Atti 1997). In 2008, Bahraini authorities for the first time set a formal measure of poverty, establishing the poverty line at a level of monthly income less than 337 Bahraini dinars (US$894). By this measure, roughly 15 to 20 percent of Bahraini households fall below the poverty line (Women Gateway 2008), compared to an estimated 18 percent of Polish households (Tarkowska 2007). A pattern of poverty distribution is also discernible in which want is concentrated in rural villages—former agricultural areas—as opposed to developed urban centers and suburbs. Even though traditional villages have experienced urbanization, they are characterized by poor infrastructure and higher rates of unemployment, and their inhabitants rely on a combination of informal-sector activities (Wilkenson and Atti 1997). Poverty in Bahrain, as in Poland, is linked primarily with unemployment. Low wages and poor working conditions deter Bahrainis from employment in the private sector and are responsible for structural unemployment among the native population.

In 2001, unemployment reached a record level of 16 percent among local Bahrainis, and rising economic demands led to an increase in social unrest in the 2000s resulting in clashes with security forces.

It is important to note that economic grievances combined with political demands have caused episodes of violent social unrest to erupt in Bahrain since the 1920s (Fearon and Laitin 2005). Levels of social unrest over economic demands are noticeably higher in Bahrain than in Poland, while poverty levels are comparable in both countries. Furthermore, income distribution in Bahrain is similar to the Polish case. Although Gini coefficient data is not available for Bahrain, the latest survey conducted in 2003 revealed the following statistics: 1) the income gap ratio between the richest and poorest 10 percent in Bahrain is 6.2; 2) the poorest 10 percent of the population accounted for 4.3 percent of total income, and the poorest 20 percent for 9.3 percent; while 3) the richest 10 percent of the population owned 26.6 percent of total income (UNDP 2003). Such income distribution indicates an average disparity similar to the socio-economic situation in Poland.

In order to explain high levels of unrest in Bahrain, it is useful to analyze the nation's complex social composition as well as the Rentier State Theory proposed by Giacomo Luciani and Hazem Beblawi (1987). Bahrain's citizens are 98 percent Muslim; Jews and Christians make up the remaining 2 percent. Shia Muslims are relatively numerous, accounting for about 60 to 70 percent of Muslims in the kingdom (PEW 2009). Clashes regularly occur between the Shia majority and the state apparatus controlled by the Sunni Al Khalifa dynasty. From the 1970s to 1990s, Shias sought greater political power by organizing a number of uprisings aimed at deposing their ruler. These rebellions were contained, however, and led to repressions and retaliation against Shias (Fearon and Laitin 2005). Controlled liberalization of the country in 2000 allowed for the participation of Shias in parliament, but perceived economic discrimination against this sect led to further violence in the following decade. No statistics are available comparing both sects according to poverty rates. In any case, the Shia population is not socio-economically homogenous (Louër 2008), nor is poverty unknown among Sunnis. A complex social composition accounts in part for higher levels of social unrest in Bahrain. Meanwhile, the Rentier State Theory suggests that "revenue from abroad dramatically improves the state's ability to buy legitimacy through allocation and increases regime stability" (Luciani 1990, 76). Oil revenues provide ruling dynasties with bargaining power, allowing them to buy the consent of citizens. State stability becomes possible since citizens find it beneficial to support ruling elites. Those who oppose the state apparatus suffer deportations and denial or retraction of citizenship. Even though the Rentier State Theory has been criticized as being simplistic (Herb 1999), it helps explain differences between the Polish and Bahraini cases. Poland, on the other hand, is not a rentier state. Consequently, expectations of citizens are considerably lower since they do not await any form of redistribution coming from oil rents. In fact, the social welfare function is mostly funded through general taxation. Bahraini society is associated with higher expectations than that of Poland regarding the role of government in promoting social welfare. Thus, when oil revenues suffer because of fluctuations in the international economy or inflation affects the prices of basic goods, redistribution fails to meet these expectations and the poorest classes—especially those who believe themselves to be discriminated against in the economic system—retaliate with economic and political demands.

Religious fundamentalism

This study on religious resurgence in Poland and Bahrain now turns to an analysis of political parties that display a fundamentalist religious character. This type of party is situated on the extreme right of the ideological spectrum. Religious values are, however, present in the ideologies of right-wing parties overall, as well as in other conservative parties. For our present purpose, we need a clear definition of extreme-right parties. Our approach involves grouping political parties that share similar ideologies (Mudde 2000). Tolz (2005) states that an extremist right-wing ideology

> includes national chauvinism, i.e., complete substitution of the rights of the individual to the interests of the 'constructed' nation, propaganda of discrimination of individuals on the grounds of nationality, religion, sexual preferences, etc. and complete rejection of democratic institutions and practices. (249)

On the other hand, Mudde (2000) enumerates various features of extreme-right parties, namely nationalism, racism (including opposition to ethno-pluralism), xenophobia, opposition to democracy and advocacy of a strong state (178). Mudde emphasizes that not all of these characteristics need to be present at the same time. This diversity of features leads to a diversity of extreme-right parties. Using the description of Minkenberg and Schain (2005), the key element of extreme-right ideology is "a myth of a homogenous nation, a romantic and populist ultra-nationalism" characterized by "the effort to construct an idea of nation and national belonging by radicalizing ethnic, religious, cultural and political criteria of exclusion and to condense the idea of nation into an image of extreme collective homogeneity" (156). Based on this definition, the authors distinguish between a fascist right, a racist right, an ethnocentric/xenophobic right and a fundamentalist religious right. For the purpose of comparing Catholic and Islamic fundamentalism, we have chosen to analyze political parties that fit within the fundamentalist religious type. The Polish extreme right is best represented by the League of Polish Families (LPR). However, the LPR is significantly influenced by its coalition partner, the initially conservative Law and Justice (PiS) party, our second party for analysis. The Bahraini extreme right is divided into Sunni (Al Asalah and the less conservative Al Menbar) and Shiite political associations (Al Wefaq). Our points of comparison include moral viewpoints, national myths and hate rhetoric.

Moral revolution

Extreme-right parties take as their starting point a re-evaluation of the state of society from a moral perspective. In their analysis, morals have been abandoned and require repair; thus these parties offer a vision in which religion is identified as the backbone of morality, and religious values need to be enforced as part of the legal system. PiS boldly announced in its political program a "moral revolution" in Polish society. Although other parties did not explicitly use the term "revolution," their programs suggest an implementation of religious morality in everyday life. There is, however, a substantial difference between the Polish and Bahraini political environments. The Bahraini constitution recognizes Islam as the dominant religion, and declares Bahrain to be a Muslim country. Meanwhile, Poland has no official state religion, although the Polish constitution makes reference to God. Bahrain's legal system is a mix of Western legal standards, tribal laws and *sharia*, a set of religious laws based on interpretations of the Quran that differ considerably between Sunni and Shia Muslims (Ahmed 2009). The Polish legal system is based on the separation of church and state, although the Catholic Church maintains a privileged position.

Bahraini political associations aim at stricter implementation of *sharia* in terms of the prohibition of alcohol and pork, traditional roles for women and the eradication of immoral behavior. Islamist political parties, for example, have stood behind a proposed ban on the sale of alcohol in public places such as restaurants, bars, clubs, hotels, duty-free shops in the airport and by the national airline. The Al Asalah bloc, for one, initiated a complete ban on the sale of pork. Islamic associations have also proposed the eradication of other supposedly un-Islamic practices, such as the display of mannequins modeling lingerie in shops (Al Wefaq); practices linked with witchcraft, sorcery and fortune telling (Al Asalah); homosexuality (Al Menbar); street voyeurism (Al Menbar); cultural events such as pop and rock concerts by certain artists (Al Menbar); mixed-gender healthcare services (Al Wefaq); and the mixing of sexes and lack of strict clothing guidelines in the only public university, the University of Bahrain (Al Wefaq).

These religion-based demands are not unlike the proposals of Polish parties. The LPR and PiS stand firmly behind the Catholic doctrine of the preservation and security of human life. Both political parties oppose elements forming the so-called modern "civilization of death," namely euthanasia, abortion, *in vitro* fertilization and the use of contraceptives (Hoffman 2007). The LPR has suggested including information about infertility risks with contraceptive pills and condoms, supposedly as a result of tests conducted by health professionals. LPR leader Roman Giertych, appointed as Minister of Education, called for a re-evaluation of the theory of evolution and suggested the possibility of its removal from the school curriculum ("Education Ministry with a Bent towards Creationism," 2006). The LPR has promoted a law to stop all trade on Sunday, since it is considered the Christian Sabbath. The PiS and LPR both support the idea of a strong state, even to the point of authoritarianism, provided that it can safeguard morality. It comes as no surprise that senior LPR member Maciej Giertych has cited the dictatorships of Francisco Franco and António de Oliveira Salazar as role models (Niklewicz 2007). The vision of Catholic and Islamist fundamentalists for society shares certain characteristics, such as a strong pro-family stand, traditional gender roles (Giertych 2008) and the eradication of homosexuality and other "immoral" elements from certain types of music (Giertych 2007).

Catholic and Islamic fundamentalism both aim at the subordination of the state system, as well as private lives, to the dictates of religion. It is important to note that both types of fundamentalism regard the community as more important than the individual. In Islam this concept is expressed by the concept *ummah* (the community of believers). Polish parties rely on the concept of the Catholic solidarity of all Poles. This stands in contrast to the individualism promoted by liberals. Catholic and Islamic fundamentalism also have in common the fact that in order to create a new type of state, they have to combat enemies who supposedly stand in the way of desired moral reforms.

Enemies of the moral order and the populist appeal

Albertazzi and McDonnell (2008) define populism as "an ideology which pits a virtuous and homogeneous people against a set of elites and dangerous 'others' who are together depicted as depriving (or attempting to deprive) the sovereign people of their rights, values, prosperity, identity and voice" (3). Polish and Bahraini religious fundamentalists make use of populist appeals to direct attacks primarily on those who are excluded from the societal mainstream on grounds of morality. The "others" include homosexuals, feminists, secular

Western liberals and all those whose behavior violates religious commandments. In addition, Polish political parties display a xenophobic character. The PiS presented an initially restrained version of nationalism that has become starker with time. The PiS did not oppose Polish membership in the EU, but promoted the sovereignty of nations within the EU, opposing federalism and the European Constitution. Subsequently, a desire to protect Polish rights led the PiS to adopt an increasingly anti-German and anti-Russian stance in 2010 (Zieniewicz 2006). Similarly, the LPR denounced the loss of national sovereignty within EU structures. The LPR presented a more radical approach than the PiS, opposing Polish membership in the EU on the grounds that it would result in unequal opportunities for Poles, the bankruptcy of Polish businesses and a selling-off of Polish land and businesses to foreigners.

Instead, the LPR favored a policy of protectionism and promoted the concept of the "True Pole," which links Polish national identity to Catholicism. This concept was devised in the interwar period by Roman Dmowski, founder of the National Democratic political camp Endecja (Pankowski and Kornak 2005). Dmowski's ideology was developed in a multinational Poland in which ethnic Poles accounted for 60 percent of the inhabitants. Dmowski was critical of minorities—especially Ukrainians, Byelorussians and Jews—and championed the idea of "Poland for the Poles." When Poland emerged as a nation-state after World War II, LPR members continued to propagate racist sentiments. To cite a few examples, LPR members denounced a perceived Jewish influence in Poland (Wise 2010), branded the election of US President Barack Obama "the end of white civilization" (Zaleski 2008), and opposed the creation of Euro regions. LPR member Maciej Giertych, under the auspices of the European Parliament, published a brochure titled "The War of Civilizations in Europe," suggesting that civilizations are locked in a conflict without any possibility of integration or multiculturalism (Giertych 2007). It comes as no surprise that the LPR would refer to the EU as the "Tower of Babel" (LPR's Political Program 2001). Until 2006, the LPR supported the All-Polish Youth (Młodzież Wszechpolska), a youth organization with clearly racist tendencies (Kurczewska, Horolets and Trojanowska-Strzęboszewska 2005).

Although religion is also a basis for differentiation within Muslim communities, the concept of religious belonging is more important than that of nationality. Becoming a member of the *ummah* ought to constitute the primary identity of a Muslim; nationality should be of secondary importance (Lewis 2003). Thus the level of open xenophobia among Islamist associations is rather limited. However, such groups sometimes associate "un-Islamic" behavior with "others" (whether conceived as specific ethnic groups, or as non-believers in general), which can ultimately lead to violence. In 2004, Bahrain was swept by Shiite riots targeting Asian businesses. The riots were mainly the result of economic discontent but also had religious overtones ("Shi'ites Riot in Bahrain against Asians, Liquor and Prostitution," 2004). Many Asians work at low-income jobs and live in shabby neighborhoods. In the past, they have been accused of illegal liquor distribution, or of running houses of prostitution. This common perception of Asian workers was reinforced by Sadiq Rahma (Al Wefaq) who stated that they make neighborhoods "dirty" (Khonji 2006). Al Wefaq proposed a law that would force manual laborers to reside in racially segregated areas. The parliamentarians argued that such workers behave in an immoral manner and should not be allowed to live in residential areas where they might corrupt family life. During the 2004 riots, tourists and Western restaurants serving alcohol were targeted by mobs as well. Sunni Islamist associations promoted a clampdown on homosexuals, calling for the deportation of gay foreigners as homosexuality remains illegal in Bahrain. Although the traditional enemies of Islamist fundamentalists are the US and Israel, the Bahraini Parliament has no influence on foreign policy, which is one reason why public statements by political associations on this topic have been limited.

Hate rhetoric

The hate rhetoric of Polish extreme-right parties combines nationalist and religious elements, while that of Bahraini Islamists operates mainly on a religious/moral level. There is also a significant difference between Polish and Bahraini fundamentalists. Islamist organizations have prominent religious figures among their leaders and members, while Polish political parties are of a secular character. However, the latter seek the support of religious figures who remain outside of the political circle. The LPR, and later the PiS, received the full support of Redemptorist Father Tadeusz Rydzyk, a powerful media figure. Rydzyk manages the radio station Radio Maryja, with some 5 to 6 million listeners; the TV channel TRWAM; *Nasz Dziennik*, a daily newspaper with a circulation of 140,0000 to 170,000; as well as the School of Social and Media Culture, an institution of higher education (Grün 2008). Close ties between LPR, PiS and Father Rydzyk have allowed members of these political parties to reach a considerable number of potential voters through Rydzyk's media.

Islamist and Catholic fundamentalists differ in their hate rhetoric. Islamists concentrate on the moral question; thus their rhetoric includes epithets related to immorality. Between 2006 and 2010, Islamist speeches in parliament contained derogatory terms relating to the "others." Homosexuals were branded "sluts" (Jones 2008); Arab pop music singer Haifa Wehbe, a "harlot"; and Michael Jackson, a "pimp" and a "child abuser" (Al A'ali 2010). Furthermore, immorality was strongly associated with "dirt." According to Al Asala, the sale of alcohol has brought "dirty money" (Toumi 2010) and turned Bahrain into a "brothel." It is also characteristic of fundamentalist rhetoric to provide unverified and oversimplified claims to prove a point. Al Asalah's leader stated, without providing any statistics, that "unclean tourism" is the main reason for the country's increased crime rates ("MPs Vote for Blanket Ban on Public Sale in Bahrain," 2009). On the other hand, Islamists refer to religious figures as well, as in the following statement against the sale of pork: "The first thing Jesus Christ—the savior of all mankind—would do is break the cross and kill the pig" ("Bahrain: MPs Call for Ban on Pork," 2009).

The PiS and LPR have also railed against perceived traitors to the nation and the national cause. During the same period, the rhetoric of the Polish extreme right—especially the PiS—described a web of conspiracy, suspicion and mistrust. Nurturing a grudge against the 1945 Yalta Conference, the PiS engaged in a political discourse distinguishing "patriots" from "traitors" and "victims" from "collaborators," calling for their reward or punishment, respectively. According to the PiS worldview, the Polish establishment is still controlled by "enemies" such as former agents of the Security Bureau (SB, the communist secret police), a "front for the defense of German interests," Stasi (the East German secret police), and the offspring of ethnic Germans who served in the Wehrmacht. As is typical among fundamentalists, anyone other than the accusers themselves is subject to suspicion. The PiS has accused such prominent figures of the Polish underground as Jacek Kuroń (leader of the opposition in 1980) and Zbigniew Herbert (a poet harassed by the communist government) of having served in the communist secret police. Father Rydzyk and the LPR focused on the erosion of Polish sovereignty and culture by Jews and the EU, claiming that "It is known that the European Union is controlled by freemasonry" and that the EU furthers the interests of "a global Jewish nation and a European German nation." (Anti-Defamation League 2006, 21). Anti-Semitic rhetoric is common on the airwaves of Radio Maryja. A "Jew" is presented as the prototype of a stranger outside of the Polish nation who secretly acts to destroy it. Rumors of an imaginary "Jewish plot" persist and attract followers as various government members and prominent culture figures have Jewish ancestry (Grün 2008). In this context, being a Jew becomes the equivalent of being a traitor. Extreme-right parties have adhered to hate rhetoric in order to create a vision of Poland under attack by "foreign" and "enemy" elements.

National myths

By itself, hate rhetoric would be ineffective without an accompanying (positive) national myth or ideological worldview, which it mirrors. It is thus important to assess the mythology and ideology of the extreme right. Extreme-right ideology offers a narrow vision of society in which oversimplified solutions are presented as a remedy for social ills. Furthermore, it discourages dialogue and the exchange of opinions, since those who question the ideology or differ in their opinions are considered enemies ("traitors," "liars," "not true Muslims," etc.). The solutions provided by right-extremists are over-simplified because they are based on false or imagined premises. The myths that are created for the purpose of promoting an ideology, however, are worth exploring.

Cultural myths relate to society and history as organizations use history to provide a vision of society to suit their needs. Their use of history is essentially creative, since facts may be considerably altered, and developments that do not fit within the desired vision are simply omitted. The PiS has analyzed modern Polish history in terms of the influence of foreign powers over the Polish nation. Their conclusion is that "the nation's natural historic progression should resume from where it had once cruelly been forced off-course in 1939" (Resende 2007, 7). Thus the period of communism constitutes a "foreign" period and should be erased from history. This ideology reinforces the theme of the unjust suffering of Poles and Poland's messianic mission developed during the early nineteenth-century Romantic Era. At that time, Poland lost its independence and was divided among three partitioning powers. The poet Adam Mickiewicz called Poland the Christ of nations:

> Just as Christ was killed for his message, an evil trinity of oppressive monarchs destroyed Poland because they feared the freedom it embodied [...]. [But] the Polish nation did not die. Its body lay in the grave and its soul had gone from the earth, that is, from public life, into purgatory, that is, into the domestic life of [those nations] suffering from slavery [...]. And on the third day the soul will return to the body and the nation will rise again and free all the peoples of Europe from slavery. (Porter 2000, 51)

Using this conception of history, one may interpret the modern history of Poland in terms of the suffering perpetuated during World War II and under communism, followed by Polish rebirth after 1989. Messianism reached its climax after the crash of the presidential airplane in Smoleńsk on 10 April 2010. The death of the presidential couple and other members of the Polish establishment occurred while en route to a ceremony honoring Polish officers murdered under Josef Stalin's orders in 1941 in Katyń. It was only in recent times that the Russian government has acknowledged responsibility for this act. Katyń had by then already become a symbol of Polish martyrdom and the object of communist propaganda blaming the incident on Nazi soldiers.

The 2010 crash was called a "second Katyń," while the deceased were referred to as having been "murdered" or as having "died in battle" (Łubieński 2010). Again, messianists portrayed this event as the bloody price paid by Poland in order to reveal the truth about the Katyń massacre to the world and to bring a final reconciliation between Poland and Russia. The deceased were declared victorious and became national heroes, while the PiS used the Smoleńsk crash to gain popular support in the 2010 presidential elections. Members of the party saw a conspiracy behind the incident, first blaming the Polish government and later the Russians for causing the crash with artificial fog, then allegedly killing off survivors. The conspiracy theory and public hysteria reached new heights with a planned removal of a cross commemorating the deceased. This makeshift cross was erected in front of the Presidential Palace in Warsaw and was due to be moved after the mourning period. Extreme-right parties together with Radio Maryja interpreted this act as a coup against the Poles and their religion, and staged a five-month rally against the government to defend the cross, whose final removal became the symbol of a conspiracy within the Polish and Russian governments.

Islamists have also created a new, distorted vision of history. In the 1980s, Islamism filled the political vacuum left after the decline and ultimate fall of the USSR. Communism failed as a counter-weight to Western liberalism and created the need for an ideology specific to the Middle East. This ideology was all the more important insofar as modern Arab history has been characterized by dependence on foreign powers, with no channel for expressing Arabs' own internal, economic and social bonds (Al-Azmeh 2009, 67). At the same time,

> [Arab] governments [...] have failed to establish or strengthen their political legitimacy. They have been criticized by opposition voices for failure to achieve economic self-sufficiency or prosperity, to stem the growing gap between rich and poor, to halt widespread corruption, liberate Palestine, resist Western political and cultural hegemony. (Esposito 2003, 72)

Islamism provided a new hope and a one-step solution: a return to religious roots and their public dimension in the form of *sharia*. Subsequently, all mistakes and problems of the Arabs were attributed to denial of the Islamic legacy. The application of *sharia* finds its culmination in the idea of an Islamic state in which gambling, alcohol, drug use, pornography, prostitution, extramarital sexual relations and homosexuality are illegal. Similarly "night clubs, dance halls, bars, and mixed swimming facilities would not be allowed" (Siddiqui 1978, 108). The core concept is that of *al asala* (authenticity), which assumes that original Islamic principles can be applied to modern times. However, as noted by Al-Azmeh, this authenticity

> contradicts historical reality. The sharia itself has evolved in parallel with the societies; and as one can tell from an objective examination of history, it is not—nor has it ever been—a unanimously accepted code, but only a collection of principles and guidelines on what is legal, deriving what unity it has from its relations with the governmental authorities in whose name it is enforced [...] The alleged return to the roots of Islam is at best metaphorical, in any case symbolic, and it involves a fair amount of falsification. (2009, 69–70)

On the other hand, Islamists concentrate on erasing the traits of *jahiliya* (literally "age of ignorance," a term that refers to the pre-Islamic pagan period). Members of Al Asalah have denounced plans for the protection of pre-Islamic mounds as historical monuments, and have subsequently called for the destruction of all pre-Islamic sites, on the grounds that these ancient cultures represent *jahiliya*. The Islamist reformer Sayyid Qutb (1906–1966) used the concept of *jahiliya* to refer to Western modernity, labelling it a modern *jahiliya*. Islamic fundamentalism in Bahrain and Catholic fundamentalism in Poland, therefore, seek to provide a vision of a homogenous society based on religious (and in case of the latter, also national) belonging. Both recreate history, using it as a tool to support their visions.

Populism's Acceptance

The success of fundamentalist religious parties in capitalist countries is attributed to a number of factors such as voters dissatisfaction with established parties, political corruption, immigration, social alienation, crime and unemployment. To begin an analysis of populism, a discussion of socio-economic conditions is necessary, since populism has been linked with high levels of poverty.

Assessment of economic conditions

Dissatisfaction with present economic conditions can easily be redirected towards a search for the vindication of the rights of common citizens. In such a political climate, parties that promise to establish justice and fairness increase in popularity. The rise of religious populism was particularly pronounced in Poland during 2004–06. Populists suffered a defeat in the 2007 parliamentary elections, but gained prominence again during the presidential elections of 2010, narrowly won by a center-right candidate. In Polish parliamentary elections in 2005 and 2007, as well as presidential elections in 2005 and 2010, strong support for right-wing parties in less-developed areas east of the Vistula River was evident. It is important to note that the PiS grew increasingly populist after 2005, when the party entered into a coalition with the LPR and the populist extreme-left Self-Defense. PiS received 33 percent of the vote, in contrast to 7 percent for the LPR and 12 percent for Self-Defense. The 2007 elections witnessed defeat for the PiS and its former coalition members, with the center-right Civic Platform (PO) winning with 45 percent of the vote. PiS received 36 percent of votes, while the LPR and Self-Defense failed to enter Parliament. The 2010 presidential elections—held after the death of President Lech Kaczyński in the Smoleńsk crash—provided a final test for the populists. PiS candidate Jarosław Kaczyński, brother of the late president, used the incident to rally his supporters. The results were similar to the parliamentary election results, revealing a division between developed and poorer regions.

The voting patterns of cities and villages indicated additional socio-economic cleavages. The PiS candidate was supported by 40 percent of urban voters and 59 percent of voters from the countryside. His rival, the center-right candidate Bronisław Komorowski, received the support of 59 percent of city dwellers and 41 percent of rural voters. The results of recent elections confirm that moderate parties gained the support of voters who are better educated, live in cities, and reside in the western part of Poland. Voter attitudes toward modernization remain the main factor affecting political choice, with the rejection of modernity combined with high religiosity accounting for the support of fundamentalist religious parties in the eastern part of Poland (Kublik 2010).

The rise of fundamentalist parties in Bahrain is no doubt linked to economic conditions. Parliamentary elections in 2002 resulted in the victory of secular and independent parliamentarians (21 out of 40 seats). It is important to note that Shia Islamists boycotted the 2002 elections. The rise of Islamists was apparent in the 2006 parliamentary elections; this was followed by a decline in support for Sunni Islamists in the 2010 elections. Instead of Al Asalah or Al Menbar, voters supported independent Sunni candidates (Al A'ali 2010). The Islamist association Al Wefaq received continuous support, winning the 2006 and the 2010 elections. However, the elections of 2006 were a turning point, bringing unprecedented success to Islamist parties. The explanation lies, no doubt, in changing economic conditions as the years preceding the elections (2003–05) were marked by a sharp increase in unemployment among Bahrainis, and a continuous rise in the number of migrant laborers. The Islamist victory could be attributed to the fact that these organizations operate in poorer districts, providing a well-organized network of charity and Islamic education centers for the masses. In the 2006 elections, socio-economic concerns were central to Al Wefaq's platform, which focused on "housing, unemployment, corruption and the discriminat[ory] allocation of resources" (Zahid and Zweiri 2007). Bahraini politics are additionally shaped by sectarian divisions, as although Al Wefaq does not claim to represent the Shiite community, its supporters are overwhelmingly followers of this branch of Islam. It is branded an opposition party to the government, which is appointed by the King.

In Bahrain and Poland alike, the rise of fundamentalist religious parties was preceded by a sharp increase in unemployment, which led to socio-economic insecurity and perceived discrimination. Voting patterns in Poland reveal a distinction between "winners" and "losers" of the economic transformation. Even though voting in Bahrain follows religious affiliation, it is the Shia population that claims to suffer economic and political discrimination. However, growing labor migration and unemployment have adversely affected the overall Bahraini population. Even though socio-economic factors have resulted in increased support for populist leaders, the rise of such figures is due to many complex forces. Indeed, by 2004 Polish economic conditions had significantly improved in comparison to the 1990s (Gadomski 2010). Therefore, the increase in populists' appeal should be attributed to additional factors, namely popular disenchantment with political elites, globalization and threats to national identity.

Additional factors

The overwhelming victory of Islamists in 2006 was attributed to "good organisational skills within the societies, to the impact of their religious message and to its strong appeal to the masses with the sectarian developments in Iraq as a background" (Toumi 2006). However, "[d]isappointment with the overall performance of the outgoing council, the first in three decades, coupled with a strong desire to influence local governance and politics" also played a part (Toumi 2006). Voter disappointment was also a factor in Poland. In the 2000s, Polish politics were marred by corruption scandals involving high governmental officials and business figures, which contributed to a social perception of an existing "deal" within power circles (Walorek 2007). Fundamentalist religious parties have based their propaganda on the concept of a "deal" corrupting Polish society since the communist era. The PiS claimed that the democratic transition in 1989 took place through an arrangement between opposition leaders, who took control of the government, and the communist elite, who remained in control of the economy (Michnik 2010). Polish populists claimed they would bring justice and a final settling of accounts with the communist era. In Bahrain, the electorate was influenced by international events in the region. Bahrain is home to a US naval base, the presence of which has been denounced by

Sunni and Shia Islamists alike. The occupation of Iraq—in which troops stationed in Bahrain took part—reverberated especially among the Shia population in Bahrain, creating an air of martyrdom (Bayat 2007).

Poland and Bahrain alike have experienced economic liberalization and the rise of consumerism. These phenomena in turn have contributed to the spread of individualism and a decrease in religiosity. It is theorized that the "salience of religious values and habitual churchgoing would be expected to erode as a society experiences the long-term transition from poorer agrarian to more affluent industrial states" (Norris and Inglehart 2004, 112). The integration of Poland into the structures of the EU and increased labor immigration and ICT in Bahrain were both seen as vehicles for contamination by foreign, "immoral" values and behavior. Economic change has led to the dissolution of social solidarity, a decrease in religiosity and a gap between an old generation adhering to traditional values and a new generation more accepting of Western ideals. The liberalization of Bahrain's economy brought a proliferation of Western-style bars, restaurants and nightclubs catering not only to an expatriate population, but also to Bahraini youth. At the same time, populists have stressed the notion of a homogenous nation with strong moral values and social ties based in part on religious principles (Michnik 2010). This notion of solidarity was also the key to the success of religious organizations in Poland such as Radio Maryja, which promoted bonds between the elderly, those with low educational attainment and the unemployed, allowing their voices to be heard. It comes as no surprise that the so-called "defense of the cross" movement provided participants with a sense of belonging, security and usefulness to the nation.

A short-lived victory

The initial success of fundamentalist religious parties in Poland and Bahrain was soon followed by disappointment. Apart from Al Wefaq, which draws its support from its reputation as the voice of Shia opposition to the Sunni government, other fundamentalist religious parties have declined in support. The emphasis on moral reform proved to be short-lived once members of these parties were involved in numerous scandals. In 2006, the daily newspaper *Gazeta Wyborcza* uncovered a scandal in which a PiS coalition member offered jobs in return for sexual services (Walorek 2007). PiS attempted to tighten control over independent media, publicized trumped-up accusations against anti-communist underground leaders and enacted anti-corruption measures that led to the unsolved death case of former MP Barbara Blida, to name but a few scandals. In general, the PiS engaged in anti-democratic manipulation of state institutions. Similarly, Sunni and Shia Islamist municipal councilors became involved in a scandal in March 2006 when they went missing in

Bangkok—a well-known destination for engaging in "immoral" activities—on an unscheduled stop from a conference in Malaysia.

The most important shortcoming that has brought about the demise of fundamentalist religious parties is their weak economic program. With their focus on morality, they have failed to offer a viable model of economic development. The 2005 PiS parliamentary elections program devoted limited space to economic questions, focusing on expected outcomes without specifying how they would be attained. At the same time, its evaluation of economic questions proved problematic. Sunni Islamists similarly focused on moral questions. Their proposals to eradicate alcohol led to an outcry among businessmen. Also, they initially supported, then later criticized as un-Islamic, certain benefits for the unemployed. Their credibility was further undermined by the socio-economic development policies of the Bahraini government, which established a Bahrain Economic and Development Board for the purpose of furthering Bahrainization and provided free vocational training under the auspices of Tamkeen. This saw Bahrain's unemployment level fall to 3.7 percent in 2010. Thus, voter disappointment with the PiS and Sunni Islamists led to the victory of alternative candidates. Despite this, Al Wefaq's image as the Shiite opposition guarantees this party the continuous support of a majority of Bahrain's population.

Conclusion

In this chapter we assessed the rise of religious populism in Bahrain and in Poland, exploring its causes as well as its negative effects. Subsequently, a number of similarities between fundamentalist religious parties in both countries were found. Christian and Islamic fundamentalists all seek to reform society from a moral perspective based on their religious ideology. Populists seek to align all aspects of society with religious standards, while directing their attacks at perceived enemies of the moral order. In both countries, populists have presented themselves as incorruptible, attracting disadvantaged supporters fearing the erosion of their lifestyle. However, without clear economic plans they have made poor decisions, mismanaged public finances, created myths to distract citizens from real problems and consequently lost popular support. Their own involvement in corruption scandals has also contributed to their downfall, leading to further delays in much-needed reforms. Given the correlation between low educational attainment, precarious economic conditions and the rise of populism, it would seem that initiatives to improve educational and other opportunities for disadvantaged groups would help dampen the appeal of populist politics and promote societal advancement over the long term.

References

Anti-Defamation League 2006. *Poland: Democracy and the Challenge of Extremism*. Online: www. adl.org (accessed December 21, 2010).

Ahmed, D. A. 2009. "Bahrain." In *Women's Rights in the Middle East and North Africa*. Ed. by S. Kelly and J. Breslin. Lanham: Rowman and Littlefield, 59–88.

Al-Azmeh, A. 2009. *Islams and Modernities*. London: Verso.

Al A'ali, M. 2010a. "Independents the biggest winners." *Gulf Daily News* (November 1): 2A.

_____. 2010b. "New plea to stop 'Jackson' concert." *Gulf Daily News* (May 21): 3B.

Albertazzi, D. and D. McDonnell. 2008. *Twenty-first Century Populism: The Spectre of Western European Democracy*. London: Palgrave Macmillan.

Bacevich, A. and E. Prodromou. 2004. "God is Not Neutral: Religion and US Foreign Policy after 9/11." *Orbis* 48: 43–54.

"Bahrain: MPs Call for Ban on Pork." 2009. *Gulf Daily News* (December 9): 2A.

Bayat, A. 2007. *Making Islam Democratic: Social Movements and the Post-Islamist Turn*. Stanford: Stanford University Press.

Borkowska, I. 2010. *Polska Polsce nierówna* [Poland Uneven Within]. Online: www.wiadomosci. polska.pl (accessed December 21, 2010).

Bowman, D. 2008. "Bahrain Witnesses Population Explosion." *Arabian Business* (February 27): 4A.

Ebrill, L. P. et al. 1994. *Poland. The Path to a Market Economy*. Occasional Paper 113, IMF, Washington, DC.

"Education Ministry with a Bent towards Creationism." 2006. (March 11). Online: http://www.spiegel.de/international/0,1518,446307,00.html (accessed December 11, 2010).

Esposito, J. L. 2003. "Islam and Civil Society." In *Modernizing Islam: Religion in the Public Sphere in Europe and in the Middle East*. Ed. by J. L. Esposito and F. Burgat. New Brunswick: Rutgers, 69–100.

Fearon, J. and D. Laitin. 2005. *Bahrain*. Online: http://www.stanford.edu/group/ethnic/Random%20Narratives/BahrainRN1.1.pdf (accessed June 10, 2000).

Gadomski, W. 2007. "Koniec rewolucji moralnej" [The End of the Moral Revolution]. *Gazeta Wyborcza* (December 22): 13.

Giertych, M. 2007. *Wojna cywilizacji w Europie* [The Clash of Civilizations in Europe]. Krzeszowice: Dom Wydawniczy Ostoja.

_____. 2008. *Gender Equality and Life Issues in the European Union*. Brussels: Maciej Giertych.

GUS. 2010. *Stopa bezrobocia w latach 1990–2010* [Unemployment Rate Statistics 1990–2010]. Online: http://www.stat.gov.pl/gus/5840_677_PLK_HTML.htm (accessed December 20, 2010).

Grün, M. 2008. *National Legacies and the Ideology of the Radical Right in Poland and the Czech Republic*. Paper presented to The Radical Right in Post-1989 Central and Eastern Europe—the Role of Legacies Workshop, New York University.

Hałabuz, N. 2010. "Dobra pensja, bow Polsce szef zarabia 10 razy więcej niż pracownicy" [Good salary since in Poland the boss earns 10 times more than the employees]. *Gazeta Wyborcza* (January 23). Online: http://wyborcza.pl/1,76842,7487076,Dobra_pensja__bo_w_Polsce__Szef_zarabia_10_razy_wiecej.html. (accessed September 5, 2012).

Herb, M. 1999. *All in the Family: Absolutism, Revolution, and Democratic Prospects in the Middle Eastern Monarchies*. Albany: State University of New York Press.

Hoffman, H. 2007. Religion and Politics in Contemporary Poland. In *Náboženství a politika*. Ed. by T. Bubík and H. Hoffmann Pantheon: Pardubice, 80–87.

Index GINI 1984–2004. Washington: World Bank.

Jones, D. A. 2008. "Bahrain Seeks Crackdown on Homosexuality. Again." Online: http://news.change.org (accessed December 20, 2010).

Juergensmeyer, M. 1993. *The New Cold War: Religious Nationalism Confronts the Secular State*. Berkeley: University of California Press.

Keane, M. P. and E. S. Prasad. 2001. "Poland: Inequality, transfers, and growth in transition." *Finance and Development* 1, no. 38: 50–53.

Khonji, T. 2006. "'No Go' Rule for Bachelor Laborers." (January). Online: http://manama-council.blogspot.com/2006/01/no-go-rule-for-bachelor-laborers-by.html (accessed April 20, 2009).

Kublik, A. 2006. "Wybory pokazały stary podział na Polskę A i B" [Elections Highlight the Old Division into Poland A and Poland B]. *Gazeta Wyborcza* (June 8): 8.

Horolets A., J. Kurczewska, M. Trojanowska-Strzęboszewska M. "Discourse Analysis of Politics. LPR's rhetoric." WP 6 Report, Institute of Public Affairs, Warsaw, October 2005 (unpublished), 8–13. Online: http://www.isp.org.pl/files/11297950200606281001164194296.pdf (accessed September 30, 2011).

Kurowska, A. 2008. *Skąd się bierze bieda* [The Source of Poverty]. Zeszyt 5. Warsaw: FOR.

Kurtz, L. 1995. *Gods in the Global Village*. Thousand Oaks: Pine Forge Press.

Lewis, B. 2003. *The Crisis of Islam: Holy War and Unholy Terror*. New York: Random House.

Longrigg, S. H. 1966. "The economics and politics of oil in the Middle East." In *Modernization of the Arab World*. Ed. by J. H. Thompson and R. D. Reischauer. Princeton: Van Nostrand, 102–14.

Louër, L. 2008. "The Political Impact of Labor Migration in Bahrain." *City and Society* 20: 32–53.

"LPR's Political Program." 2011. *Prawica Polska*. Online: http://www.prawicapolska.pl/wybory_programy_lpn.shtml (accessed April 20, 2009).

Luciani, G. 1990. "Allocation vs. Production States: A Theoretical Framework." *The Arab State*. Berkeley: University of California Press, 65–84.

Luciani, G. and H. Beblawi. 1987. *The Rentier State*. New York: Croom Helm.

Łubieński, T. 2010. "Nie wińcie naszych romantyków" [Do Not Blame Our Romantics]. *Gazeta Wyborcza* (April 17): 17.

Maciejewicz, P. and M. Kokot. 2010. "Na Podlasiu nie jest źle" [It Is Not that Bad in Podlaskie Voivodeship]. *Gazeta Wyborcza* (March 1). Online: http://wyborcza.pl/1,76842,7610816,Na_Podlasiu_nie_jest_zle.html (accessed September 5, 2012).

Michnik, A. 2008. "Mowa pogrzebowa nad grobem IV Rzeczypospolitej" [A Funeral Speech on the Tomb of the Fourth Polish Republic]. *Gazeta Wyborcza* (January 1). Online: http://wyborcza.pl/1,101421,4797110.html. (accessed September 5, 2012).

Minkenberg, M. and M. Schain. 2005. "The Front National in Context: French and European Dimensions." In *Right-Wing Extremism in the Twenty-first Century*. Ed. by P. H. Merkl and L. Weinberg. London: Taylor and Francis, 155–84.

Moghadam, V. M. 2003. *Modernizing Women: Gender and Social Change in the Middle East*. Boulder: Lynne Rienner Publishers, Inc.

"MPs Vote for Blanket Ban on Public Sale in Bahrain." 2009. *Gulf Daily News*. (May 6): 4B

Mudde, C. 2000. *The Ideology of the Extreme Right*. Manchester: Manchester University Press.

Nasr, V. 2006. *The Shia Revival: How Conflicts within Islam will Shape the Future*. New York: W. W. Norton and Company.

Niklewicz, K. 2007. "Maciej Giertych znów szokuje eurodeputowanych" [Maciej Giertych Shocks the Euro MPs again]. *Gazeta Wyborcza* (February 16). Online: http://wyborcza. pl/1,76842,3923332.html (accessed November 29, 2008).

Norris, P. and R. Inglehart. 2004. *Sacred and Secular: Religion and Politics Worldwide*. Cambridge: Cambridge University Press.

Pankowski, R. and M. Kornak. 2005. "Poland." In *Racist Extremism in Central and Eastern Europe*. Ed. by C. Mudde. New York: Routledge, 156–80.

PEW Research Centre. 2009. "Mapping the Global Muslim Population." The PEW Forum on Religion & Public Life. Online: http://www.pewforum.org/uploadedfiles/Orphan_ Migrated_Content/Muslimpopulation.pdf (accessed April 29, 2011).

Porter, B. 2000. *When Nationalism Began to Hate: Imagining Modern Politics in Nineteenth-Century Poland*. New York: Oxford University Press.

Resende, M. 2007. *Divide and Rule: Nationalism and the Failure of Christian Democracy in Poland*. Presented at Escola de Verão do IPRI.

Riesebrodt, M. 1990. *Pious passion: The Emergence of Modern Fundamentalism in the United States and Iran*. Berkeley: University of California Press.

Robbins, P. 1994. "Can Gulf Monarchies Survive the Oil Bust?" *The Middle East Quarterly* 10, no. 4: 51–63.

Rutkowski, J. 1998. *Welfare and the Labor Market in Poland*. Washington: World Bank.

"Shi'ites Riot in Bahrain against Asians, Liquor and Prostitution." 2004. *World Tribune* (March 15). Online: http://www.worldtribune.com/worldtribune/WTARC/2004/ me_gulf_03_14.html (accessed April 24, 2009).

Siddiqui, Z. 1978. "Other Aspects of Daily Life." In *The Islamic Tradition*. Ed. by L. Smith and W. Bodin. Allen, TX: Argus Communications, 111–16.

Tarkowska, E. 2007. *Oblicza polskiej biedy.* [The Faces of Polish Poverty]. Warsaw: Instytut Filozofii i Socjologii PAN.

Tolz, V. 2005. "Right-wing Extremism in Russia." In *Right-Wing Extremism in the Twenty-first Century*. Ed. by P. H. Merkl and L. Weinberg. London: Taylor and Francis, 243–62.

Toumi, H. 2010. "Call to Civil Society, Upper Chamber to Support Alcohol Ban Move in Bahrain." Online: http://www.habibtoumi.com/2010/03/14/call-to-civil-society-upper-chamber-to-support-move-to-ban-alcohol-in-bahrain (accessed December 20, 2010).

_____. 2006. "Islamists Hail Huge Election Victory." *Gulf News* (November 27): 2A.

United Nations. 2010. *International Human Development Indicators*. Online: http://hdr.undp. org/en/statistics/ (accessed January 6, 2010).

UNDP. 2003. *Bahrain: MDG Survey*. Online: www.undp.org.bh/Files/MDG03/Goal1.pdf (accessed December 19, 2010).

Walorek, J. 2007. "Zjawisko korupcji politycznej w Polsce w latach 2000–2007" [The Phenomenon of Political Corruption in Poland 2000–2007]. In *Raport o korupcji*. Online: http://www.transparency.pl/files/7768cb2ff94865c380e16d8701960021.pdf (accessed December 17, 2010).

Wilkenson, B. and A. Atti. 1997. *UNDP Microfinance Assessment Report for Bahrain*. United Nations Capital Development Fund. Online: http://www.uncdf.org/english/ microfinance/uploads/country_feasibility/bahfinaldb.pdf (accessed August 28, 2007).

Wise, K. A. 2010. Civilizational Boundaries in Christian-Jewish Relations. *Studies in Christian-Jewish Relations* 5, no. 1: 1–22.

Women Gateway. 2008. "News" (May). Online: http://www.womengateway.com/enwg/ News/2008/May/nws.htm (accessed December 5, 2010).

Zahid, M. and M. Zweiri. 2007. *The Victory of Al-Wefaq: The Rise of Shi'ite Politics in Bahrain*. Athens: Research Institute for European and American Studies (RIEAS), Research Paper 108.

Zaleski T. 2008. "Poseł PiS: Obama to koniec białej cywilizacji" [PiS MP: Obama Means the End of White Civilization]. (November 8). Online: http://fakty.interia.pl/fakty_dnia/news/news/posel-pis-obama-to-koniec-bialej-cywilizacji,1208377 (accessed April 6, 2009).

Zieniewicz, A. 2006. *Retoryka agresywnego populizmu?* [Rhetoric of Aggressive Populism]. [Radio interview]. (August 30). Online: http://blogfm.blox.pl/2006/08/Retoryka-agresywnego-populizmu.html (accessed September 13, 2009).

Part Three

RELIGION IN TAIWAN

Chapter 8

RELIGION IN THE MEDIA AGE: A CASE STUDY OF DA AI DRAMAS FROM THE TZU CHI ORGANIZATION

Pei-Ru Liao
University of Leeds, United Kingdom

Introduction

Tzu Chi (Fojiao Ciji Gongdehui, the Buddhist Compassion Relief Foundation) was founded in 1966 by Master Cheng Yen (Zhengyan), originally as a group of 30 laywomen and several nuns in Hualian, a town on Taiwan's eastern coast. Today Tzu Chi is one of the largest civic organizations in Taiwan, with a membership in the millions, and operates state-of-the-art hospitals, schools and mass media facilities. One of these, the Da Ai (Great Love) TV channel, stands out among public broadcasters not only for its religious focus but also for the depth and variety of its programs. These include Da Ai dramas, Buddhist teachings by Master Cheng Yen, information and educational programs, children's programs, cultural programs, medical information and news shows (in Mandarin Chinese and English). Da Ai dramas, adapted from the real-life stories of senior Tzu Chi members, are broadcast during prime time (8:00 to 9:00 PM). Despite a competitive market, they have managed to climb to a leading position, according to ACG Nielsen ratings. With their religious themes and intricate storylines, the dramas provide a rich source for examining media representations of religion and gender in a contemporary Confucian society.

This chapter examines the religious themes implicit in Da Ai dramas, and how gender roles are constructed in this specific religious medium. Through an interdisciplinary analysis based on insights from gender theory, media studies and religious studies, I explore gender and religious issues from the perspective of the audience. Intertextuality between the media and everyday life is also an important concern. This approach offers a fresh perspective on religious broadcasting and attitudes of its audiences, and more broadly, on religion and gender in an East Asian context.

Let us begin by situating the topic within existing theories on religion and gender in relation to Buddhism, before moving on to a detailed analysis of one Da Ai drama, *Love from the Valley*.

Feminist Buddhism

At the end of my first year of PhD study, one of the examiners asked me whether meditation practice in Humanistic Buddhism differs from other kinds of Buddhism. I was stunned by the question—not because I lack knowledge of Humanistic Buddhism, which is a popular form of Buddhism in contemporary Taiwan, but because it had never occurred to me that meditation practice ought to play an important role in Buddhism. Although my father is a pious Buddhist who has studied the scriptures all his life, I seldom see him meditate or visit temples. Many people around me identify themselves as Buddhists, but have never practiced meditation in their lives. Only very recently, when I encountered feminist works on Buddhism, did I come to appreciate how the term "Buddhism" is interpreted in diverse ways across cultures.

Just as we should not assume Buddhism to be a homogenous ideology, so should we avoid viewing women and their experiences in a monolithic fashion. Kwok (2000) argues that Western scholars of China have often constructed stereotypes of Chinese women as universally subjugated under Confucian patriarchy. In the same way, early feminist theorists ignored differences among women across and within cultures but, assuming the privileged position of a white middle-class, portrayed women elsewhere as victims (Kwok 2000, 2002). To ignore such differences, notes Spivak (1988), is to deny women historical agency and to suppress their individual voices. Scholars should consequently re-examine their stance in order to construct theories that are closer to women's actual lived realities.

Above all, specific cultural and social contexts must be analyzed if we are to properly understand the situation of particular women. One common error is to assume analyzing institutionally sanctioned or official religious texts to be sufficient for understanding the experiences of Buddhist women. On this issue, Schneiderman (1999) is right to criticize Western feminist Buddhists such as Klein, Shaw and O'Halloran for ignoring Asian Buddhist women's divergent experiences with the justification that Western Buddhists expect "textual-based, institutionally oriented forms of Buddhism" (222, 224). In Asia, Buddhism is a religion characterized by far more diversity and dynamism than such an approach acknowledges.

Under the influence of Christian traditions which emphasize the role of texts and institutions, Western scholars have neglected the practices of lay Buddhists whose perspective does not fit this model (Cooey 1990). One leading feminist Buddhist, Rita M. Gross, suggests that Buddhism faces serious structural problems as a lay tradition because the laity lack time to spend in meditation practices (Gross 1993, 277). Her call to establish an institution in which laypeople can engage in meditation practices and study Buddhist philosophy, assumes an institutionally oriented type of Buddhism to which Western feminists can better relate. While the experiences of Western feminist Buddhists of course cannot be ignored, neither can those of Asian Buddhist women. The need for a more context-specific approach for understanding Buddhist women in Asia should be readily conceded, as women from various cultures derive different worldviews and roles from the social structures they inhabit (Schneiderman 1999, 227). Diversity and difference, however, are rarely discussed in English-language Buddhist scholarship, because Western Buddhist women are unwilling to describe the reality of Asian Buddhist women, fearing that their unequal roles might threaten or "challenge Buddhism's egalitarian potential in the West" (Schneiderman 1999, 233). However, the inequality faced by most Asian Buddhist women is rooted in cultural patriarchy, not in Buddhism per se. To argue for gender equality in Buddhism, we cannot avoid bringing cultural and historical contexts into discussion.

As just mentioned, the study of Buddhism in the East and the West is biased toward the study of texts. Scholars like Gross (1993) and Diana Paul (1985) view Mahayana textual traditions as a means of empowering women. While this is certainly a worthwhile pursuit, their reliance on canonical texts presents several problems. First of all, contemporary debates on gender and Buddhism are based on an earlier feminist Buddhist framework which overemphasizes Pali texts relative to Sanskrit ones (Collet 2006, 83). Thus, there is a taxonomy of value in the canonical texts being studied. Moreover, a Protestant-influenced evaluation of Buddhist texts tends to misrepresent women in Buddhism, especially when reliable English translations are unavailable (Collet 2006, 65). Secondly, the validity of canonical texts needs to be questioned (Derris 2008). Some of the scriptures popular in Chinese Buddhism are pseudepigraphal works composed specifically for Confucian contexts. It is therefore necessary, as Collet (2006) suggests, to re-contextualize earlier texts and reposition them within their ancient setting. A further re-contextualization of Buddhist women across cultures is also essential to understanding the real experiences of Buddhist women.

Limiting the analysis of gender in Buddhism to canonical texts is also problematic because "Buddhism cannot be abstracted from its cultural context as if it existed alone" (Lefferts 2000, 63). In the Greater China region (consisting of China, Hong Kong, Taiwan, and other areas dominated by Chinese culture), Buddhism has been transformed by the dominant secular ideology of Confucianism—a process known as the domestication of Buddhism in China (Goodman 2008, 31). Since the term or the concept of "religion" first entered China in the nineteenth century, through contact with Western cultures, "Buddhism" as a subject of study is a modern invention. Unfortunately, this textually based study of Buddhism fails to reflect the complexity and diversity of Buddhism, whether in its Mahayana or Theravada traditions, or how they are experienced differently in various cultures. Rather than being fixed subjects, Asian Buddhist women have adapted their religious beliefs in tandem with social changes such as modernization or globalization (Lefferts 2000). The social context in which they live includes political structures. Modernists tend to see religion as belonging to the private realm (Casanova, 1994), and therefore treat religion and politics as two separate spheres (Harris 2001, 1). However, an examination of the interrelationships between religion and politics in different cultures helps us to understand how Buddhist institutions work differently across Asia (and elsewhere). Such an understanding is essential to a discussion of Asian Buddhist women, while textually based Buddhism can at most supplement our understanding. Scholars should thus be aware of the social context of the women for whom they speak, including the adaptation of their religions to modern technology. After all, religions change, and today are expressed through advanced media technologies such as the Internet, television and radio. In this regard, an analysis of Da Ai dramas enables us to not only better understand women's individual social contexts but also their unique roles in Buddhism.

Religion and the Media

The fact that contemporary religions have adapted to the media age raises many important questions regarding Buddhism and women. Nowadays, religions can be circulated through media other than written texts or oral traditions, rendering a mono-medium approach to understanding religion "ill-suited to the variety of phenomena which make up this complex and media diverse tradition" (Arthur 2004, 22–3). However, amid society's ever-greater dependence on mass-media communication and computerized communications technology, media studies as a discipline neglects religion as unworthy of scholarly attention (Hoover 1997, 4). In cultural studies as well, religious topics are rare compared to studies on gender, sexuality, race or class, perhaps because religion is deemed to belong to a separate field. Moreover, sociologists of religion have also largely failed to acknowledge the influence of media on religions, or to analyze how religions have changed in the media age.

Since religion represents an integral component of human cultures, it should be taken more seriously in media and cultural studies, especially now that religious movements are actively adopting new technologies to promote their interests (Meyer and Moors 2006).

Religious use of popular media first attracted academic interest in the 1950s and 1960s as religious broadcasting began to grow. More recently, conventional studies on televangelism have assumed that mediated religious activities threaten "authentic" (i.e., institutionalized) religions, a view that ignores changing social and cultural patterns (Bruce 1990; Hadden 1988; Horsefield 1984). These studies have focused on the audience of religious programs and on governmental policies toward religious broadcasting. Televangelism, a common topic in the literature, is treated as a phenomenon specific to North America and the Christian world. Meanwhile, scholars have rarely used theories from media studies or audience research to explore the relationship between media, religion and audience. Yet as television has increasingly become a part of daily life, a diverse variety of religious programs have appeared other than Christian televangelism. Finally, earlier studies on religious television tend to be quantitative, aimed at finding out who the audience was and why they watched particular shows. Not until very recently have scholars begun to examine religion's appearance in the media as a contradiction to the modernist assumption that religion will retreat back into the private realm under modernizing pressures (Wilford 2009).

Entering the public sphere and commercial world, religions manifest themselves in various forms of mediation. The adoption of electronic media blurs the line between the "sacred" and "mundane," bringing new influences into religious development. More recent media studies of religion have broadened their scope to religious representations in the secular media, such as music videos (Mackee and Pardun 1999), prime-time dramas (Robinson and Skill 1994), news and journalism (Scheufele, Nisbet and Brossard 2003; Winston 2007) and fan culture as a "pop religion" (Hoover 2006). This chapter is concerned with the religious use of media; therefore, debates on religious representations in secular media do not concern us here.

Studies on American Puritanism in the public sphere remind us that the re-articulation of religion in the public sphere runs contrary to the modernist narrative of the decline of religion in public contexts (Meyer and Moor 2006, 6). Although the modern world assigns religions to the private sphere, the public sphere of the media has become a sacred place (Martin-Barbero 1997), a virtual altar for laypeople. The public presence of religions worldwide is not a return to the repressed past; rather, globalization is reshaping the relationship between religion and the media. The religious adoption of electronic media represents a new form of religious mediation

(Meyer and Moor 2006). Religions, then, spread their messages faster and more widely under globalization. If a religious tradition is understood as a system or reservoir of symbols, including "manifestations in belief, patterned behavior, written records, ceremonial performances, iconography, traces in human memory, and so forth" (Babb 1995, 1), it would be worthwhile to discuss religions' use of new technology, for religious symbols are embedded in everyday global media communications.

As the above literature review suggests, studies on media and religion in the Christian world have moved from analyzing a certain type of religious media—televangelism—to various secular media. However, Buddhist broadcasting represents a new and intriguing area of research. In Taiwan, a limited number of studies have been conducted on Chinese-language religious broadcasting (Bai 2009; Lee 2006; Wu 2000; Yu 2002). Most of these are concerned with the marketing strategies of Buddhist TV networks, rather than the study of religious meaning within the secular media. Research into how religious meaning or practices have changed in recent times as a result of new media technologies is conspicuous by its absence. This chapter on Da Ai dramas, therefore, analyzes society as represented in the dramas in order to better understand gender roles in Taiwanese society, as well as the important role played by Tzu Chi as one of the most important Humanistic Buddhist organizations in Taiwan.

Globalization and the Media

Da Ai is a non-profit TV network broadcast globally to more than 25 countries in Asia, the Americas, Africa and Europe, via terrestrial and satellite broadcast signals, and webcasting. In Indonesia, Da Ai TV is localized as the Da Ai Indonesia TV network, established in 2007, with a potential audience of 20 million people. Although it is common for Taiwanese commercial dramas (especially so-called "idol dramas") to achieve success in Asian countries, especially in the Greater China region (Chan 2005; Thomas 2000), a religious TV network like Da Ai seldom enjoys success abroad. A brief look into media globalization helps to explain Da Ai's media environment, as several newly arisen but rarely discussed media forces can be observed in East Asia. Furthermore, many works on Asian media studies apply Western methodologies and epistemologies to "local texts." The biggest flaw in Asian media studies is a deliberate neglect of Asian contexts (Erni and Chua 2005). A better understanding of these contexts can help us understand the emerging markets for Da Ai TV and other religious networks. In this regard, the Taiwanese TV industry provides a useful starting point for discussing the potential of Da Ai TV, the first Buddhist TV network to enjoy global success.

Globalization is often characterized as a "compression" of the world as a whole (Robertson 1992), with early scholars of globalization tending to view it as a powerful homogenizing force threatening cultures and cultural minorities worldwide. As such, globalization was seen as a threat, because powerful media exporters in America and Great Britain seemed poised to eliminate local media industries, especially in developing nations (Tomlinson 2002, 36). However, it is now acknowledged that global exporters of significance can emerge in different parts of the world, not just in the West. That is, the flow of globalization should be seen as multidirectional (Curran and Park 2000, 6). Moreover, local adoption is now seen as crucial to the success of global media enterprises, whatever their home nation (Croteau and Hoynes 1997). In other words, local cultures have the ability to reproduce their own meanings while engaging with global media flows, and it is impossible for global media flows to control how local consumers reinterpret or repurpose imported symbolic content (Ang 1996). Underlying the debates of cultural imperialism is the image of globalization as a giant and localization as a dwarf. Yet in reality, globalization produces a hybrid cultural product "in which the global and the local are inextricably intertwined" (Ang 1996, 154). That is, media representations in global products interact with local experiences. Most Western globalization scholars fail to notice the powerful flow—i.e., regionalization—that mediates between globalization and localization (Chan 2005).

Although differences across Asian cultures should not be ignored, common cultural elements exist as well, which Asian media industries constantly blend to construct "a synthesized 'Asian culture'" (Moeran 2001, 13) in the form of media products with pan-Asian content (French and Richards 2000; Moeran 2001, 5). This pan-Asian identity offers an alternative to globalization or westernization (Chuan 2008). In East Asia, Confucian influences are still visible in most countries due to ancient ties with China. These countries share the common experience of "Asian modernity," a unique process of modernization found in East Asian countries (Tu 1996). Under the influences of globalization, "Asian modernity" is seen as a hybrid product of globalization and localization. This kind of regional cultural proximity helps promote the consumption of Japanese dramas in East Asian countries (Iwabuchi 2005). US cultural hegemony has gradually been replaced by regionalization, "defined by geographical locations and cultural proximity" (Chan 2005, 190). In particular, East Asian youth participate in an emerging regional popular culture that blends traditional values with Western chic (Tamney and Chiang 2002). However, regional flows of media and popular culture happen mostly in urban areas, and economically deprived people are always excluded from this experience of Asian modernity (Ganguly Scrase 2006, 47).

Media products popular among Asian countries often represent a middle-class and urban lifestyle that is not experienced equally by all Asians. However, Da Ai dramas are deemed more traditional in that they represent "ordinary" people's lives, and approach their audiences (mainly Chinese communities around the world) via cultural proximity based on ordinary people's life experiences. Instead of a form of resistance aimed at protecting local cultures against globalization, regionalization is better viewed as an expression of local needs in an area where people share similar cultural backgrounds and experiences of modernization (French and Richards 2000). Where younger generations share common experiences of modernization, older generations find nostalgic comfort in Da Ai dramas. Regionalization can be seen as a revival of traditional values in a non-traditional way, in which "tradition" is not a fixed concept, but changes according to time and place. Pan-Asian identity is forged through the circulation of popular culture and media products among East Asian countries. It reflects a unique process of Asian modernity that blends traditional values and modernity into media products.

Taiwanese Buddhism and Tzu Chi

In the 1930s and 1940s, the Japanese colonial government repressed Taiwanese culture in order to "Japanize" its subjects. Temples with Chinese or Taiwanese features were destroyed, while the erection of Japanese-style temples was encouraged. Japanization policies did not last long, however, as Taiwan was taken over in 1945 by the Nationalist Chinese Kuomintang (KMT) government (Jones 2003; Katz 2003; Laliberte 2003; Weller 2007).

Two important historical events molded the subsequent course of Buddhism in Taiwan. First, in 1949, the Chinese Communist Party (CCP) took over mainland China, forcing the KMT regime to retreat to Taiwan. Many prominent Buddhist *sangha* members fled to Taiwan in order to escape religious repression on the mainland (Chandler 2006; Xu 1998). One of the most influential of these monastic refugees was Master Yinshun, a disciple of Master Taixu. In the 1920s, Master Taixu introduced a modernized, reformed Buddhism called *Rensheng Fojiao* (Buddhism for Human Life). It represents a Chinese Buddhist response to attacks from the West, as well as from within Chinese culture. Master Yinshun later modified the phrase to *Renjian Fojiao* (Buddhism for the Human World). Both terms are commonly translated into English as "Humanistic Buddhism" or "This-worldy Buddhism" (Chandler 2006; Laliberte 2004), and suggest an emphasis on this-worldly affairs over other-worldly concerns (Shi 1999; Yang 2000). In Taiwan, Master Yinshun's approach was taken up by two of his most prominent disciples, Master Hsing Yun (Xingyun) and Master Cheng Yen.

The second important event was the 1987 lifting of martial law, which led to Taiwan becoming a liberal democracy (Chandler 2006; Feuchtwang 2001; Jones 1999; Laliberte 2003, 2004). Local Buddhist organizations flourished in tandem with the rapid economic growth of the 1980s and 1990s, contradicting theories of modernity which expected economic growth to lead to a decrease in religious activity (Weller 2007). The largest and most prominent Buddhist organizations are Foguangshan (Buddha's Light Mountain), led by Master Hsing Yun; and Tzu Chi, led by Master Cheng Yen. The latter has a larger female population, and female members play more active role relative to males in the organization (Jiang 2003, 9). In addition to its matriarchal characteristics, Tzu Chi is also distinct for its leadership by lay Buddhists (Laliberte 2004).

As will become evident, Da Ai dramas explicitly promote Tzu Chi's Buddhist agenda among the viewing audience. Master Cheng Yen blends the Humanistic Buddhism of Master Yinshun with the Mahayana Buddhist ideal of the Bodhisattva, the compassionate person who chooses to halt his or her final progress to enlightenment for the purpose of enlightening and saving all living beings. For Tzu Chi members, the most prominent Bodhisattva is Guanyin/Avalokiteśvara, who is also the most popular divinity in Taiwanese folk Buddhism (Dong 2008, 266). Shi (2006) points out that Taiwanese Buddhists link their identities as Buddhists with the worship of Guanyin, who is seen as answering prayers and saving people from suffering (3–5). As an enlightened being, a Bodhisattva such as Guanyin is thought to adopt a this-worldly focus out of compassion for all living beings (Reed 2003, 199; Weller 2007, 356). Tzu Chi is not a textually oriented Buddhist institution—instead of reciting sutras, Tzu Chi members focus on virtuous actions (Wu 2007, 165–6). Indeed, Master Cheng Yen encourages her followers to follow the Bodhisattva path through practicing the discipline of compassion, and by participating in social welfare and charity work (Huang and Weller 1998). Her practice of Humanistic Buddhism has elevated it to an international level, disseminated through various forms of print and broadcast media. In this way, Tzu Chi transforms Buddhism from a complicated philosophy based on difficult scriptures, into the sphere of daily practice. For this reason, a textually based study of Buddhism is insufficient for understanding what Buddhism means to contemporary Taiwanese society.

Da Ai Drama

Da Ai TV began broadcasting in 1998, with the stated aims of promoting harmony, ending corruption, countering excessive individualism and materialism, and inspiring viewers with Buddhist ideals. It is a non-commercial station that relies on audience donations, as well as profits from Tzu Chi's environmental projects (such as its recycling initiatives). Although Da Ai is categorized as a religious TV channel because it is run by the Tzu Chi organization, with the popularity of Da Ai dramas, more and more people have come to regard it as a normal television channel. Unlike prime-time dramas broadcast on commercial channels, Da Ai dramas assume a docudrama form. All the stories in Da Ai dramas are based on the lives of senior Tzu Chi members, with each drama telling the story of a particular Tzu Chi member's life. Although Da Ai does not take ACG Nielsen ratings into consideration, in 2004 it numbered among the top twenty most popular TV channels in Taiwan.

At the end of each 50-minute show, there is a 10-minute interview session in which the audience is introduced to the producer, director, actors and actresses, and the real people on whom the dramas are based. During these interviews, the actors and actresses are typically asked about their personal feelings and interpretations of the characters, while their real-world models are asked to reflect on the events of their lives, as broadcast in the dramas. The authenticity of Da Ai dramas is also reinforced through reconstructed historical scenes. The viewing experience is subsequently less melodramatic than that of prime-time dramas on commercial channels. Since Da Ai dramas are based on the lives of senior Tzu Chi members, the timeline of the stories spans the twentieth century.

Da Ai dramas fall into a unique genre, in that they are at once religious programs and reality-based adaptations. As such, they can be categorized as docudramas. A "documentary drama" is, in Corner's (1999) words, "essentially a form of *play*" that refers to "specific real events" or events that appear to have taken place (35). Dovey (2000) mentions other characteristics of docudramas, such as "the combination of commentary, editing and camera style which work together to create an ideal, unified point of view for the audience" (142). Family related issues are most often the focus of Da Ai dramas, though they also promote Tzu Chi's activities in the fields of healthcare, international volunteering, education, and so on. Thus, the production of Da Ai dramas furthers Tzu Chi's agenda not only in terms of the values presented, but also in relation to the organization's actual work.

According to Wu (2000), Da Ai narratives usually focus on the role played by Tzu Chi in the protagonists' lives. More often than not, the characters experience hardship before learning about Tzu Chi. Religious themes are tied to the character's involvement with Tzu Chi's volunteer work (the action component of Humanistic Buddhism). The narrative structure of Da Ai dramas resembles Reed's (2003) concept of the Guanyin narrative found in many areas of Asia. According to Reed, this narrative has been constructed through folk legends and Buddhist scriptures; at the same time, lay Buddhists have constructed their own narratives in which Guanyin helps them persevere during times of difficulty. In Da Ai dramas, Tzu Chi is presented as a savior figure, like Guanyin in the lay Buddhist narrative. In the standard narrative structure, the leading characters suffer in the second stage of their life (often in marriage), endure many crises and seek deeper answers to life's questions. Not until they discover Tzu Chi do they find solace, becoming devoted Tzu Chi members in the process.

However, the narrative of Da Ai dramas does not end here. Being a devoted Tzu Chi member means *doing* Tzu Chi. Reed further proposes a "Guanyin counter-narrative" used by Master Cheng Yen, which encourages followers to learn from their sufferings in order to help themselves and others. Rather than waiting passively to be saved, Tzu Chi members embody the image of Guanyin and help each other by doing good works through the Tzu Chi organization. Thus in a Da Ai drama, the story does not end at the third stage; rather, the protagonist begins a new, more spiritual life.

Love from the Valley

The Da Ai drama *Love from the Valley* (*Xigu Ama*, literally "Silicon Valley Grandma") premiered in September, 2008, and continued for a total of 50 episodes. The series was directed by Deng Anning, who also directed *Caoshan Chunhui* ("Spring's Sunlight from Mt Cao"), one of the most popular Da Ai dramas of 2005. *Love from the Valley* tells the story of one of the very first Tzu Chi members in the United States, Hsiu-Chin Lin-Wang (Lin Wang Xiuqin), whose life story spans the twentieth century. In order to attract a broader audience, the lead male role was given to popular actor/singer Eli Shih (Shi Yinan), and the lead female role to Golden Bell Award-winning actress Huang Caiyi. A star-studded supporting cast was recruited from the television, music and modeling industries. Since Hsiu-Chin's story is an important part of Tzu Chi's history in North America, the film crew worked closely with members of the San Jose, California branch. As a result, the contents as well as the production of the drama were highly globalized, revealing a global flow of religion which departs from the common scholarly view of globalization as a form of Western cultural imperialism.

Plot summary

Wang Hsiu-Chin was born in 1917, as the youngest of five children (she had four older brothers) in a rich family which ran one of the biggest tea-trading businesses in Taiwan. Growing up under Japanese colonial rule, Hsiu-Chin and her brothers received a Japanese education, with most of them pursuing higher education in Japan. Despite their wealth, one brother fought for the equality of Taiwanese people in Japanese-ruled Taiwan (he later fell victim to KMT martial law); another was one of the first on the island to start a home for the poor; and the youngest brother became a volunteer doctor in rural Japan (where he died). Surrounded by such public-spiritedness, Hsiu-Chin dreamed of organizing charity work from her adolescence. In an era when society was not open to marriage based on romantic love, she followed her heart and married Lin Chunsheng, who was from a poor peasant family but had aspirations of studying in Japan. In 1937, soon after their marriage, the couple moved to Dalian, China, where they had five children. Eleven years later, in 1948, civil war broke out as Dalian was attacked by Japan and Russia. Fleeing to Taiwan with her husband and family, Hsiu-Chin experienced life as a beggar and witnessed the darkest side of humanity.

In Taiwan, Chunsheng struggled in business while Hsiu-Chin, a housewife, did her best to support the family. As time went by, each of their children received a higher education, and most of them emigrated to the United States. At the age of 61, Chunsheng died of a heart attack. In order to help Hsiu-Chin (then 53 years old) overcome her grief, her daughters encouraged her to volunteer at an orphanage and hospital. In 1977, she immigrated to the United States. In 1984, on a visit to the Tzu Chi headquarters in Hualian, she was invited to chat with Master Cheng Yen, who assigned her the task of establishing Tzu Chi in the United States. As soon as Hsiu-Chin returned to northern California, she began recruiting members from her and her daughter's social network of Taiwanese immigrants and students. Through her diligence and leadership, she succeeded in founding a Tzu Chi branch in San Jose, and came to be respected as "everyone's grandmother" because of her generosity and kindness to others. She died in 2003, ten years after the establishment of the San Jose branch.

Marriage and Family in *Love from the Valley*

Some scholars argue that rather than biology determining gender, "the process of genderization in the familial kinship system is intertwined with the process of ritualization within which all unequal social roles are differentiated" (Rosenlee 2006, 73). Historians of women in China believe that the modern Chinese term for "women" (*nuxing*) appeared during and after the May Fourth Movement (1919), a reform movement that severely attacked Confucianism for being conservative and outdated (Huanglin 2004; Rosenlee 2006). Before this, another term (*funu*) was used. Beyond the bare meaning of "women," it reflected a discourse of gender in pre-modern China whose legacy endures today. The older term served to bind women in families (*jia*), with their social status linked to their social relations as embodied in familial roles (Tamney and Chiang 2002). Marriage for women meant increased and more demanding duties. Before marriage, women were simply daughters, to be prepared for marriage and motherhood. In other words, women were viewed as having been born to be wives and mothers, with marriage always assumed to represent a turning point in a woman's life. After marriage, women became wives and daughters-in-law (among other roles), with each role associated with different obligations. At a later stage, women became mothers and mothers-in-law, thereby achieving a higher and more powerful position in the Confucian hierarchy. The analysis below focuses on these social roles, and how they define women in the Taiwanese context, helping clarify the power dynamics behind the Confucian family hierarchy.

The drama begins with the diminutive figure of Hsiu-Chin standing next to the Golden Gate Bridge with her friend Meili, the drama's narrator. Meili tells the audience that Hsiu-Chin is affectionately known as "Ama" (grandmother) for her caring attitude towards everyone she knows. The smell of jasmine tea in a tea shop inspires Hsiu-Chin to reminisce about her past in Taiwan. As a teenage girl in the 1920s, she differed from other girls because of her rich family and her education. She had no worries in life, and enjoyed more freedom than the poor peasant girls who had to labor at household chores. In this way, the first few scenes situate the story in a global context, and carry the audience back to the early twentieth century.

Marriage and modernization

Modernity in Taiwan is largely associated with Japanese colonization, since many Taiwanese intellectuals were educated in Japan. Although Japan was itself influenced by westernization, it left its own imprint on the areas it colonized, and spread a unique form of modernization. *Love from the Valley* begins in Japanese-ruled Taiwan after Hsiu-Chin's brothers finish their education in Japan, bringing back certain new and then-controversial ideas. Notably, the brothers have come to believe arranged marriages to be wrong— men and women, they insist, ought to be able to choose their own partners based on feelings of romantic love. They also criticize the complexity and cost of traditional wedding rituals. Rituals are important in Confucian society, since they signify social standing and the appropriate role of every individual (de Bary 1998). The marriage of Hsiu-Chin and Chunsheng thus embodies tensions between tradition and modernization.

The scene of their first meeting (in Episode 1) establishes Hsiu-Chin's kindness and generosity, which will pave the way for her future practice of the Bodhisattva path. In the scene, Chunsheng watches Hsiu-Chin assisting a disabled couple. Seeing her through his eyes, the audience understands why Chunsheng would then break off his arranged marriage with a peasant girl named A-yue. Hsiu-Chin is also distinguished by her interest in the poetess Shi Liyu—not only as a demonstration of literacy, but also because Shi Liyu had controversially divorced her husband and married a man ten years younger than her. Chunsheng and Hsiu-Chin praise her for her modern values and willingness to defy tradition. (As shown in Episode 4, Shi had been born during a period when foot binding was commonplace. For intellectuals who had received modernized education, foot binding was a bodily symbol of "traditional values," and this was the reason she was respected—she was confined in a body disciplined by traditional Chinese virtues, while brave enough to break through the confinement.) Even today, women in Taiwan often think in a "modern" fashion, while outwardly conforming to traditional patriarchal custom (Quah 2008, 127).

The concept of marriage based on romantic love did not exist in pre-modern China. In Confucian society, women were confined to their inner chamber, unable to choose a person to fall in love with. Meanwhile, men rarely had a chance to meet well-educated women due to the gender segregation rules associated with Confucianism. It was common for marriages to be arranged by matchmakers. During the May Fourth Movement, Chinese intellectuals who had studied abroad called for an end to the practice, and promoted romantic love as the basis for marriage. Similar ideas were brought to Taiwan through intellectuals who studied in Japan (like Chunsheng, Hsiu-Chin and her brothers). However, marriages based on romantic love were not common until the mid-twentieth century. Chunsheng's arranged marriage was typical of earlier Taiwan. It was common practice for peasant families to view their young daughters as future brides who might bring large dowries. Women were treated like commodities, traded from one family to another for the sole purpose of reproduction, since Confucianism emphasizes the continuity of patrilineal blood lineage. As modernization took hold, however, women were more often treated as individuals. This kind of conflict between Confucian traditions and modern notions of womanhood is a frequent theme in women's life stories as represented and reconstructed by Da Ai dramas.

In *Love from the Valley*, the story of Hsiu-Chin's marriage shows how tradition is reshaped, but not erased, by modernization. The audience sees that love-based marriage does not necessarily grant women absolute freedom from patriarchal control. Though in love, the couple must ask their parents' permission to get married (Episode 4). At first, Chunsheng's parents refuse because they prefer A-yue; this obstacle is overcome when A-yue marries someone else. At this point Chunsheng is allowed to propose. However, Hsiu-Chin's mother worries that Hsiu-Chin will suffer from having to do too many household chores (Episode 6). Weary of the obstacles to their marriage, Chunsheng realizes that marriage is not just about two individuals, but also involves their families (Episode 7). He and Hsiu-Chin are eventually able to marry, in large part because his mother promises her mother not to overwork Hsiu-Chin. Finally the love-marriage takes place, with the approval of both sets of parents. The power and authority of older generation thus endure.

The same process is also visible in the marriages of Hsiu-Chin's children, several of whom bring their fiancé(e)s home to seek her approval. For the most part, she does not raise any objections. However, on being informed of her eldest son's divorce, she criticizes him for not taking proper care of his family (Episode 29). Like many Taiwanese parents, Hsiu-Chin tries to use her parental authority to persuade her son not to get divorced (Episode 30). Although married children are considered adults—as shown when Chunsheng tells his eldest son to shoulder his responsibilities "like an adult" once he is married (Episode 23)—parental authority and control do not end with their children's marriages. Rather, adult children are expected to obey their parents, who in turn have a duty to guide their children onto the right path. Chang (1998) discusses the concept of *fen*, which implies mutual obligations: the absolute obedience of the person in the subordinate position is linked to the fulfillment of obligations on the part of the superior. However, Hsiu-Chin's children notice a change in their mother after she becomes a Tzu Chi member. When one of her daughters decides to marry an American, Hsiu-Chin does not object, but tells her children that they must decide how to live their own lives. Through Tzu Chi, the older generation learns to abandon its insistence on hierarchical power.

Kitchen and community

The domestic kitchen, belonging to the private sphere, is important in that the whole family has meals in this setting, and married women spend much of their time preparing meals there every day while the men work outside the home. Also, it is in the kitchen that women pass down homemaking knowledge from generation to generation. The dining table is a central place where men talk about their work, and women talk about their daily lives. On most days, the dining table serves as a gathering place for Hsiu-Chin's nuclear family, while at other times it becomes a meeting area for the Taiwanese students and workers of Tzu Chi's San Jose branch. One particular kitchen scene, discussed below, is especially important for the message it conveys.

Before her marriage, Hsiu-Chin often goes into the kitchen to chat with her mother or sister-in-law. She watches them prepare meals, not needing to help with household chores. Unlike other women, she is not confined to the kitchen and her inner chamber, but is instead allowed to help in her brother's office, to study abroad, to manage the family tea trade, etc. After she marries, however, she has to learn how to do household chores, since keeping house is part of the duties of a daughter-in-law, at least according to Hsiu-Chin's mother (Episode 6). On the day after her wedding, when tradition requires that she visit her natal family, Hsiu-Chin sits in the kitchen with her sister-in-law, learning how to prepare meals. Her sister-in-law shares her experiences as a daughter-in-law, to let Hsiu-Chin know that she will have to learn much and work hard. As becomes evident, although notions regarding the qualities of an ideal daughter-in-law are subject to the interpretation of each parent-in-law, housework and kitchen chores are seen as essential duties. On this occasion, Hsiu-Chin's mother gives her advice on how to be a good daughter-in-law (Episode 7). Hsiu-Chin must fulfill her duties quietly, without arguing with anyone. Marriage will add to the roles which she must fulfill. Besides being a daughter, she now has to learn the duties of a daughter-in-law.

Soon after marriage, Hsiu-Chin moves to Dalian with her husband. A kitchen scene from this time shows her being helped by her sister-in-law (i.e., the wife of her brother, who is living with them), with whom she chats about life (Episode 7). Apart from Hsiu-Chin, women are seldom shown in the public sphere, but are mostly depicted in the kitchen or bedroom. Although not strictly confined to the private sphere, they are portrayed as busy with chores, while men are rarely present in the private sphere apart from a few intimate moments. The kitchen, then, becomes a place where private and public worlds converge.

When Hsiu-Chin returns to Taiwan during the war, she begins living with Chunsheng's family. As a daughter-in-law, she is expected to help in the kitchen, even though she knows little about cooking. Hsiu-Chin's mother-in-law teaches her how to do kitchen chores, while her sister-in-law helps her with the laundry. In Episode 10, her father-in-law becomes upset because "he has never seen a mother-in-law who treats her daughter-in-law like Mazu" (a popular goddess). By this he means that a mother-in-law ought to tame or discipline the daughter-in-law, and make her handle the household chores. This accords with the patrilineal tradition of Confucianism, in which a woman, regardless of her status in her natal family, must learn to cope with the patrilineal family she marries into. Conflicts between mothers-in-law and daughters-in-law often emerge in this area. Although the mother-in-law is also a woman, her incorporation to the patrilineal family grants her authority over newcomers. Having already adapted to the rules of the patrilineal family, it is her duty to teach these rules to a new daughter-in-law, so the younger woman can become part of the family.

Chunsheng and Hsiu-Chin eventually move out to start a new life as a nuclear family. The narrator states that Hsiu-Chin will now manage her own household (Episode 12). The couple's new life begins with a scene where Hsiu-Chin, Chunsheng and their children gather around the dining table to have a meal. From this point on, Hsiu-Chin becomes the central figure at the dining table. Here she prepares meals, and discusses important issues with her husband. It soon becomes apparent that she has mastered kitchen work, and gained power in the family. This development illustrates how the role of a wife within the private sphere can be understood as complementary to the role of the husband within the public sphere. The narrative of women being confined in the inner chamber thus underestimates the power and importance of women's horizontal ties in the private sphere (Weller 1999, 35). As Hsiu-Chin's daughters mature, they start to help with food preparation. The dining table is depicted as a place where women learn to be virtuous, dutiful daughters and daughters-in-law (Episode 18). As members of the younger generation grow up, they take over duties in the kitchen so that the older generation can relax and enjoy retired life. (For housewives, retirement means having daughters-in-law to help with household chores.) Although Hsiu-Chin is depicted as in control of her own kitchen, her nuclear family is still subject to the authority of parents and parents-in-law. Her mother-in-law comes to live with them; and her father-in-law visits quite often, as does her mother from time to time. On these occasions, Hsiu-Chin's mother and mother-in-law sit beside one another at the dining table, talking about family matters (Episode 16). Thus the dining table becomes a place where women meet—not only to informally pass down housekeeping tips, but also to share stories. Although the dining table and kitchen belong to the private sphere, in this case the private sphere empowers the public sphere. In Episode 8, when Chunsheng and Hsiu-Chin face difficulties during the war, they both sit in front of the dining table. Instead of positioning the camera in front of the actor and actress, the camera angle shows Chunsheng from behind, embracing Hsiu-Chin, who is cradling an infant. At that moment, Hsiu-Chin becomes a source of spiritual support for Chunsheng and the family. Instead of portraying women as victims for being mostly confined in the private sphere, Da Ai dramas emphasize their contributions and support in the private sphere, without challenging existing traditions and values.

When Hsiu-Chin emigrates to the United States, the dining table transforms from a gathering place for her nuclear family into a gathering place for Taiwanese students and workers. During her first stay with her eldest son, she cooks many meals for him and his Taiwanese students (Episode 29). When she stays with her youngest daughter and her husband, she prepares traditional dishes for them as well. Hsiu-Chin comes to be treated as "everyone's mother," even by those outside the family (Episode 31). Overcoming her initial ignorance of cooking, with time she gathers more and more people together around the dining table. The dining table not only strengthens ties among family members, but establishes horizontal ties among people from other families and backgrounds.

Tzu Chi discourse reveres motherhood as a form of strong, selfless love. Instead of seeing women as inferior and weak, Da Ai dramas—relating stories from a female point of view—tend to empower women and motherhood. As director Deng states in an interview, this is a drama that shows how strong women can be, and how they can provide crucial support for their husbands and families (Episode 8). From the perspective of media communication, Tzu Chi's use of media confronts the existing value system without challenging it. Chang and Leung's (2005) study, for example, demonstrates how Tzu Chi uses media to critique existing social discourses on body donations. As a Buddhist organization, Tzu Chi cleverly reframes the issue by emphasizing the positive nature of charitable acts. In this way it commandeers the existing value systems of its audience, in order to encourage acceptance of alternative viewpoints.

The kitchen scene motif is also extended to the Tzu Chi organization. When the branch in San Jose first opens, the kitchen and dining table provide important spaces for networking and recruitment. As one of the early members recalls, members often went to the kitchen during their lunch breaks to enjoy meals prepared by Hsiu-Chin and other female members. For Taiwanese workers in the US, these meals helped combat homesickness and encouraged recipients to learn about Tzu Chi. For the women who were not employed outside the home, preparing these meals together provided an opportunity to bond with others in similar situations. In Episode 41, Meili is shown preparing meals with a divorced woman; they share their life stories as single mothers in a foreign country. While preparing meals, Tzu Chi members talk about difficulties in their lives and marriages, and in the process create a support network. Tzu Chi is thus shown to attract housewives because it extends the private sphere into the sphere of religion, in which women feel comfortable. The private leads the public, and blurs the boundary between the private and the public. As Weller (1999) points out, women are able to generate informal capital through their networks or ties with other women (35). Tzu Chi is a good example of women's powerful informal ties in the public sphere. Setting aside its religious agenda, Tzu Chi is by far the most powerful matriarchal organization in Taiwan, more powerful than any feminist organization or women's movement.

Family

We have already seen how Tzu Chi media approaches the issue of women's contributions in the family. Rather than powerless victims, women maintain the patriarchal tradition as they climb higher in the hierarchy. Understanding the private sphere (with the dining table at its center) as complementary to the public sphere, often associated with men, I would now like to explore how the concept of family is understood in the secular context, and how it is extended to the Tzu Chi organization in a religious sense.

Familial discourse is an important aspect of Confucianism. The ideal form of the Asian family is an "extended family" that includes at least three generations: parents, married children and their spouses, and grandchildren (Quah 2008, 2). While gender provides an important focus for discussing family issues, feminist analysis of the family often ignores other factors such as age and the relationships among different family members (Morgan 1996, 9). Consequently, power dynamics within the Asian family are more multifaceted than contemporary gender theory acknowledges. In this regard, examining how the family is represented in Da Ai dramas can help us better understand the family, and how definitions of the family in Asia may change over time.

How gender is constructed in Asian cultures must be explored within specific contexts, since it is "constituted through historical and cultural practice" and "acquires meaning through cultural texts as well as social practices" (Evans 2008, 70). Problems occur, however, when social scientists trained in Western academic traditions employ feminist theory to identify and criticize Confucianism as a source of patriarchy and female subordination (Yamashita 1996). Quah's (2008) study of families in Asian countries, for example, uses centuries-old literary sources to blame Confucianism for the contemporary oppression of East Asian women (102). Confucianism is seen by Quah as representing a sexist tradition for such reasons as the lack of women in Confucius' *Analects* (Quah 2008, 106–7). Even as a text-based study, her analysis fails to acknowledge that Confucianism draws on many literary sources other than the *Analects*, some of which are more relevant. Works by female literati, such as Ban Zhao's *Nujie* (Lessons for Women), once served as key texts for instructing women in appropriate moral conduct. Although the *Nujie* states that women are born inferior to men and that men are meant to dominate women, Rosenlee (2006, 106) proposes a progressive reading of Ban Zhao and her text, suggesting that her literary achievements contradict the views of gender propriety expressed in the *Nujie*. In any case, a reliance on Confucian texts ignores the question of how illiterate women interpreted and enforced prevailing values in their daily lives. Dorothy Ko's (1994) study of women in seventeenth-century Jiangnan (southern China) shows that "commentators at the time were all too aware of the incongruity between realities in this floating world and the idealized Confucian order frozen in terms of such binaries as high/low, senior/junior, or male/female" (33). King (1994) explains that in Western symbolic logic, the categories A and non-A (e.g., male and non-male) are assumed to be mutually exclusive; however, Yin-Yang philosophy regards them as interdependent and complementary. Whether the domestic sphere to which women are confined is thought to be inferior, or equal, to the male-dominated public sphere, depends on such considerations.

There are many other reasons why gender issues must be culturally situated. Such factors as age and generational affiliation, for example, cannot be ignored when discussing gender oppression in the Confucian tradition. Moreover, as Rosenlee (2006) argues, the oppression of Chinese women "runs deeper than Confucianism as a state ideology" (121), a common focus in feminist studies on Chinese women. Confucianism is not merely a state ideology that influences social and political elites; rather, Confucian familial ethics—such as an emphasis on filial piety, ancestor worship and continuity of the family name—"are more of a way of life," and lie at the root of women's oppression in China. Rosenlee sees Confucianism not as an institution, but as a source of moral guidance. Even when institutional Confucianism gives way to modernization at the state level, it retains its role in the daily life of most Chinese people. The state might become democratic and modernized but prevailing beliefs remain wedded to traditional Confucian values.

In East Asian contexts, the central role of women within the family is pronounced. In *Love from the Valley*, Chunsheng says that no matter what happens in the future, everything will be fine as long as the family stays together (Episode 12). This idea that family members must not separate is mentioned several times in the drama. During wartime, for instance, Hsiu-Chin insists on fleeing with Chunsheng and their children because she believes the family should remain together (Episode 8). When one of her brothers is arrested by the KMT government, another brother says that they cannot afford to lose any brothers, and that as long as the family members stay together, they can overcome any difficulties (Episode 12). On another occasion, while starting a new life as a nuclear family and running their own business, Hsiu-Chin and Chunsheng face financial problems. Chunsheng manages the business with his friends, while Hsiu-Chin grows vegetables, raises chickens and engages in trade in order to make ends meet. The narrator praises her strength in supporting the family and working closely with her husband through hard times (Episode 13). Hsiu-Chin's attitude towards family unity can also be shown by her anger on learning that one of her sons has gotten divorced without consulting her (Episode 29). Since the core values of Confucianism are oriented towards the family, a divorce naturally means a "broken" or "incomplete" family, which does not accord with the Confucian familial ideal (Tamney and Chiang 2002).

The importance of family further extends to the Tzu Chi organization, where it serves as a metaphor for the bonds of affection among members. For example, the Mandarin title of the drama is *Xigu Ama*, which means "Silicon Valley Grandma." The narration of Episode 1 states that Hsiu-Chin is the "grandma" of Tzu Chi members in the Silicon Valley area; the sentiment is repeated by her son in Episode 46. As the drama moves on to Hsiu-Chin's life in the US, the stories of other Tzu Chi members are included. These reveal how Tzu Chi is not only a religious organization but also a social network in which Taiwanese, Malaysian Chinese, and others who speak the same language and share similar cultures can obtain a sense of religious and cultural belonging in a foreign land. Various scenes show male members leading meetings, while female members clean and cook for everyone (Episode 40). Female members thus extend their nurturing roles from the private realm of their families, to the public sphere of the Tzu Chi family, where their selfless love can be diffused to a broader public. The gendered division of labor in the family extends to the organization, where members continue doing what they are good at or familiar with. Two stories feature mothers who find support and comfort in the San Jose branch. Before joining Tzu Chi, they worked for a living and took care of their children. They find a welcoming community space through Tzu Chi, even after their children have grown up and moved away. For retired people, entering Tzu Chi is also depicted as a way to meet and socialize with people of the same age. Similarly, a student says that thanks to the warmth of the other members, she is never homesick (Episode 42). The San Jose branch is like a smaller version of the Tzu Chi organization, where everyone treats one another like family, and their common spiritual home is Tzu Chi headquarters in Hualian.

By using terms like "dharma relatives" and "dharma family," Master Cheng Yen unites Tzu Chi members into a huge household, of which she is the head. Adapting secular familial values to the Tzu Chi organization, followers learn to "love broadly" (the literal meaning of *Da Ai*). In the metaphorical family of Tzu Chi, Hsiu-Chin's role as a Bodhisattva is an extension of her role as a mother. Her care towards Taiwanese students and workers in the Valley area establish her as "everyone's mother" or "everyone's grandmother." Although what she offers is ordinary meals, what she provides is comfort. Instead of challenging existing societal discourses of gender and family, Tzu Chi ascribes to them religious meaning, and encourages followers to extend their selfless love from the family to a broader public. As an organization largely composed of female members, Tzu Chi does not challenge the prevailing patriarchal ideology, but inverts standard gender discourses by emphasizing women's efforts to maintain the family as a unit. This discourse calls upon men to appreciate women's efforts to strengthen family bonds. Instead of seeing women as inferior and weak, Da Ai dramas, by telling stories from women's point of view, aim to empower womanhood and motherhood within contemporary norms. Instead of liberating women from the patriarchal family or urging a reformation of patriarchal tradition, Tzu Chi rewrites gender discourse without contradicting tradition.

Religion in *Love from the Valley*

Tzu Chi as a religion

The first turning point, marriage, leads the main character into adulthood (transitioning from carefree daughter to dutiful wife and mother). The second turning point comes through her participation in the Tzu Chi organization. With the loss of her husband, Hsiu-Chin turns to charity work as a way to find comfort and counter her confusion.

One of the most important scenes occurs when the lead characters join Tzu Chi. Several years after Chunsheng's death, Hsiu-Chin moves to the US to live with her youngest daughter and son-in-law. At one point she joins a tour to Hualian. After sightseeing, Hsiu-Chin is brought to the Tzu Chi headquarters and is shown bowing before the building, where she then spends the night (Episode 31). Through Hsiu-Chin's eyes, the audience sees the simple, understated architectural style, and how Master Cheng Yen and her ordained disciples live independently of any financial donations from lay followers. (All donations to Tzu Chi go to charitable works and medical services.) This contrasts with most Buddhist organizations in Taiwan, which rely on donations from adherents who believe that their karma can be improved through such meritorious acts (Falk 2000, 51).

Through Hsiu-Chin's first visit to Tzu Chi headquarters, and later participation (along with her companions) in Tzu Chi activities, the docudrama introduces the organization's charity work, as well as its concept of the Bodhisattva path. Hsiu-Chin and other US members decide to pay regular visits to a San Jose sanitarium which is reported to have the fewest resources. They visit all the residents, regardless of religious belief. On learning that a patient has converted to Christianity, Hsiu-Chin expresses happiness for him and treats him no differently than anyone else. She later explains that they can help such people in a Buddhist spirit, as opposed to a Buddhist form (Episode 38). In a voiceover, Meili tells other members that "compassion is shown in respecting the patients' religious beliefs and giving them what they need" (Episode 42). By visiting and volunteering at the sanitarium, the Tzu Chi volunteers experience an essential doctrine of Buddhism, "Life is bitterness" (Episode 42). Out of compassion, they strive to help as many people as possible regardless of ethnicity, nationality or religious beliefs. As compassion is an essential element of the Bodhisattva path, the characters learn how to be compassionate by helping others.

In order to advertise and explain Tzu Chi's activities, Da Ai dramas usually devote several episodes to the protagonists' activities after joining the organization. Of the 50 episodes of *Love from the Valley*, the last 20 cover Hsiu-Chin's career with Tzu Chi. In the process, many details about the organization and its history emerge. In Episode 31, on their first meeting, Master Cheng Yen assigns Hsiu-Chin the mission of spreading Tzu Chi's message in America. Although Hsiu-Chin at first doubts her abilities, she is eventually persuaded that nothing is impossible if one is determined enough. One of the most cited phrases in *Love from the Valley* is "where there's a will, there's a way." Supporting this idea are stories about IT engineers, retired émigrés, housewives and divorcees who overcome tragedies and setbacks. These stories not only reveal how Tzu Chi provides a spiritual home for people from all walks of life, but also serve to depict Hsiu-Chin as a leader of the Tzu Chi family in America. For the general television audience with no knowledge of Tzu Chi, the drama provides an introduction to its main beliefs. For Tzu Chi members, the drama strengthens their group identity and prompts them to re-assess their behavior according to the organization's standards. *Love from the Valley* is particularly significant as it depicts Tzu Chi as a global organization. Tzu Chi appeals to Chinese communities in the Silicon Valley area as it provides a forum for people of similar cultural backgrounds to forge friendships and other ties within the context of a larger host culture (Episode 46). Rather than merely being synonymous with American cultural imperialism, *Love from the Valley* shows how globalization consists of multidirectional exchanges in which America itself is influenced and enriched by external cultural influences, and in which minority groups need not succumb to complete assimilation into American society. *Love from the Valley* ends with the San Jose branch celebrating its tenth anniversary. In this final episode, a musical in sign language based on the *Filial Piety Sutra* is performed (group "singing" in sign language being a common Tzu Chi activity). Its main message is that children should respect their parents, since parents sacrifice so much for their children. Hsiu-Chin, who is revered as the grandmother of Tzu Chi members in the Valley area, is then invited onto the stage. The drama ends here.

Conclusion

The narrative structure and aims of *Love from the Valley* are typical of Da Ai dramas. These invariably depict the Tzu Chi organization as a savior figure like Guanyin, helping the protagonists (Tzu Chi members) out of difficulties. Da Ai dramas also serve to encourage Tzu Chi followers, and invite the audience to practice Buddhism by doing charity work.

As a matriarchal organization, Tzu Chi uses Da Ai dramas to celebrate women's resilience and strength in adverse situations. Rather than attract controversy by challenging prevailing discourses on gender, Da Ai dramas praise women's contributions to the family. This perspective in *Love from the Valley* is best exemplified through its kitchen scenes. The women in the story are often shown working in the kitchen, and family members are shown gathering around the dining table. The dining table symbolically bridges the private sphere (ruled by women) and the public sphere (dominated by men). Rather than showing opposition between the public and the private spheres, women's contributions to the private sphere are lauded and depicted as a crucial complement to men's success in the public sphere. In this particular drama, the kitchen and the dining table not only connect Hsiu-Chin's biological family members, but also take on religious significance by grounding activities of her "dharma family" at Tzu Chi's branch in San Jose.

There are two turning points in the narrative of the typical Da Ai drama: the first is when a lead character marries; the second, when the character finds Tzu Chi. The depiction of family and marriage in Da Ai dramas resembles women's reality in daily life; therefore, to observe how family is represented in the dramas helps us to understand women in the Taiwanese context. *Love from the Valley* demonstrates that a woman's gender roles multiply after marriage. To understand gender roles, it is necessary to locate an individual within his or her network of familial relationships. With increasing gender roles as a wife, daughter-in-law, and mother, a woman's obligations and duties increase. Their fulfillment is necessary, and grants women power in the family. As the analysis shows, women gain more power when they become mothers or mothers-in-law, and often become keepers of the patriarchal tradition. A closer examination of the power dynamics in this specific cultural context shows that women are not necessarily victims under patriarchy. This is underscored by the social and cultural contexts of Buddhist women, in which women can be empowered "by sharing what lies beyond patriarchy in our own traditions" (King 1994, 70)

The concept of family is important not only to understanding an individual's gender roles, but also in understanding women's roles in the Tzu Chi organization. The central symbols of the kitchen and the dining table in *Love from the Valley* can be understood as an extension of the gender roles of female family members. Joining Tzu Chi is the most convenient way for female members to extend their gender roles as mothers into the public sphere, after fulfilling their roles as housewives. The easiest way to understand the Buddhist concept of compassion is to focus on these women and their broadening sense of selfless love emerging from their roles as mothers. Through their extension of the caring and nurturing features of motherhood, female members learn to do charity work, which is seen as crucial to the path of the Bodhisattva. In this way, sophisticated Buddhist concepts are embedded in the daily experiences of mothers.

Tzu Chi's approach to women and their daily life experiences differs from those of other institutionally oriented Buddhist organizations that encourage meditation and scriptural study. This shows the insufficiency of text-based approaches and the importance of social context, especially for the study of women in Buddhism. As different social contexts harbor diverse gender issues, Buddhism may not be the only influential factor in the situation of women in a given Buddhist tradition. Moreover, religious organizations are increasingly turning to other types of media than written texts to spread their messages in the contemporary world. In this regard, new media technologies have the potential to reach a broader public and bypass once-insurmountable geographical constraints, resulting in new interpretations of religious thought and practices.

References

Ang, I. 1996. *Living Room Wars: Rethinking Media Audiences for a Postmodern World*. London: Routledge.

Arthur, C. 2004. "Media, Meaning and Method in the Study of Religion." In *Religion: Empirical Studies*. Ed. by S. J. Sutcliffe. Chippenham: Antony Rowe Ltd., 19–32.

Babb, L. A. and S. S. Wadley. 1995. *Media and the Transformation of Religion in South Asia*. Philadelphia: University of Pennsylvania Press.

Bai, H. 2009. "Organizational Culture Impacts on the Producing Principles of Religious Channels: A Case Study on Tzu Chi Da Ai Drama 'Spring in the Grass Mountain.'" MA dissertation. Tzu Chi University, Taiwan.

Berkwitz, S. C., ed. 2006. *Buddhism in World Cultures: Comparative Perspectives*. Santa Barbara: ABC-CLIO.

Biersdorfer, J. D. 2002. "Religion Finds Technology." *New York Times* (May 16). Online: http://www.nytimes.com/2002/05/16/technology/circuits/16CHUR.html?pagewanted=1 (accessed March 21, 2010)

Bruce, S. 1990. *Pray TV: Televangelism in America*. London: Routledge.

Casanova, J. 1994. *Public Religions in the Modern World*. Chicago: University of Chicago Press.

Chan, J. M. 2005. "Trans-border Broadcasters and TV Regionalization in Greater China: Processes and Strategies." In *Transnational Television Worldwide: Towards a New Media Order*. Ed. by J. K. Chalby. London: I. B. Tauris, 173–95.

Chandler, S. 2006. Buddhism in China and Taiwan: The Dimensions of Contemporary Chinese Buddhism. In *Buddhism in World Cultures: Comparative Perspectives*. Ed. by S. C. Berkwitz. Santa Barbara: ABC-CLIO, 169–94.

Chang, H. and K. Leung. 2005. "'Be a Teacher after Death': The Message Strategies of a Body Donation Campaign in Taiwan." *Media Asia* 32, no. 2: 99–105.

Chang, W. 1998. "The Confucian Theory of Norms and Human Rights." In *Confucianism and Human Rights*. Ed. by W. T. de Bary and W. Tu. Chichester: Columbia University Press, 117–41.

Chuan, B. H. 2008. "East Asian Pop Culture: Layers of Communities." In *Media Consumption and Everyday Life in Asia*. Ed. by Y. Kim. Oxford: Routledge, 99–113.

Collet, A. 2006. "Buddhism and Gender: Reframing and Refocusing the Debate." *Journal of Feminist Studies in Religion* 22, no. 2: 55–84.

Corner, J. 1999. "Drama Documentary Origins and Developments." In *Why Docudrama? Fact-Fiction on Film and TV*. Ed. by A. Rosenthal. Carbondale: Southern Illinois University Press, 35–46.

Cooey, M. 1990. "Emptiness, Otherness, and Identity: A Feminist Perspective." *Journal of Feminist Studies in Religion* 6, no. 2: 7–23.

Croteau, D. and W. Hoynes. 1997. *Media/Society*. Thousand Oaks: Pine Forge Press.

Curran, J. and M. Park. 2000. "Beyond Globalization Theory." In *De-Westernizing Media Studies*. Ed. by J. Curran and M. Park. Oxford: Routledge, 1–20.

de Bary, W. T. and W. Tu. 1998. *Confucianism and Human Rights*. Chichester: Columbia University Press.

Derris, K. 2008. "When the Buddha Was a Woman: Reimagining Tradition in the Theravada." *Journal of Feminist Studies in Religion* 24, no. 2: 29–44.

Dong, F. 2008. *The Religions in Taiwan*. Taipei: Qianwei publisher.

Dovey, J. 2000. *Freakshow: First Person Media and Factual Television*. London: Pluto.

Dumoulin, H., ed. 1976. *Buddhism in the Modern World*. London: Collier Macmillan.

Erni, J. N. and S. K. Chua. 2005. *Asian Media Studies*. Oxford: Blackwell Publishing.

Evans, H. 2008. "Gender in Modern Chinese Culture." In *Cambridge Companion to Modern Chinese Culture*. Ed. by K. Louie. Cambridge: Cambridge University Press, 68–90.

Falk, M. L. 2000. "Women in Between: Becoming Religious Persons in Thailand." In *Women's Buddhism, Buddhism's Women: Tradition, Revision, Renewal*. Ed. by E. B. Findly. Somerville: Wisdom Publications, 37–57.

Farris, C. S. 2002. "Women's Liberation under 'East Asian Modernity' in China and Taiwan: Historical, Cultural, and Comparative Perspectives." In *Women in the New Taiwan: Gender Roles and Gender Consciousness in a Changing Society*. Ed. by L. Anru, C. Farris and M. Rubinstein. London: M. E. Sharpe, 171–98.

Feuchtwang, S. 2001. *Popular Religion in China: The Imperial Metaphor*. Richmond: Curzon.

French, D. and M. Richards. 2000. *Television in Contemporary Asia*. London: Sage.

Ganguly Scrase, R. and T. J. Scrase. 2006. "Constructing Middle-Class Culture: Globalization, Modernity and Indian Media." In *Medi@sia: Global Media/tion In and Out of Context*. Ed. by T. Holden and T. J. Scrase. Oxford: Routledge.

Goodman, C. 2008. "Consequentialism, Agent-Neutrality, and Mahayana Ethics." *Philosophy East and West* 58, no. 1: 17–35.

Gross, R. M. 1993. *Buddhism after Patriarchy*. New York: State University of New York Press.

Grossberg, L. and C. Nelson, eds. 1988. *Marxism and the Interpretation of Culture*. Basingstoke: Macmillan Education.

Hadden, J. and A. Shupe. 1988. *Televangelism: Power and Politics on God's Frontier*. New York: Henry Holt.

Harris, I., ed. 2001. *Buddhism and Politics in Twentieth-century Asia*. London: Continuum.

Hill, G. 1989. "The Commoditization of Chinese Women." *Signs* 14, no. 4: 799–832.

Hoover, S. M. 2006. *Religion in the Media Age*. London: Routledge.

Hoover, S. M. and K. Lundby. 1997. *Rethinking Media, Religion, and Culture*. London: Sage.

Horsefield, P. 1984. *Religious Television: The American Experience*. New York: Longman.

Huang, C. J. and R. Weller. 1998. "Merit and Mothering: Women and Social Welfare in Taiwanese Buddhism." *Journal of Asian Studies* 57, no. 2: 379–96.

Huanglin, Z. B. 2004. *Zhongguo nu xingzhuyi* [Feminism in China]. Gilin City: Guangxi shi fan da xuechu ban she.

Iwabuchi, K. 2005. "Discrepant Intimacy: Popular Culture Flows in East Asia." In *Asian Media Studies*. Ed. by J. N. Erni and S. K. Chun. Oxford: Blackwell Publishing, 19–36.

Jiang, C. 2003. *Taiwan jindaifojiao de biangeyufansi* [The Revolution and Reflection on Contemporary Buddhism in Taiwan]. Taipei: Tongdai Publishers.

Jones, C. B. 2003. "Transitions in the Practice and Defense of Chinese Pure Land Buddhism." In *Buddhism in the Modern World: Adaptations of an Ancient Tradition*. Ed. by S. Heine and C. S. Prebish. New York: Oxford University Press, 125–42.

Katz, R. 2003. "Identity Politics and the Study of Popular Religion in Postwar Taiwan." In *Religion and the Formation of Taiwanese Identities*. Ed. by R. Katz and M. A. Rubinstein. Houndmills: Palgrave Macmillan, 157–80.

King, U. 1994. *Feminist Theology from the Third World: A Reader*. New York: Orbis Books

Ko, D. 1994. *Teachers of the Inner Chambers: Women and Culture in Seventeenth-Century China*. Stanford: Stanford University Press.

Kwok P. 2000. *Introducing Asian Feminist Theology*. Sheffield: Sheffield Academic Press.

Kwok, P. and L. E. Donaldson, eds. 2002. *Postcolonialism, Feminism and Religious Discourse*. London: Routledge.

Laliberte, A. 2003. "Religious Change and Democratization in Postwar Taiwan." In *Religion in Modern Taiwan: Tradition and Innovation in a Changing Society*. Ed. by P. Clart and C. B. Jones. Honolulu: University of Hawai'i Press, 158–85.

Laliberte, A. 2004. *The Politics of Buddhist Organizations in Taiwan: 1989–2003*. Oxford: Routledge Curzon.

Lee, M. 2006. "Humanities and Creative Elements in Da-ai Drama." MA dissertation. National Taiwan Normal University.

Lefferts, H. L. 2000. "Buddhist Action: Lay Women and Thai Monks." In *Women's Buddhism, Buddhism's Women: Tradition, Revision, Renewal*. Ed. by E. B. Findly. Boston: Wisdom, 63–80.

Liu, R. 2000. *Jin dai Zhongguo nu quanlunshu* [Feminism in Modern China]. Taipei: Taiwan xue sheng shuju.

Lu, H. 2002. "Imagining "New Women," Imagining Modernity: Gender Rhetoric in Colonial Taiwan." In *Women in the New Taiwan: Gender Roles and Gender Consciousness in a Changing Society*. Ed. by L. Anru, C. Farris and M. Rubinstein. London: M. E. Sharpe, 76–98.

Martin-Barbero, J. 1997. "Mass Media as a Site of Resacralization of Contemporary Cultures." In *Rethinking Media, Religion, and Culture*. Ed. by S. M. Hoover and K. Lundby. London: Sage, 102–116.

McKee, K. B. and C. J. Pardun. 1999. "Reading the Video: A Qualitative Study of Religious Images in Music Videos." *Journal of Broadcasting and Electronic Media* 43, no. 1: 110–22.

Meyer, B. and A. Moors. 2006. *Religion, Media, and the Public Sphere*. Bloomington: Indiana University Press.

Moeran, B. 2001. *Asian Media Productions*. Surrey: Curzon Press.

Morgan, D. 1996. *Family Connections and Introduction to Family Studies*. Cambridge: Polity.

Paul, D. Y. 1985. *Women in Buddhism: Images of the Feminine in Mahayana Tradition*. London: University of California Press.

Quah, S. R. 2008. *Families in Asia: Home and Kin*. London: Routledge.

Reed, B. E. 2003. "Guanyin Narratives—Wartime and Postwar." In *Religion in Modern Taiwan: Tradition and Innovation in a Changing Society*. Ed. by P. Clart and C. B. Jones. Honolulu: University of Hawai'i Press, 36–47.

Robertson, R. 1992. *Globalization: Social Theory and Global Culture*. London: Sage

Rosenlee, L. 2006. *Confucianism and Women: A Philosophical Interpretation*. Albany: State University of New York Press.

Scheufele, D. A., M. C. Nisbet and D. Brossard. 2003. "Pathways to Political Participation? Religion, Communication Contexts and Mass Media." *International Journal of Public Opinion Research* 15: 300–324.

Shi, S. 1999. "Renjianfuojiao de renjiaojingtu" [This-Worldly Pure Land in Humanistic Buddhism]. *Chung-Hwa Buddhist Studies.* 3: 1–17.

Shi, Z. H. 2006. *Renpusaxing de li shizulu* [Historical Footprints of the Path of Human Bodhisattva]. Taipei: Fajie Chu ban.

Schneiderman, S. 1999. "Appropriate Treasure? Reflections on Women, Buddhism, and Cross-Cultural Exchange." In *Buddhist Women across Cultures: Realizations.* Ed. by K. L. Tsomo. Albany: State University of New York Press, 221–39.

Skill, T., J. D. Robinson, J. S. Lyons and D. Larson. 1994. "The Portrayal of Religion and Spirituality on Fictional Network Television." *Review of Religious Research* 35, no. 3: 251–67.

Spivak, G. C. 1988. "Can the Subaltern Speak?" In *Marxism and the Interpretation of Culture.* Ed. by C. Nelson and L. Grossberg. Basingstoke: Macmillan Education, 271–316.

Tamney, J. B. and L. H. Chiang. 2002. *Modernization, Globalization, and Confucianism in Chinese Societies.* Westport: Praeger Publishers.

Thomas, A. O. 2000. "Transborder Television for Greater China." In *Television in Contemporary Asia.* Ed. by D. French and M. Richards. London: Sage, 91–110.

Tomlinson, J. 2002. *Cultural Imperialism: A Critical Introduction.* London: Continuum.

Tu, W., ed. 1996. *Confucian Traditions in East Asian Modernity: Moral Education and Economic Culture in Japan and the Four Mini-dragons.* London: Harvard University Press.

Weller, R. 1999. *Alternate Civilities: Democracy and Culture in China and Taiwan.* Boulder: Westview Press.

Weller, R. 2007. "Identity and Social Change in Taiwanese Religion." In *Taiwan: A New History.* Ed. by M. A. Rubinstein. London: M. E. Sharp, 339–65.

Winston, D. H. 2007. "Back to the Future: Religion, Politics, and the Media." *American Quarterly* 59, no. 3: 969–89.

Wu, W. 2000. "The Representation of Meanings in Religious TV Programs: An Example of Da Ai Series." MA dissertation. Shih Hsin University, Taipei, Taiwan.

Xu, S. 1998. "Zhonggiofuojiaozaitaizhifazhanshi" [The History of Chinese Buddhism in Taiwan]. *Chung-Hwa Buddhist Studies* 2: 289–98.

Yamashita 1996. "Confucianism and the Japanese State." In *Confucian Traditions in East Asian Modernity: Moral Education and Economic Culture in Japan and the Four Mini-dragons.* Ed. by W. Tu. London: Harvard University Press, 132–154.

Yang, H. 2000. "Cueng Yin-shun de renjianfuojiao tan taoxinyu she yuxiandaichan de zongjiaofazhan" [Analysis of Religious Development of Society for a Buddhist Renaissance and Modern Zen through the Lens of Master Yin-Shun's Humanistic Buddhism]. *Taiwan Buddhist Studies,* 5: 275–312.

Yu, C. 2001. *Kuan-yin: The Chinese Transformation of Avalokitesvara.* Chichester: Columbia University Press.

Chapter 9

"TECHNO DANCING GODS": COMICIZED DEITY IMAGES AS EXPRESSIONS OF TAIWANESE CULTURAL IDENTITY

Thzeng Chi Hsiung

National Yunlin University of Science and Technology, Taiwan

Tsai Chin Chia

National Yunlin University of Science and Technology, Taiwan

Introduction

Images of gods are typically treated with solemnity. Recently, however, devotees in Taiwan have taken to producing playful images of deities to increase the friendliness of the visual environment and to lessen the social distance between gods and their worshippers. This chapter explores the transformation of deity images into comicized forms (i.e., with the exaggerated neoteny associated with cartoon or manga styles) and its meaning for Taiwan as a "glocalizing" society. Our focus is the contemporary phenomenon known as *Dianyin Santaizi*.

Santaizi is the name of a Chinese god whom Taiwanese temple fairs often portray in the form of giant, human-occupied puppets. *Dianyin* means "electronic music," i.e., techno dance music. The combined name therefore refers to the innovation of making the god-puppets dance to pop songs, or techno remixes thereof.[1]

Dianyin Santaizi performances have recently grown in popularity as part of the *Taike* ("Taiwan hick") trend. Outside of temple fairs, they may also be encountered through television programs, video-sharing websites, promotional campaigns or company parties. Unlike traditional Santaizi puppets, the *Dianyin Santaizi* are not formally invested with the deity's power (although some people respect them as if they were) and are only used in non-religious public-relations activities.

Dianyin Santaizi were featured at the opening ceremony of the 2009 World Games in Kaohsiung, as well as the opening and closing ceremonies of the 21st Summer Deaflympics in Taipei that same year.[2] Both performances recalled, in caricature, the street processions associated with local temple fairs. This chapter will analyze the differences between their respective presentations of Taiwanese culture.

Origins

Li Nuozha is a deity of the Chinese folk religion, a guardian of justice said to offer protection against evil spirits and fierce gods. A figure of popular Buddhism as well as Daoism, he is mentioned in the Ming Dynasty novels *The Journey to the West* and *The Investiture of the Gods*. Among his titles are "Marshal of the Central Shrine and Supernatural General," "Divine Commander of the Central Encampment," "Noble Prince of the Jade Emperor" and Santaizi or "Third Prince," as he is the youngest of three brothers. His votive statues are customarily placed next to those of the goddesses Guanyin and Mazu, since all three are thought to bless traffic and transportation. Nuozha is also the patron deity of children. In Taiwan, most statues of him resemble a heroic yet diminutive warrior. He can be identified by the flying disk ("Wheel of Wind and Fire") under his right foot; the red-tasseled spear ("Fiery Sharp Spear") in his right hand; the hoop-like weapon ("Heaven and Earth Ring") in his left hand, held at the chest; and the sash of "Heaven-Confusing Silk" draped over his armor, billowing behind him. Nuozha is often seen in the company of his brothers Jinzha ("Golden Face"), who holds two swords; and Muzha ("Wooden Face," but actually black), who holds two maces.

Human-occupied Santaizi puppets lead the way in processions at temple fairs, when the gods conduct their inspection tours. They often perform comic routines designed to appeal to onlookers, especially children. However, a Santaizi is not usually easy to approach when he is performing the "Step of the Seven Stars," since there are always temple volunteers on hand to hold back bystanders who might be harmed by his supernatural weapons.

Yu Zhongbing, the leader of the Beigang Taizi Association, recounts the origin of the *Dianyin Santaizi* phenomenon:

One night we had to wait far too long to enter a temple. Our members grew bored, so while wearing their Santaizi costumes, they began humorously dancing to Mavis Fan's [children's exercise song] "Three Circles on the Left, Three Circles on the Right" and Aya's "Shaved-Ice

Dessert Dance." Their dance unexpectedly attracted public attention. Everyone kept watching and calling for encores, so that our members had to dance for almost two hours. (Personal interview, January 8, 2009)

In the beginning, some traditionalists felt this behavior to be sacrilegious. Yu however argues that such performances attract people who would not otherwise attend a temple fair, making them a good way to promote traditional culture.

Traditional Santaizi march to the accompaniment of firecrackers, reed instruments and percussion. *Dianyin Santaizi* invariably dance to pop songs— some 2009 favorites were "Sorry, Sorry" by the Korean boy-band Super Junior and "Nobody" by the Wonder Girls (another Korean group)—and are particularly associated with techno music. A change of songs signals the beginning of a new dance performance. From the perspective of the audience, the introduction of techno music suggests approachability, departure from tradition and a lack of solemnity. In fact, electronic music has long been used in Taiwanese temple fairs, which commonly feature synthesizer-enhanced performances of Chinese opera, or scantily clad women dancing and singing (with karaoke-like acoustics) atop flower-covered floats.

Dianyin Santaizi performances came into vogue as part of the *Taike* (or TK) subculture, which celebrates stereotypically "Taiwanese" culture. Three of the TK Rock Festivals held between 2005 and 2008 have had a significant influence, defining the so-called "Taiwanese style." During this time, *Dianyin Santaizi* rose to become one of the most important elements of the *Taike* trend. A number of *Dianyin Santaizi* troupes were formed during this period, of which four stand out. While numerous other troupes exist, they tend to follow the lead of these four, which are managed along the lines of cultural or artistic institutions:

First is the aforementioned Beigang Taizi Association, honored as the founders of the phenomenon. While the group itself is two decades old, their switch to the *Dianyin Santaizi* style came only in 2006, after their premier on the stage of the TK Rock Festival. They participate in various promotional activities, for example, appearing as pitchmen on TV commercials for the electronic game Santaizi Online.

The Puzi Dianyin Santaizi Folk Art Group comes from Puzi City, in Jiayi County. This group often performs at temple fairs in Tainan and Jiayi. They have also appeared on several well-known television shows. Famous for their creative performances, they regularly release videos with new dance routines. Their director is Zhang Qiyuan.

The Nuozha Hall Dianyin Taizi Group is located in Fengshan City, in Kaohsiung County. This is the group that performed for the 2009 World Games in Kaohsiung. They are noted for having the smallest-sized Santaizi figures in Taiwan. Their shows feature stage lighting, elaborate props such as cars, and Santaizi with faces of five different colors. Director Zeng Huaide is glad that instead of being limited to the subculture of temple fairs, they are now able to promote the spirit of Taiwan to the wider world.

Finally, the Qiang Yuan Chi Religious Hall Dianyin Tongzi Practice Group is located in Pingdong County. Founded in 2007, it is the only group in Taiwan to feature *Shentong* (divine youths; also called *tongzi*) in place of (*San*) *taizi* characters. They mostly perform for temple fairs in southern Taiwan. Since the *Shentong* are not so august as other divinities, they feel more free to adopt exaggerated sunglasses, hairstyles and other comic features. A very lively group, they invite audiences to dance with them for the finale of their show. Their director is Cheng Yinliang.

Design Features

Traditional Santaizi hold weapons that establish them as sacred and unapproachable. In contrast, *Dianyin Santaizi* are given comic accoutrements such as sunglasses or Mickey Mouse gloves to distinguish them as humorous figures. When they ride motor scooters or bicycles, this playfully recalls the original iconography in which Santaizi stands atop his "Wheel(s) of Wind and Fire." Both types of Santaizi performer try to adopt the god's character and personality. They refer to the traditional Santaizi using the respectful expression *Taiziye* ("noble prince") and to the comic version as *don-a* ("kiddo" in Taiwanese).

Dianyin Santaizi puppets vary according to their morphological features. In terms of frame type, in addition to the normal Santaizi frame, smaller frames are used for *shentong* figures, while larger ones are needed for other deities (such as the tall demonic attendants of the goddess Mazu). Cartoon characters and event mascots may require custom-designed bodies. Color may be added to the basic Santaizi face to distinguish his two brothers or between the members of the "five [directional] guardians" whose faces are respectively red, yellow, blue, black and white. Variations also occur in the design of the eyes, eyebrows, sideburns and hair. Turning to accessories, we find pacifiers, sunglasses, plastic "diamonds," eye shadow, gloves, hats, neckties, etc. as well as various vehicles (e.g., tricycles, kangaroo bikes, motor scooters, music cars) used to transport the deities. Characters borrowed from folk stories, animated cartoons or mascots all require their own adaptations.

Except in the case of *shentong* puppets—who are usually made by craftsmen and workshops specializing in woodcarving or paper sculpture—most of the groups mentioned above construct and dress their own Santaizi figures. This results in different designs and styles for the different teams. For example, the Beigang group starts by casting a mold of the head, and then contracts with local craftsmen to produce it. Sometimes they add clay to the figure's head to change the facial features. They make the costumes and decorations themselves. Director Yu explains that the gods are happy to dress in new clothes when they go on inspection. As a former sculptor, he is fastidious about their construction. The Kaohsiung group uses Santaizi costumes designed by the director's wife, who reports being inspired by women's fashion magazines. For example, she outlines the eyes with little beads. The Pingdong group uses materials that can be found at beauty shops, such as hair accessories and ties.

Appearances at International Sporting Events

In the wake of the 2008 Beijing Olympics—the opening ceremony of which glorified Chinese culture, collectivism and the beauty of mass synchronization—Taiwan hosted two international sporting events: the 2009 World Games in Kaohsiung and the 21st Summer Deaflympics in Taipei. Such international mega-events are typically treated as opportunities for the host country to promote its cultural and political identity under the gaze of the international media. They may also serve as platforms for the reversal of certain stereotypes, and the introduction of new cultural identity symbols. To researchers of design, the arrangements and applications of these symbols are especially important.

Cultural commentator Chan Wei-hsiung (2009) observes that opening and closing ceremonies have become an arena in which countries compete to provide spectacle and publicize the cultural symbol of their "national narrative." For example, the opening ceremony of the 2000 Sydney Olympics aimed at replacing the old image of Australia as a place where Britain sent convicts into exile, with one of a glorious land of nature, sunshine and freedom. Similarly, the pageantry of the Beijing Olympics was aimed not at promoting Chinese culture to the world, so much as at making a certain impression upon the Chinese people themselves. Thus, its cultural narratives were ones which foreigners would not be familiar with.

Both Taiwan events used religion—including modernized images of divine beings—to represent the island's cultural identity. The second act of the opening ceremony of the World Games, "Prayer of the People" (literally "Prosperity of the Multitudes"), featured a performance of *Dianyin Santaizi*, 32 of whom circled into the venue on motor scooters. Led by the aforementioned Nuozha Hall Dianyin Taizi Group, they wore large eyeglasses or goggles and embroidered armor, all outlined in LED lights. Tzong-Ching Ju, chief director of the opening and closing ceremony of the 2009 World Games, explains that the LED lights represented the Taiwanese passion for technological products,

Figure 9.1. *Dianyin Santaizi* performance for the opening ceremony of the 2009 World Games in Kaohsiung, Taiwan.

Source: Screen capture from *We Totally Love the World Games Show! The Opening and Closing Ceremony Performances of the Kaohsiung World Games.*

while the motor scooters recalled a common scene in the daily life of local citizens (See Fig. 9.1).

A variety of other figures then marched into the venue. These included a large group of divine generals, the "twelve scholars" (*jishi*), parasol-carrying attendants called *huagai*, flag-bearers and teams carrying sedan chairs—most of them empty, but one containing a statue of Cheng Huang Ye (the "City God") from the nearby Shen Huang Temple. His appearance was particularly appropriate, since the venue of the World Games was located in the area of Zuoying, which falls under his spiritual jurisdiction. Thus the performance qualified as a genuine inspection tour with prayers for prosperity, like a temple fair adapted for the stage. For foreigners, such events reveal unique aspects of the local culture. The act also accorded with the custom of reverencing heaven, Earth and the gods at the commencement of an event.

The TV broadcast of the opening ceremony was very well received for its upbeat atmosphere and suggestion of a rich local culture, bringing new visibility to the *Dianyin Santaizi*. The closing ceremony did not include any

Figure 9.2. *Dianyin Santaizi* performance for the opening ceremony of the 21st Deaflympics in Taipei, 2009.

Source: Screen capture from 2009 Taipei Deaflympics opening ceremony as covered by CTV (China Television) News Channel. Online: http://www.youtube.com/watch?v=koxpRMuLQYg (accessed February 20, 2011).

gods, but did feature the song "You Are My Flower," by Wu Bai, which Santaizi troupes often perform for temple fairs. At a retrospective exhibition held after the Games, photo-imprinted commodities featuring *Dianyin Santaizi* were offered for sale as part of a major visual communication campaign.

Unlike the *Taike* style of the World Games performances, which reflected the life of the common people through folk and popular culture, the Deaflympics focused on high culture for a more theatrical effect. Deity images from the opening ceremony included the goddess Mazu, portrayed by model/actress Patina Lin (Lin Jiaqi); a Thousand-Armed Guanyin performance by the China Disabled People's Performing Art Troupe; and hovering above the stadium, god-shaped helium balloons.

Act 6 ("Heartbeat of a City"), Part 2 ("Festival") incorporated a procession of modernized god-puppets boasting spherical heads with smiling faces printed on the fabric and costumed bodies with a width-to-height ratio of one to two. They were both male and female, and of numerous types (See Fig. 9.2). Where the *Dianyin Santaizi* from the World Games wore embroidered armor, hand-made by traditional craftsmen, their Deaflympics counterparts were designed and produced using computers. Their presence was not central to the performance—after a brief circuit, the god-puppets soon yielded the stage to hip-hop dancers and masked acrobats.

The closing ceremony featured a pageant called "100 Celestial Beings Give Blessings" (literally translated "Congratulations of a Hundred Immortals"). Surrounded by balloons, god-puppets and parasol-bearers, diva Sun Tsui-Feng, in the role of General Tian Du, led actors portraying gods and other auspicious beings in formal toasts to heaven, earth and the assembled athletes. The ensemble cast combined the talents of the Hong-Sheng Lion Dance Theater and the Ming Hwa Yuan Taiwanese Opera Troupe, *inter alia*. The performance concluded with an "outdoor banquet" at which the athletes were served various traditional delicacies.

General director Stan Lai (Lai Shengchuan) explains that he sought to create an atmosphere of the gods descending from heaven and joining the athletes in a "banquet of champions," as a perfect conclusion to the event. In traditional Taiwanese drama, however, an "Immortals Play" is usually performed prior to the main play, in order to ensure that the performance will be peaceful and successful. Aside from its entertainment value, it constitutes an expression of gratitude to the gods and a prayer for blessings. By moving it to the end, the Deaflympics weakened the drama's sacredness and turned it into more of an international carnival-style performance.

In general, the contrasts between the two events may be summarized thus:

World Games (Kaohsiung)	Deaflympics (Taipei)
Glocalization	Globalization
Domestic recognition	International recognition
Connecting with tradition	Departure from tradition
Taike and popular culture	High culture
Postmodern baroque style	Modernized logo design

In other words, the World Games performance was more reflective of a specifically Taiwanese cultural identity (hence "glocalization") than the Deaflympics shows, which abstracted the Santaizi tradition almost beyond recognition.

Comicization and Tiers of Sacredness

In Taiwan, the phenomenon of *Dianyin Santaizi* constitutes part of a wider trend towards comicization—i.e., its translation into a "cute" (*Q* in Taiwanese

Fig. 9.3.

RECEIVED · PERCEIVED

Source: S. McCloud, *Understanding Comics: The Invisible Art* (New York: Harper Perennial, 1993), 49.

Mandarin) visual style associated with comics and cartoons—in advertising, branded products and Visual Identity Systems (VIS). From a design perspective, comicization involves omission, exaggeration, transformation and simplification. It reduces complex visual forms to symbols composed of lines and perhaps color, selecting certain features to emphasize qualities such as friendliness. (The possibility of solemn cartoon images requires further research and sample collection.) McCloud (1993) illustrates the logic behind this process (see Fig. 9.3). In this way abstract, half-figurative images stand for concrete objects. Note also the progression towards childlike imagery expressive of humor and approachability.

As part of a society suffused with comicized multimedia characters (e.g., Hello Kitty, Doraemon, Pikachu, Astro Boy, Sakura Maruko, Winnie the Pooh, Snoopy, SpongeBob SquarePants, Pleasant Goat), Taiwan's temple festivals have naturally gravitated to a similar style in their creation of mascots and peripheral commodities. The authors' research (conducted 2008–09) found redesigned deity images being used as souvenir figurines; on posters and flyers; on identifying clothing (t-shirts, reflective vests and/or caps) worn by festival workers; as two- or three-dimensional mascot images mounted on the lead vehicle of a street parade; and as logos. (For example, some *Dianyin Santaizi* troupes have their own cartoon mascots.) Two more categories might be listed—customized god-puppets depicting such minor deities as Huye ("Lord Tiger") or the door guardians in a cartoon style; or story-themed *Dianyin Santaizi* (e.g., the Pingdong group created a special set of god-puppets based on characters from *The Journey to the West*)—but whether they will become popular remains to be seen.

In this era of the "pictorial turn," mascot design serves to promote image identity and strengthen focus. The same morphological evolution can be observed in numerous gods, not only in Santaizi. Most god mascots are visible only in connection with religious festivals. Created by computer graphic software and guided by the designer's interpretation of the god's role, the modernized images follow precise linear patterns and use bright colors, in sharp contrast with traditional deity images crafted using older technologies and materials. The shift in media (e.g., from temple mortar to print) also affects the underlying symbolic meaning.

When applied to religious images, the usual result of comicization is desacralization. According to Émile Durkheim, the sacred is marked by reverence, fear and respect, and distinguished from the profane (i.e., everyday life or the secular) by special taboos and/or rites such as ceremonies, prayers and sacrifices. While traditional Santaizi figures are regarded as divine, *Dianyin Santaizi* weaken this sense of sacredness by substituting modern dance steps for the "Step of the Seven Stars," by adopting comic accoutrements in place of their traditional weapons, and by allowing onlookers to dance with them or to have their photo taken with them. On the other hand, the expressions of mutual joy and interaction between spectators and performers are not merely spectacle, but forms of ritual performance in their own right. Owing to his childlike nature, Santaizi lends himself relatively easily to these shifts in representation.

Johan Huizinga (1955) describes a rite in terms of *dromenon* or performance behavior. The content of *dromenon*, called drama (i.e., that which is performed), "re-presents" the sacred on stage (broadly conceived as any performance space)—not simply as imitation but as a form of devotion. As with secular drama, costume signals a conscious deviation from the routine of everyday life. However, different types of *dromenon* produce different effects. For example, differences in costume signal whether a rite is to be solemn or game-like, as in a masquerade. A solemn rite transports its participants into the realm of the sacred, either by demonstration or invocation, and thus brings about "re-enchantment." Game-playing rites likewise inspire certain emotional effects on the part of their devotees, typically in the form of fun or "crazed" behavior; and result not in re-enchantment, but in affinity. Within this reading, both traditional Santaizi and *Dianyin Santaizi* performances qualify as *dromenon*. Each involves a hierarchical transformation in which participants are transported between the realms of the sacred and profane. Adapting Victor Turner's (1995) approach to ritual process analysis, we may distinguish between three tiers of sacredness, among which qualities are uploaded or downloaded:

(1) A transcendent tier in which ritual performance relates primarily to the sacred functions of divine beings, not to the human world. This may take the form of messages to or from the gods, acts of worship, etc. Divine beings are set apart through sacred spaces and sacred objects. For example, traditional Santaizi are associated with temple altars and street processions (their position in the parade being a kind of "space"), and carry identifying supernatural weapons, all of which serves to warn against trespass.

(2) An immanent tier in which the distance between ritual performers and their audience is narrowed and divine beings are transformed into amicable, approachable figures, such as the *Dianyin Santaizi*. The aim is to cultivate a

sense of collective experience and *communitas*. Rather than sacred spaces, we should speak of stages or performance arenas, with secular objects replacing sacred ones.

(3) An abstract, symbolic tier in which divine images are simplified into a merely visual experience. Here "worship" may take the form of the purchase of commodities (symbolic consumption). The arena is removed to the communications medium or exhibition counter, while objects are reduced to symbolic representations.

The World Games performance retained the sanctity of the gods, albeit softened and made more approachable through comic elements. In contrast, the puppets used at the Deaflympics failed to evoke a sense of the sacred for their audiences and so lacked the transitional quality of the *Dianyin Santaizi*.

Conclusion

From their origins on the margins of traditional religion and culture, *Dianyin Santaizi* performances have emerged as an important element of Taiwanese cultural identity, to the extent that they have been chosen to represent the island at international events that amount to global rituals. This new popularity is intimately related to visual communication design issues such as comicization. Through the process of hierarchical transformation, Santaizi and other gods reconcile their local religious roles with the wider forces of globalization. Their future evolution deserves watching, as the gods take on new forms for the benefit of people in the secular world. An interesting question is whether Taiwan's religious festivals are able to avoid losing their cultural identity in the course of these adaptations.

Notes and References

1. YouTube hosts numerous videos of Taiwanese street parades as well as *Dianyin Santaizi* performances. For footage of a typical street parade with Santaizi, see:
    http://www.youtube.com/watch?v=sSXux4pnwbs&feature=related (accessed December 13, 2012).
    For examples of *Dianyin Santaizi* in a street parade and on television see:
    http://www.youtube.com/watch?v=mL6X1SrxMtk (accessed February 20, 2011)
    http://www.youtube.com/watch?v=32G28t201SA (accessed February 20, 2011)
2. Videos of these performances may be viewed on YouTube. For the portion of the World Games opening ceremony featuring *Dianyin Santaizi* and other gods, see:
    http://www.youtube.com/watch?v=G41_8qo0NvA&feature=related (accessed February 20, 2011)
    http://www.youtube.com/watch?v=xLSKPxxmLrk&feature=related (accessed February 20, 2011)

For parts of the Deaflympics opening and closing ceremonies discussed here, see:
http://www.youtube.com/watch?v=koxpRMuLQYg (accessed February 20, 2011)
http://www.youtube.com/watch?v=q2VLHgpFlWk&feature=related (accessed February 20, 2011)
http://www.youtube.com/watch?v=dqOTAPt1yII&feature=related (accessed February 20, 2011)

Anonymous. 2009. 眾神加持 世運好閃 [Thanks to the Assistance of Numerous Gods, the World Games Shine Brightly]. 中國時報 [*China Times*, Taipei] (July 14): A1.

Barnard, M. 1998. *Art, Design, and Visual Culture: An Introduction*. London: Palgrave Macmillan.

Barnard, M. 2001. *Approaches to Understanding Visual Culture*. London: Palgrave Macmillan.

Baudrillard, J. 2006. *The System of Objects (Radical Thinkers)*. London: Verso.

Cai Wenting. 2005. 台灣民俗筆記 [Taiwan Folk Customs Notebook]. 光華雜誌 [*Guanghua Magazine*, Taipei].

Character Marketing Project. 2001. 図解でわかるキャラクターマーケティング−これがキャラクター活用のマーケティング手法だ! [Understanding Character Marketing with Pictures—This Is the Marketing Method which Utilizes Characters!]. 日本能率協会マネジメントセンター [Japan Association of Efficiency Management Center], Tokyo.

Chen Xiaoyi. 2003. "哪吒人物及故事研究" [Research into the Character and Story of Nuozha]. Unpublished MA thesis. Feng Chia University, Taizhong.

Griswold, W. 2004. *Cultures and Societies in a Changing World*. Thousand Oaks: Pine Forge Press.

Hall, S. 1997. *Representation: Cultural Representations and Signifying Practices*. London: Sage.

He Dingjiao. 2009. 運動賽事 文化符號競技 [Sports Games, Cultural Codes, and competition]. 聯合報 [*United Daily News*, Taipei] (September 6): A4.

He Mingchuan and Guo Wenzong. 1997. 產品文化識別之探索 [The Discovery of Product Culture Identity]. 國立雲林技術學院學報 [*Journal of National Yunlin College of Science and Technology*] 6, no. 3: 253–63.

Huizinga, J. 1955. *Homo Ludens: A Study of the Play-element in Culture*. London: Routledge & Kegan Paul.

Jian Zongxiu. 2004. "台灣民間哪吒太子信仰研究---「以新竹市為例」" [Research into Taiwan Folk Beliefs about Prince Nuozha: The Example of Xinzhu City]. Unpublished MA thesis, National Sun Yat-sen University, Kaohsiung.

Kagan, M. S. 1973–4. *Lekstii po istorii estetiki* [Lectures on the History of Aesthetics]. St Petersburg: Izdatel'stvo Leningradskogo Universiteta.

Lai Shenchuan (dir.). 2009. 第21屆聽障奧運閉幕大典 [Closing Ceremony of the 21st Deaflympics]. Taipei: 中視 [China TV] (September 15).

———. 2009. 第21屆聽障奧運開幕大典 [Opening Ceremony of the 21st Deaflympics]. Taipei: 中視 [China TV] (September 5).

Li Fengmao. 2008. 文化識別：從事馬來西亞華人宗教研究的經驗 [Cultural Identity: The Experience of Researching Religious Studies among Chinese Malaysians]. 亞太研究論壇 [*Asia-Pacific Research Forum*] 41: 2–30.

Li Yajie, He Mingchuan and Lin Fangsui. 2008. 圖像造形之文化識別研究--以奧林匹克運動會為例 [Research into Culture Identity in Images and Design: The Example of the Olympic Games]. 科技學刊(人文社會類) [*Technology Periodical (Humanities and Social Studies)*] 17, no. 3: 221–34.

McCloud, S. 1993. *Understanding Comics: The Invisible Art*. New York: HarperPerennial.

Smith, P. and Riley, A. 2008. *Cultural Theory: An Introduction*. London: Wiley-Blackwell.

Sturken, M. and L. Cartwright. 2009. *Practices of Looking: An Introduction to Visual Culture*. Oxford: Oxford University Press.

Tezuka Osamu. 1996. マンガの描き方–似顔絵から長編まで [How to Draw Manga—From a Composite Drawing to a Long Story]. Tokyo: Kobun sya.

Tu Huijen. 2004. "那吒故事及信仰之研究" [Research into the Stories and Beliefs about Nuozha]. Unpublished MA thesis, National Hualian Normal College.

Turner, V. 1995. *The Ritual Process: Structure and Anti-structure*. Piscataway: Aldine Transaction.

Wang Meizhen. 2006. "文化「台」風意味著什麼？-「台客文化」的社會想像與認同形構" [What Does "Cultural *Tai*-phoon" Mean? Social Imagination and Identity Construction in "*Taike* Culture"]. Unpublished MA thesis, National Chengchi University, Taipei.

Ye Jun'gu. 2005. "兒童神的敘事：以孫悟空與李哪吒為主的考察" [Stories of Child Gods: Research into Sun Wukong and Li Nuozha]. Unpublished MA thesis, National Chengchi University, Taipei.

Zhang Jiemao. 2006. "從次文化看工業設計：以改裝車的台客次文化為例" [Subcultural Approaches to Industrial Design: The Example of Remodeled Cars in the *Taike* Subculture]. Unpublished MA thesis, Shi Chien University, Taipei.

Zhang Weifeng (producer) and Zhu Zongqing (dir.). 2009. 我們超愛世運秀！高雄世運開閉幕秀現場實錄 [We Totally Love the World Games Show! The Opening and Closing Ceremony Performances of the Kaohsiung World Games]. Kaohsiung Organizing Committee for the 2009 World Games.

Zhang Yating. 2004. "台灣陣頭鑼鼓之研究" [Research into Taiwan's Religious Processions and Gong/Drum Ensembles]. Unpublished MA thesis, Nanhua University, Jiayi County.

Zhen Yaxin. 2004. "儀式象徵與地方感呈現" [Displays of Ritual Symbolism and a Sense of Place]. Unpublished MA thesis, National Yunlin University of Science and Technology.

Zhou Xian. 2008. "視覺文化的转向" [New Directions in Visual Culture]. Beijing University Press.

Chapter 10

RITUALS OF IDENTITY IN *ALID* BELIEF: SIRAYA RELIGION IN TAIWAN SINCE 1945

Tiaukhai Iunn
St Andrew's University, United Kingdom

Introduction

The Siraya are an Austronesian aboriginal group in Taiwan whose status is unrecognized by the Republic of China (ROC) government controlling the island. Sinification has impacted the Siraya since the beginning of Chinese rule in 1662, but accelerated after World War II and the 1949 retreat of Nationalist forces to Taiwan. In the midst of this sinification, the Siraya revival movement in recent years has aimed at persuading the government to recognize the group's distinct ethnic identity and indigenous status.

Like other Formosan aboriginal groups, the Siraya are classified as Austronesians. Some scholars (Chaw 2001; Huang 1996; Sim 2003) believe Taiwan to be the prehistoric source of Austronesian peoples elsewhere in the Pacific. Following twentieth-century Japanese ethnography, aboriginal Formosans are divided into two main categories: *Takasago-zoku* (mountain tribes) and *Peipo-zoku* (plains tribes). The Siraya belong to the Peipo group and are divided into three subgroups: Siraya proper (or the main group of Siraya), Makattao and Teivorangh (also known as Taivoan) (Hsieh 2006). I use "Siraya" for all three, although some members of the Makattao and Teivorangh consider themselves to belong to different ethnic groups.

Although numerous records attest to the historical existence of the Siraya, the ROC government refuses to recognize contemporary Siraya either as indigenous or as a distinct ethnic group. At issue is whether the Siraya have retained enough of their culture and identity to claim continuity with their forebears, or can be considered as having assimilated to the Han. To make the case for a Siraya identity, the Siraya revival movement therefore aims to document the people's history, language and culture.

As an element of culture, religion plays an important role in the Siraya revival movement. During centuries of sinification, many Siraya gradually abandoned their traditional religious practices in favor of the Chinese folk religion, while others have converted to Christianity, especially in the form of the Presbyterian Church in Taiwan (PCT). To counteract the negative impact of these trends, many Siraya since the 1990s have been trying to reconstruct their former religion and its central practice, the Alid ritual.

The Siraya regard their traditional religion as monotheistic. In the Siraya language, Sinckansche, "God" is called *Alid*. This is both the generic word for a monotheistic deity and a proper name (analogous to "Yahweh"). It is used not only by followers of the traditional Alid ritual, but also by Siraya Christians. Both groups agree that they are worshipping the same God. For this reason, I refer to the religion of both groups as Alid belief, although, on inspection, their concepts of Alid turn out not to be the same. I call the non-Christian worshippers of Alid, whose rituals are held in a community *konkai* (shrine or temple), "ritualists."

The Alid ritual is thought to provide ritualists with a feeling of unity, bringing them closer to their Austronesian roots and contemporary social identity (Aguilar 2009, 36). (I use the term "Austronesian" instead of "Siraya" because some elements of the contemporary Alid ritual are believed to have been adopted from other aboriginal groups in Taiwan.) Today, however, some ritualists argue that only they are true Siraya—that those who do not worship Alid, or who worship the Christian God as Alid, are not really Siraya. Of course, others do not agree (and neither do I).

In sinified Siraya communities, the *konkai* is usually part of a Chinese temple in which Alid is worshipped alongside Chinese deities. Chinese ritual forms are normally used. Private rituals are also performed before home altars. Although Alid is still worshipped, the offerings and ceremonies are entirely Chinese. Such rituals play no role in the Siraya revival movement and should be classified as a form of the Chinese folk religion. However, not all private Alid rituals have been completely sinified. Liu (1998) notes several cases in which the practitioners of such rituals have resisted Chinese attempts at land-grabbing; these Siraya strengthen their self-confidence with stories crediting Alid with defending them against the Chinese.

Although a few ethnic Chinese have adopted the Alid ritual, they retain their Chinese identity and their religious practices blend into those of the Chinese folk religion. For them, Alid is only one of many gods rather than the only god, or at least the highest god, as most of the Siraya claim. However, because I am interested in the Siraya as an ethnic group, I focus on those who identify themselves as Siraya.

Chuen-rong Yeh, a scholar in Taiwan's Academia Sinica who specializes in the Siraya and Chinese religions, distinguishes four forms of interaction between the Alid ritual and other religions: coexistence, compartmentalization, syncretism and conversion (Yeh 2006, 133). By "coexistence," Yeh means a situation in which the Alid ritual and another religion exist in close proximity without mixing or influencing one another. "Compartmentalization" places Alid belief under the umbrella of the other religion. "Syncretism" means that worshippers practice Alid rituals and the other religion on an equal basis. Finally, "conversion" involves the ritualists totally abandoning the Alid ritual and converting to another religion. This last category is more likely to be applied to the case of a Siraya who becomes a Christian; the situation of a Siraya who worships Chinese deities is more difficult to define (Yeh 2006, 134).

I would add that, in most places today, the relationship of the Alid ritual to the Chinese folk religion should be described as either compartmentalization or syncretism. In compartmentalized rituals such as those of the communities of Baccaluangh[1] and Kabuasua, Alid is worshipped together with Chinese deities and ghosts, and is no longer seen as the highest god. On the other hand, rituals in which Alid is considered as the highest (or only) god, or as equal to the highest Chinese deity, can be defined as syncretism. This term especially applies to the rituals of communities in Pak-thau-iunn and Khau-sia-liau. I analyze these in detail later in this chapter.

Jordan (1993) views conversion to the Chinese folk religion as both "conditional" and "additional" (289–94). By "conditional" he means that Chinese worship is conceived not as an absolute duty, but as a means of obtaining certain benefits; "additional" means that new deities tend to be added to those already worshipped, rather than replacing them. Yeh (2006) accepts the "conditional" category, though he denies that "additional" conversions qualify as conversion, defining these instead as examples of compartmentalization or syncretism (133). Jordan (1993) does not consider ethnicity as "an issue in conversion" to the Chinese folk religion (289), but emphasizes "pantheon interchangeability" as well as the attractions of glyphomancy and healing (290–2). However, pantheon interchangeability indicates that the concept of "conversion" is inapplicable here. It is quite common for Chinese folk religionists to periodically add to or reduce the number of deities they worship.

In addition, Jordan's theory is contradicted by Koxinga's (seventeenth-century) policy of forcing non-Chinese to set up home altars to deities of the Chinese folk religion. This policy demonstrates that worshipping Chinese deities was considered a symbol of Chinese identity. Therefore, ethnicity is actually an issue in conversion. It also applies to contemporary Siraya who worship Chinese deities and ghosts. At the same time, the fluidity and pantheon interchangeability of the Chinese folk religion has in some cases opened doors to the compartmentalization or syncretism of these two bodies of belief.

As mentioned above, many Siraya communities have been trying to reconstruct the "original" Alid ritual (Duan 2004; Duan 2007; Twu 2002). However, the form of the ritual identified as "original" varies from community to community, with some versions even boasting scholarly endorsement (Hsieh 2006; Liu 1998; Liu 2001; Twu 2002). According to my observations, most of these rituals are too sinified to be considered traditional. In this chapter, I discuss several different forms of the Alid ritual and how each ritual has influenced the ethnic consciousness of its community.

Ritual Practices and Siraya Identity

I begin with the settlement of Soulangh, which considers the Kabuasua form of the Alid ritual to be the most authentic. For this reason, it has figured prominently in the Siraya revival movement. Soulangh's relative remoteness is the basis of this claim, which is accepted by several outside ritualists and scholars.

Soulangh can be divided into eight communities according to the locations of its *konkai* (Twu 2002). Among these, the most noteworthy are Pak-thau-iunn, Tham-khian, Hoan-a-un and Kabuasua, which are the most well-known today.

Although Pak-thau-iunn managed to preserve its original Alid ritual until the end of Japanese rule, the practice was abandoned after 1945 due to harsh discrimination against the Peipo and the pressures of sinification. By the beginning of the revival movement in the 1990s, the ritual had been completely lost. To recover the ritual, people in Pak-thau-iunn instinctively thought of their "brother community" of Kabuasua, famous for its ritual practice. In 1999, Huan-jhih Su (then a legislator, and from 2002 to 2010 the mayor of Tainan County) accompanied some Alid believers and specialist scholars to Kabuasua. With the approval of Alid, a dance teacher and an *inibus* (priestess of the Alid ritual) were sent to teach their practices to Pak-thau-iunn (Twu 2005).

The principal reason why Kabuasua was able to maintain its ritual is the community's exclusivity. Because Kabuasua is surrounded by Lak-teng-khe (a Teivorangh community), Dorco (another Peipo settlement) and some Han communities, the Alid ritual served to reinforce its distinct identity (Duan 2004). Thus, most of its inhabitants became ritualists. For this reason, the Siraya in Kabuasua claim their Siraya consciousness is the strongest and hail their *konkai* as the paragon example of the Alid ritual.

Their ancestors originally lived in Pak-thau-iunn, where they were forcibly sinified during the Qing dynasty. At that time, the Peipo communities in Dorco and Lak-teng-khe (in the northern part of Tainan County) were not quite so sinified, and so were considered "savage" by the Chinese. In addition, there were several Chinese communities in the vicinity of those two communities, and the conflicts between Peipo and Chinese were seen as serious problems by the Qing government. For this reason, a group of Soulangh people were resettled in Kabuasua to act as a buffer between the Peipo and the Chinese. The Qing government also hoped that their example would encourage the Peipo in Dorco and Lak-teng-khe to assimilate and sinify. This is, in fact, what occurred.

However, conflicts between the Peipo and the Chinese drew in the Siraya in Kabuasua as well. They faced a dilemma: on the one hand, the Qing government wanted them to adopt a Chinese lifestyle, to sinify Dorco and Lak-teng-khe. On the other hand, Kabuasua experienced conflict with the real Chinese surrounding their community. Thus, their "cultural isolation" arose from this situation (Aguilar 2009, 57).

For this reason, the Siraya in Kabuasua felt they had to maintain a Siraya identity in their dealings with the Chinese and a Chinese identity when dealing with the Peipo in Dorco and Lak-teng-khe. Because Alid belief was seen as a symbol of Siraya identity and Chinese religion as a symbol of sinification, elements of Chinese religion were adopted into Kabuasua's Alid ritual. Later, Chinese deities came to be worshipped as well. This conflation allowed the Alid ritual to be preserved in Kabuasua. However, as sinification pressures became stronger, Alid ceased to be regarded as the only god, or even the highest god. Kabuasua's claim of superior authenticity for its Alid ritual is therefore ironic.

Like Pak-thau-iunn, Kabuasua was forced to abandon its Alid ritual between World War II and the 1990s. The current Alid is believed to have been "invited" from another Soulangh community called Hoan-a-un, which then belonged to a village called Tok-ka. It is because of this that the form of Alid ritual practiced by Kabuasua is commonly called the Tok-ka Alid. Because Hoan-a-un no longer belongs to Tok-ka today, it is generally suggested that the name of the ritual should be changed to "Hoan-a-un Alid" to reflect the community's "jurisdiction" (Chen 2005). Consequently, Tham-khian's distinct tradition was able to survive, although its ritual has been simplified due to the low population of believers (Twu 2002, 44, 49).

Another argument against the authenticity of the Kabuasua form of the Alid ritual lies in the behavior of its *inibus*. The *konkai* in Kabuasua has the appearance of a Daoist temple. Although neither joss sticks nor *kim-choa* (paper money) are used when worshipping Alid, some ritual practices resemble those associated with the Chinese folk religion. In addition, Chinese deities are worshipped by the local Siraya, even those who are faithful Alid ritualists. For instance, when the previous *inibus* was asked who her successor should be, she replied that it would depend on the decision of Alid. Thereafter, Alid would have to seek permission from heaven and the underworld. Chinese deities choose their mediums using exactly the same procedure.

This was unusual for another reason: even among the sinified Siraya, Alid is still regarded as the highest (though not necessarily the only) god. The status of Alid ought to be equal to, if not higher than, that of Thinn-kong (Tian Gong, the Lord of Heaven; a.k.a. Yuhuang Dadi, the Jade Emperor), the highest Chinese god (Liu 2001; Twu 2002). This being the case, why would Alid need to seek permission from other deities (or ghosts) before choosing an *inibus*? The influence of the Chinese folk religion is obvious. Furthermore, the former *inibus* actually worshipped Chinese deities, offering them paper money and joss sticks every day while she was alive (Liu 2001, 275). Today, therefore, the question of the sinification of the Alid ritual is widely discussed (Liu 2001, 276).

The attitude of the *inibus* suggests that the Siraya of Kabuasua have adopted a dual identity as both Siraya and Han Chinese (or Hok-lo, the major local Chinese sub-ethnicity). How could this have happened? As mentioned above, the ritual now practiced in Kabuasua was adopted from the community of Hoan-a-un (Twu 2002, 111), whose ritual is totally sinified. Most obviously, joss sticks and paper money are used, and the items offered to Alid by the local people are consistent with Chinese ritual practice. In contrast, ritualists from outside the community offer items in accordance with Siraya tradition or a mixture of Siraya and Chinese items. In addition, Hoan-a-un's *konkai* building has been constructed in a Chinese style: one would not recognize it as a Siraya *konkai* unless one entered and took care to note what god was being worshipped (Twu 2002, 56). Furthermore, this *konkai* functions as a shrine not only for Alid, but also for several Chinese deities and ghosts (Twu 2002, 59–60).

Clifford (1982) describes the possibility of dual identity among the Canaque people of New Caledonia, who can be Canaque and French simultaneously (as well as Austronesian and Methodist). When applied to the Alid ritual, this principle suggests how a ritualist might observe Chinese religious practices while retaining his or her Siraya identity. Moreover, Chinese folk religions do not normally forbid their followers from worshipping other deities or joining other religious groups (though this did happen several times in Chinese history, e.g., in seventeenth- and eighteenth-century Taiwan).

As the former *inibus* explained to Liu (2001), she did not feel any contradiction in being Siraya and Han at the same time. She explained that Alid chose her to become an *inibus* not because she was Siraya, but simply because her family name is Li, the same as Thai-siong Li Lo-kun (Taishang Li Laojun, the divinized Laozi), one of the highest Daoist gods. In a paper on the Vezo people of Madagascar, Astuti (1995) reports that the Vezo are not really an ethnic group; instead, they are Vezo only when they are fishing. For Astuti, being a Vezo is an activity, not an ethnic identity. The testimony of the *inibus* suggests that this theory also applies to the Siraya in Kabuasua. The *inibus* thinks of herself as a Siraya only when worshipping Alid; at other times, she is indistinguishable from a Han.

Notwithstanding their sinified Alid ritual and *konkai*, the people of Kabuasua are eager to promote the Siraya language, Sinckansche. Although opportunities to speak it are very limited, the Siraya people of Kabuasua make an effort to retain it in their religious life, including ritual use. This desire is unusual among the Siraya communities.

It is important to understand that many Taiwanese aboriginal languages are either dead or moribund. Therefore, language activism has been a key element of the revitalization of Austronesian Formosan cultures. The ROC government has tended to support mother-tongue education among Takasago students, while neglecting the Peipo. Nevertheless, attempts to revive Sinckansche have been ongoing since the late twentieth century.

In Kabuasua, the priestess of the Alid ritual is called (in Sinckansche) an *inibus*, *inibs* or *mipus*, while most of the other communities call her an *ang-i*. In most of the ritualist communities today, men can also serve as priests, normally called *tang-ki* (from the Hok-lo term for a spirit medium). Some communities also call their priests *ang-i*, although in the past this term applied only to women. In Kabuasua, priests are normally called (in Sinckansche) *siga buatau* or *alak* (Duan 2007). In addition, *konkai* is also believed to be a Hok-lo loan word because the Chinese characters for this term (*gongjie*) mean "public office" or "government building." In addition to its role as a religious center, the *konkai* also serves as a place where the public affairs of the community are managed. In Kabuasua, this kind of building is normally called *kuwa*, which means "house of spirit" (Duan 2007).

Tham-khian, another Soulangh community, is described as a "comparatively traditional Peipo *konkai*" (Twu 2002, 44). According to Twu (2002), the *konkai* today looks nearly the same as when another scholar, Prof. Pin-hsiung Liu, described it in the 1960s, even though it has been rebuilt in a different position and with different materials (44–9). The *ang-a* ("jars" or "bottles") for the ritual have also been replaced because children destroyed the old ones several years ago. Today, the only relic remaining from the earlier *konkai* is the stone representing Alid. The items used in the ritual are all traditional: for example, betel nuts, rice wine and *bah-tsang* (a.k.a. *zongzi*, a pyramid-shaped mass of glutinous rice wrapped in leaves). In accordance with tradition, *i-hing* (Japanese eupatorium) is also offered. Neither paper money nor joss sticks are used. Most importantly, only Alid is worshipped in the *konkai*; no other god is present.

Although the *konkai* today is still very traditional, Twu reports that its rituals have been simplified since the 1950s. For example, the traditional sacrifice of a pig is omitted today. While it is unfortunate that the traditional Alid ritual will probably not be passed on to future generations, the fact that the *konkai* has managed to remain active at all is noteworthy in view of the many aspects of the traditional Siraya religion that have been destroyed.

Because Tham-khian is closer to Pak-thau-iunn than Kabuasua, why did the ritualists of Pak-thau-iunn turn to Kabuasua instead of Tham-khian for the revival of their Alid ritual? According to my observations, although Tham-khian has preserved its traditional ritual, the people there lack a strong ethnic consciousness. For example, they did not take part in the May 2009 demonstrations demanding that the government recognize the Siraya. Meanwhile, the ritualists in Kabuasua have a strong identity as Siraya, despite their sinified ritual. (One of the leaders of the demonstration was from Kabuasua.) Furthermore, the ritualists in Tham-khian have never been interested in reviving Sinckansche.

Among Alid ritualists, it is widely assumed that the more sinified their ritual the less interest its practitioners show in their mother tongue. I disagree with this claim. As indicated above, I surmise that in Kabuasua, Sirayaness is seen as an activity, not as an ethnic group. This activity includes the promotion of Sinckansche. Notwithstanding the sinification of their ritual and *konkai*, when worshipping Alid they are Siraya.

Conversely, although the ritual and *konkai* in Tham-khian are traditional and Alid is the only god represented in the *konkai*, there is no direct evidence that the ritualists in that community see Alid as the only god. It is common in Taiwan for people to worship many deities simultaneously, and, as mentioned before, Chinese folk religion today does not usually prohibit its religionists from worshipping the deities of other religions. In addition, it is very common in the Chinese folk religion for each deity to have his/her own temple or shrine. Presumably, the people of Tham-khian worship Alid in the *konkai* during the festivals of Alid, while worshipping other deities on other days. Besides, the Alid ritualists in Tham-khian do not have a very strong Siraya identity.

Their earlier willingness to abandon their Alid ritual to the *konkai* of Pak-thau-iunn suggests that the people of Tham-khian intended to become totally sinified. They have continued with the ritual not of their own free will, but only in order to avoid punishment by Alid. Furthermore, they worship Alid only when they must (e.g., during the festivals), and otherwise avoid the Alid ritual, as well as Siraya identity in general.

Shiun-wey Huang (2003) sees the adoption of the Chinese and Japanese languages by the Amis (another indigenous Taiwanese group) as a form of modernization or "borrowing from the dominant outsiders" (269). Many people have applied this theory to other Austronesian Formosans, especially the Peipo. In the case of the sinified Siraya ritualists, however, the relationship between ritual and language identity suggests another explanation.

Feuchtwang (2001) theorizes that a god is celebrated "as a reminder of a larger, or of a former, place of origin from which settlers not only here but in neighboring localities trace their ancestry" (25). It is likely that his theory also applies to the Siraya. After many decades of Kuomintang (KMT) propaganda, the sinified Siraya have been persuaded to think they are Chinese—that their ancestors are from China, exactly like the Hok-lo and Hakka. Perhaps this is why they prefer the Hok-lo language. (In the next section, I describe some Siraya rituals that imply a Chinese identity.)

Another well-known Soulangh community is Pak-thau-iunn. Although its Alid ritual was copied from Kabuasua in the 1990s, it later became quite different. For instance, after the original *inibus* passed away, the ritual came to be led by a *tang-ki* who serves a Chinese temple next to the *konkai*. (Actually, the *konkai* falls under the administration of the temple, although the shrine of Alid is separate from those of Chinese deities.) Thus, for the ritualists of Pak-thau-iunn, Alid is not the only god.

However, in this community it is likely that Alid is seen as the highest god. For example, the name of the temple literally means "Alid the Long-Standing and Well-Established." According to local ritualists, the Chinese temple was established with the permission of Alid (Twu 2002, 27–8). Furthermore, Alid is always worshipped before the other deities (Twu 2002, 41). The ritual in Pak-thau-iunn is very traditional compared to most of the other communities because, although joss sticks and paper money are used when worshipping the Chinese deities in the temple, they are not used when worshipping Alid, and the gifts and food offered to Alid during the festival are entirely traditional.

The ritualists in Pak-thau-iunn are very active in the Siraya revival movement (indeed, some of the leaders of the aforementioned demonstration were from this community), and are also keen to revive Sinckansche. In my experience, most learners of the language are Christians. My half-Siraya friend and I used to learn Sinckansche in the Presbyterian churches in Khau-pi and Poa-be. While doing fieldwork in Pak-thau-iunn several years ago, we were once asked to teach Sinckansche to the ritualists in their *konkai* during the Alid festival. Unfortunately, we were unable to agree on a time. Nevertheless, we still managed to instruct the *alak* (*tang-ki*) and other ritual officiants in the language privately.

Ritual Practices and Chinese Identity

Since the rebirth of Siraya consciousness in the 1990s, many ritualists (not only those from Soulangh) came to view the Alid ritual practiced by Kabuasua—the Tok-ka Alid, also known by the phonetic variation *Chhou-ka* (Twu 2002, 210)—as the most authentic. Therefore, many communities also "invited" this Alid (Chen 2005; Duan 2007; Twu 2002). Interestingly, the ritualists in Hoan-a-un have never called their own Alid by these names. Instead, the official name of the *konkai* in Hoan-a-un is "Hoan-a-un Alid Temple" (*Fanzaiwen Alizu Miao*) (Twu 2002, 56–8). Without question, the rituals of those communities contain many Chinese elements to a greater degree than even Kabuasua. Also, as in Kabuasua, Alid is worshipped alongside other gods in many of the Hoan-a-un *konkai*.

One of the most noteworthy of these communities is Thau-sia, another Tainan-area Siraya community that belongs to the settlement of Bacclouangh. Thau-sia has become famous for its Alid ritual, which was "invited" from Kabuasua in 1980 (Chen 2005). For this reason, every year before the Alid festival, two votive statues of Alid are invited from Soulangh into the *konkai* of Thau-sia. Pigs are then sacrificed and offered to Alid. Because Thau-sia now serves as the capital of Bacclouangh, its ritual has influenced many other communities in this settlement.

The community *konkai* was originally divided into three rooms that belonged to and represented the three villages of Thau-sia. Each village had its own altar. After the *konkai* was rebuilt, the three altars were combined although the *konkai* continued to be shared by the three villages.

Its original name was "Thau-sia Konkai," but during the 1990s this name was changed to "Thau-sia Thai-siong Liong-thau Tiong-gi Temple" (*Toushe Taishang Longtou Zhongyi Miao*). Why would they choose a name that sounds like that of a Chinese temple, at the very moment when Siraya consciousness was emerging, and many communities were trying to undo the effects of sinification? I once asked this question to the man responsible for the Alid ritual there. He told me that it was feared that without sinification, Alid belief could not survive.

Although I do not agree with him, his words have a basis in fact. When community leaders tried to register Thau-sia Konkai with the ROC Ministry of the Interior as a religious building, their application was rejected on the grounds that "*konkai*" did not appear on the list of categories of religious buildings (Twu 2002). Thus, after the *konkai* was rebuilt with new materials, it was given a new name to make it resemble a Chinese temple.

Some of its ritual elements are purely Peipo, such as the use of *ang-a*, *i-hing*, and the skull of a pig. However, many Chinese ritual elements are present as well, such as joss sticks and paper money. According to tradition, Alid likes cleanliness and dislikes smoke and fire. (For this reason, the pigs should not be cooked.) In the Chinese folk religion, joss sticks serve as a bridge between human beings and the gods, while paper money is considered the best gift to offer a god (Twu 2002, 187). Twu sees Thau-sia's ritual as a synthesis of Chinese and Peipo traditions (Twu 2002, 160, 494).

In addition, Chinese gods are also worshipped in Thau-sia's *konkai*. Before worshipping Alid, ritualists must first worship Thinn-kong (Tian Gong), the highest Chinese god. This indicates that Thinn-kong outranks Alid (Twu 2002, 182). This practice is followed even during the Alid festival, when most Siraya communities consider it unnecessary to worship any other god.

Thau-sia was sinicized very early. According to a photograph shown to me by Dr Chuen-rong Yeh, men have been acting as *ang-i* since the 1930s, when Taiwan was still under Japanese rule. However, Twu (2002) describes these men not as *ang-i* but as *tang-ki*, using the general Hok-lo term for a spirit medium in the Chinese folk religion (160).

Today, the rituals are conducted by a *tang-ki*, though the man I interviewed sometimes describes him as an *ang-i*. When I mentioned that the term *ang-i* normally applies to women, and a man doing that job should be described as an *alak* (quoting the words of the people in Kabuasua), my informant said he could not agree with this definition.

Another famous *konkai* in Thau-sia is the one at Pi-a-kha, also in the Tainan area. (Nowadays, all three *konkai* in the settlement of Bacclouangh are located in the same district.) After being rebuilt, it was renamed "Tok-ka Liong-ho Temple" (*Dujia Longhe Miao*). Its outward appearance is quite similar to the *konkai* in Thau-sia except for being quieter, cleaner and more like a park. It is associated with a sub-temple, Tok-ka Seng-ho Temple (*Dujia Shenghe Miao*). These names indicate that the two temples are both named for the Tok-ka Alid. Though customary elements such as *i-hing*, flowers, ritual dances and rice wine are retained, the ritual itself has become sinified. Apart from the names of the *konkai*, joss sticks and paper money are used, and there is a large furnace for the ritualists to burn paper money offered in the ritual (Twu 2002, 189).

In the past, the ritual in Pi-a-kha Konkai was very simple, using neither joss sticks nor paper money. These elements were introduced because the original *inibus* of this community served simultaneously as a *tang-ki* of Moniang Lin, the Chinese goddess commonly known as Mazu. Thus, Moniang Lin came to be worshipped in the *konkai*. At first, joss sticks and paper money were offered only to Moniang Lin, not to Alid (because, as noted above, Alid dislikes fire). However, ritualists later began offering these to Alid, as still happens today.

Although the votive statue of Moniang Lin has been returned to the house of the *tang-ki*'s grandson, its incense burner remains in the *konkai*. The *tang-ki* claims that where the incense burner is, there is the goddess; therefore, she believes that Moniang Lin is still in the *konkai* (Twu 2002, 193–4).

There is another *konkai* in the same district, whose official name is now Tok-ka Liong-heng Temple (*Dujia Longxing Miao*). As the name implies, it too is named after the Tok-ka Alid. Today, it is administered by a Chinese temple devoted to the Bodhisattva Guanyin. This *konkai* was traditionally called "Sio-hoe-a Konkai" (*Shaohuizi Gongjie*) after the name of its community, and this name is still commonly used by scholars.

This *konkai* was set up by the *tang-ki* of Thau-sia *Konkai*, and its decorations and altar are exactly like those at Thau-sia. Its ritual is relatively traditional compared to Thau-sia and Pi-a-kha. For example, betel nuts are offered when worshipping Alid. A local elder once scolded people for using joss sticks instead of betel nuts, explaining that Alid does not like fire (Twu 2002, 198). Even so, paper money is still burned and offered to Alid. Other Chinese elements in Sio-hoe-a Konkai include a religious flag emblazoned with the phrase, "The Flag of the True (or Righteous) Tok-ka Alid" and a seal that reads "The Seal of Tok-ka Alid" (Twu 2002, 198).

At Sio-hoe-a, unlike Thau-sia, Alid is seen as the highest god. This is reflected in the fact that during the festivals of other Chinese gods, the community will not make offerings of meat because animals are offered only to Alid during the festival of Alid.

An interesting question concerns the gender of Alid. According to a *tang-ki* of Bacclouangh, because Alid is considered the king of the Siraya, he must be male (Twu 2002, 157). This reflects the fact that the ritual in Bacclouangh is normally conducted by men, unlike in most other Siraya communities, in which this role is held by women. It also indicates that owing to sinification, Bacclouangh has become a patrilineal society, unlike most of the other settlements that are still matriarchal. In matriarchal Siraya communities, Alid is generally believed to be female. Even in sinified, patriarchal Siraya communities most people believe Alid to be female although some individuals consider Alid to be male.

The name-changes of the *konkai* in Thau-sia, Pi-a-kha, and Sio-hoe-a are believed to have been instigated by the *tang-ki* at Thau-sia, who originally "invited" their Alid rituals from Kabuasua. From the history of this *konkai*, described above, one can easily understand why the ritualists in Thau-sia would insist that their *konkai* should be named in the style of a Chinese temple. The fact that Kabuasua calls its ritual the Tok-ka Alid has led all three of these communities to name their *konkai* after Tok-ka. Thus, it is important to ascertain the origins of this name and what it actually means.

Owing to the fame of the Tok-ka Alid, many people mistakenly assume Tok-ka to be a Siraya community. Chen (2005) describes this as a "false truth."

In fact, Tok-ka is a traditional Chinese village. Alid is not worshipped by the people there, and the temples in Tok-ka are those of traditional Chinese religions. The Tok-ka Alid was first invited to Kabuasua from Hoan-a-un, a Siraya community that at that time fell in the same administrative division as the village of Tok-ka. According to Chen, the man who first introduced the Alid ritual to Kabuasua did not clearly distinguish Hoan-a-un from Tok-ka and claimed to be from "Hoan-a-un, Tok-ka," according to the name of the administrative division. Therefore, this form of the Alid ritual came to be called the Tok-ka Alid. The ritualists in Kabuasua did not necessarily suppose that Tok-ka was a Siraya community, but as the Tok-ka Alid came to be introduced into other Siraya communities that did not understand this history its provenance became garbled (Chen 2005).

I disagree with Chen's view, however. Instead, I suggest that the name "Tok-ka Alid" is used to demonstrate sinification or Chinese identity or, perhaps, to give the impression that the Alid ritual is a Chinese belief. (As my informant in Thau-sia explained, he did not think that Alid belief could survive without being sinified.)

As Feuchtwang (2001) informs us, a god is worshipped "as a reminder of a larger, or of a former place of origin" (25). In Chinese religion, it is not unusual for the name of the place where the cult originated to be added in front of the god's or goddess's name. The most famous example is Moniang Lin, a.k.a. Mazu. Because her cult was introduced to Taiwan from Meizhou (in northern Fujian), Moniang Lin is commonly described as Meizhou Mazu. Today, many temples in Taiwan are named after Meizhou Mazu.

The history of the ritual in Thau-sia suggests that its ritualists purposely chose to be sinified, even as ritualists in other communities were seeking the pure, original Alid ritual. Indeed, from that time on, more and more Chinese elements have come to be adopted. Furthermore, the names of the *konkai* in Thau-sia, Pi-a-kha and Sio-hoe-a all include the Chinese character *liong* (dragon). Dragon totems are often seen in Chinese temples and are associated with the Bodhisattva Guanyin. Because even Hoan-a-un Konkai, the fountainhead of Tok-ka Alid, is decorated with dragons and described as a "temple" (*miao*), this indicates that its Alid ritual has been deeply sinified (Twu 2002, 56–8).

In brief, "Tok-ka" in the name of the Tok-ka Alid is designed to make the ritual appear more like a Chinese religion, and mislead outsiders into supposing that Alid is a Chinese god from Tok-ka. Most importantly, this name demonstrates that the ritualists consider themselves to be Chinese. Hence, the ritualists in Thau-sia are unlikely to accept Chen's suggestion that the ritual was renamed the "Hoan-a-un Alid" on the grounds that they are no longer in the same village today and that Tok-ka is a Chinese village. Also, because

Thau-sia has a strong influence on other Bacclouangh communities, it is also unlikely that they will accept this suggestion either, at least for now.

Another noteworthy aspect concerning Thau-sia is that although its ritualists recognize that they are Siraya, they are not very active in the Siraya or other Peipo revival movements. The aforementioned Thau-sia leader told me in the interview that he would never want to see the Siraya recognized by the government as an indigenous ethnic group, as he does not believe the Siraya can survive without being sinified. In other words, he is happy about being Han and wants to apply this designation to all his fellow Siraya. Indeed, the same man lamented the successful application of the Kavalan, another Peipo group who recovered their indigenous status in 2002. These findings indicate that the ritualists of Thau-sia, like those of Kabuasua, consider "Sirayaness" to be an activity, not an ethnicity.

Interestingly, Christianity is not strong in either community. Although there is a Presbyterian church in Thau-sia, its congregation is small. The Presbyterian leadership once described Thau-sia as a "community of idolatry." They could not have been unaware that both the Alid ritualists and Siraya Christians believe that they are worshipping the same deity. Instead, I suspect that the main issue was that the Alid ritual as practiced in Thau-sia and Pi-a-kha has become very sinified, and Alid is no longer the only god. (In the Thau-sia *konkai*, Alid has even lost his status as the highest god.) Also, Presbyterian ministers hired from elsewhere might easily be misled by the new sinified names of the *konkai* in Thau-sia, Pi-a-kha and Sio-hoe-a, and assume them to be Chinese temples.

Bacclouangh was at first settled from the coastal area of Tainan where Siraya who resisted sinification were forced to abandon their lands and flee inland. The name Thau-sia literally means the "first" or "leading" community and because of the role of Thau-sia in inviting the Tok-ka Alid to Bacclouangh, Thau-sia is believed to be the first settled community in Bacclouangh. Interestingly, this community also became the first in Bacclouangh to introduce Chinese elements into the Alid cult. Even more ironically, the ritualists in Thau-sia today blame other communities for failing to adopt Chinese elements, dismissing their rituals as inauthentic. In addition, the ritualists in Thau-sia show no interest in recovering Sinckansche. (The same man I mentioned above told me that he did not feel it necessary.)

In Thau-sia, it is strongly believed that there are five Alid, and they are sisters. This belief suggests that Thau-sia is not a single community but a combination of five communities. (The opinion of its *tang-ki* that Alid is male probably only represents the *tang-ki*'s personal viewpoint.) This appears to reflect the teaching of the Chinese folk religion in which the deity of each temple is believed to have its own soul or spirit, even when the votive statues represent the same god. For example, every year during the Mazu festival, the Mazu of Tai-ka (Dajia) is brought to visit the Mazu of Sin-kang (Xingang), though they are actually the same deity. However, as Chinese folk religionists believe that the deity of each temple has its own soul/spirit, the Mazu believers of these two places believe that their Mazu have different spirits.

Twu (2002) thinks that the use of Chinese elements reflects the sincere beliefs of the ritualists, even if they do not reflect Siraya custom (494). However, he concedes the case of Bacclouangh—whose ancestors moved there to escape sinification, only later to embrace it—to be a bit ridiculous (Twu 2002, 219).

Two other communities deserve mention: Khau-sia-liau and Ji-liau, both of which belong to the settlement of Sinckan (and are located in the same district, according to present-day administrative divisions). The Siraya language, or Sinckansche, is named after this settlement.

Surprisingly, most of the ritualists in Khau-sia-liau are either Chinese or sinified Siraya. Most of the community members who claim to be Siraya are Christians today. Therefore, the shrine of this community is called not a *konkai* but an altar (*tan/toann*), as at several small Chinese temples nearby (Twu 2002, 273–5). Most importantly, the altar is actually part of a Chinese temple. Its rituals are led by the *tang-ki* of the temple, and most of the ritualists are actually the temple's worshippers. However, the design of the altar and ritual are very traditional, even more so than those of Kabuasua, and the offerings are also purely Siraya.

I once talked with a temple manager who thought it ironic that while the Chinese have become faithful worshippers of Alid, the Siraya themselves do not *gia hiunn* (burn joss sticks in their worship). In the interview, she declared the rank of Alid to be at least equal to that of Shangdiye (Xuantian Shangdi, the Emperor of Dark/Mysterious Heaven), the main god of that temple.

However, I must challenge the view that the local Siraya do not believe in Alid. Since Siraya Christians also call God by the Sinckansche word *Alid*, and Sinckan is one of the places where Christian mission has been very successful, I suggest that Siraya Christians are actually worshipping Alid in a different building and with a different kind of ceremony.

The Ji-liau *konkai* is located on private land but open to the general public. Although rebuilt in 1994, the structure is still "purely Siraya" (Twu 2002, 302). Joss sticks and paper money are forbidden, and Alid is considered female. Most importantly, Alid is the only deity worshipped in the *konkai*. However, its ritualists (like those of Tham-khian) do not express any interest in Siraya consciousness, let alone the revival of Sinckansche.

In other Sinckan communities, Alid is usually worshipped together with Chinese deities such as Moniang Lin, Xuantian Shangdi and Tudigong. This practice reflects the fact that sinification occurred very early among the Siraya there. Xuantian Shangdi was the main god worshipped by the government of the Tang-leng (Dongning) kingdom. His cult was introduced to Taiwan from Fujian by Koxinga's forces in 1662. At the time, he was considered the highest god among the Hok-lo. Moniang Lin was awarded the title Tianhou (Heavenly Empress) by the Qing government, and many of her temples bear the name Tianhou Gong (Heavenly Empress Temple). Tudigong, the earth god, is very common in the Chinese folk religion, and nearly every Chinese community in Taiwan has a Tudigong shrine. The cults of these Chinese deities reflect the influences of the Chinese colonizing powers.

Another noteworthy settlement is Lak-teng-khe, which belongs to the subgroup of Teivorangh. The structure of its *konkai* is quite traditional, and the foods offered to *Alid* are also "purely traditional" (Twu 2002, 429). In addition, the ritual is conducted by a female *inibus*. However, the ritual itself has been sinified, and other deities are worshipped. As in Thau-sia, Alid is described as "five sisters" (Twu 2002, 429). Furthermore, the *konkai* of this community is divided into two shrines, with one consecrated to a Chinese god described as "the true *konkai*" (Twu 2002, 432), indicating that this other god enjoys a higher rank than Alid. This reflects the influence of Thau-sia, whose *tang-ki* initiated the ritual's revival there. Although the ritual in Kabuasua and Lak-teng-khe is conducted in Sinckansche, ritualists in Lak-teng-khe show no interest in the language.

Conclusion

Having a form of godliness, but denying the power thereof: from such turn away.
(II Timothy 3:5)

In this chapter, I have argued—contrary to certain commonly accepted scholarly theories—that being an Alid ritualist does not entail being an ethnic Siraya or having a strong Siraya consciousness. In Khau-sia-liau, most of the ritualists are Chinese. The ritualists in Kabuasua see themselves as simultaneously Chinese and Siraya, though they demonstrate a strong Siraya consciousness and are eager to learn Sinckansche. Although the ritualists in Thau-sia recognize that they are Siraya, their behavior demonstrates that they are very eager to be sinified, and they show no interest in either government recognition or the revival of Sinckansche. The cases of Kabuasua and Thau-sia suggest that, for them, "Sirayaness" is not so much an ethnic group as an activity. Ironically, the ritualists of these two communities maintain that those who do not worship Alid as they do are not true Siraya or true Alid believers.

Concerning Tham-khian and Ji-liau, though the rituals of these communities are plausibly "purely traditional" and "purely Siraya" (Twu 2002) the ritualists do not express any Siraya consciousness and play no role in the Siraya revival movement. Just as having a traditional ritual does not mean having a strong Siraya consciousness, so must we also reject the view that the more sinified the ritual the less interest its participants show in the revival of Sinckansche. This view is disproved through the cases of Tham-khian and Ji-liau, on the one hand, and Kabuasua and Pak-thau-iunn, on the other.

As mentioned at the beginning, Alid belief has played an important role in the Siraya revival movement and is a symbol of Siraya identity. Aguilar (2009) confirms the historic importance of monotheism for Siraya "self-perception" (153). Yet in most Siraya communities today, Alid is worshipped alongside other deities and, in places, is no longer considered even the highest god. In Kabuasua and Thau-sia, ritualists ordinarily worship Chinese deities except during the Alid festival. In Tham-khian and Ji-liau, although Alid is the only god in the *konkai*, there is no reason to suppose that the ritualists there are not also worshipping other gods.

This suggests that the Alid ritual cannot reflect Siraya identity very effectively. The Tok-ka Alid—in which Alid can easily be misinterpreted as one of the Chinese gods—is especially unsuitable for this purpose. Recall that the *inibus* of Kabuasua felt no problem with being simultaneously Siraya and Chinese. In many Siraya communities, the Alid ritual reflects just such a dual identity. To the extent that it becomes assimilated into the Chinese folk religion, the Alid ritual loses its meaning for those with strong Siraya consciousness. Just as conversion to Islam has effected cultural changes among the Oromo in Waso Boorna (Aguilar 2009, 61), so has sinification among the Siraya.

Because Siraya identity cannot be properly expressed through the Alid ritual, no matter how traditional in form, it is incapable of attracting people with a strong Siraya consciousness. To become a faithful Alid believer and a true Siraya, another kind of ritual is needed: one that reflects the monotheistic basis of the pre-Chinese Alid belief.

Though Christianity was originally also a foreign religion, being monotheistic and having no other god but Alid worshipped in church buildings, it eventually constituted an act of Siraya consciousness through another kind of ceremony. Furthermore, because of the enculturation of Christianity (especially the PCT), adopting that religion eventually became "the only way to protect the [society] from the growing threat of [Chinese]" (Hefner 1993, 112) and fight against Chinese culture making use of Western domination (Yeh 2006). Therefore, though many Takasago tribes today pursue social reconstruction on the basis of their folk religions, for most Peipo it is actually the indigenized (contextualized) Christianity that opens the door to the revitalization and the maintenance of their ethnic identity. Because Christianity is monotheistic, worshipping Alid in church qualifies as an expression of Siraya consciousness through a different kind of ceremony.

Appendix

Sinckansche	Mandarin (Hànyǔ Pīnyīn)	Taiwanese (Hok-lo)	Chinese	Other
Bacclouangh	Mù jiā liū wān		目加溜灣	Baccaluangh
	Pí zǐ jiǎo	Pi-a-kha	埤仔腳	
	Shāo hūi zǐ	Sio-hoe-a	燒灰仔	
	Tóu shè	Thau-sia	頭社	
Soulangh	Xiāo lǒng		蕭壠	
	Fān zǎi wēn	Hoan-a-un	番仔塭	Fān zǐ wēn
	Dǔ jiā	Tok-ka	篤加	
Kabuasua	Jí bèi shuǎ		吉貝耍	交破所
	Běi tóu yáng	Pak-thau-iunn	北頭洋	
	Tán jiǎn	Tham-khian		Tán qián
Sinckan	Xīn gǎng	Sin-kang	新港	Zincan
Tavakan	Dà mù jiàng		大目降	Tavocon, Tavokon
	Kǒu pí	Khau-pi	口埤	
Baksa	Mù zhà	Bak-cha	木柵	
	Gāng zǐ lín	Kong-a-na	岡仔林	
	Bá mǎ	Poa-be	拔馬	
	Kǒu shè liáo	Khau-sia-liau	口社寮	
	Guāng hé	Kong-ho	光和	
	Chéng shān	Teng-san	澄山	
	Èr liáo	Ji-liau	二寮	
Mattauw	Má dòu		麻豆	蔴荳
Teivorangh	Dà wǔ lǒng		大武壠	Taivoan, 大滿 (Dà mǎn)
Tapani	Jiāo bā nián	Ta-pa-ni		Tamai, Daobali
	Lìu chóng xī	Lak-teng-khe	六重溪	
Makattao	Mǎ kǎ dào		馬卡道	
Dorco	Dūo lúo gūo		哆囉嘓	

Notes and References

1 The Taiwan locations discussed here are known by various names; see Appendix for a list of other-language equivalents.

Aguilar, M. I. 2009. *The Politics of God in East Africa: Oromo Ritual and Religion*. Asmara, Eritrea: The Red Sea Press, Inc.

_____. 1995. "African Conversion from a World Religion: Religious Diversification by the Waso Boorana in Kenya." *Africa: Journal of the International African Institute* 65, no. 4: 525–44.

Astuti, R. 1995. "'The Vezo Are Not a Kind of People': Identity, Difference, and 'Ethnicity' among a Fishing People of Western Madagascar." *American Ethnologist* 22, no. 3: 464–82.

Campbell, W. 2006. *A Dictionary of the Amoy Vernacular Spoken throughout the Prefectures of Chin-chiu, Chiang-chiu, and Formosa*. Tainan: The Taiwan Church Press and PCT Press.

Chen, Y. 2005. *Dujia alizi yu fanzaiwen alize de misi* [The Myth about Tok-ka Alid and Hoan-a-un Alid]. Online: http://siraya.tnc.gov.tw/modules/tinyd0/index.php?id=92 (accessed December 14, 2009).

Chou, W. 2001. *Taiwan lishi tushuo—shiqian zhi 1945 nian* [Illustration of the History of Taiwan—From the Pre-historical Era to 1945]. Taipei City: Linking Press.

Clifford, J. 1982. *Person and Myth: Maurice Leenhardt in the Melanesian World*. Berkeley: University of California Press.

Duan, H. 2007. *Guanyu jibeishua—Jibeishua de jidian* [Concerning Kabuasua—The Rituals in Kabuasua]. Online: http://siraya.tnc.gov.tw/modules/tinyd0/index.php?id=88 (accessed December 3, 2009).

_____. 2004. *Guanyu jibeishua—Jibeishua de xinyang liliang* [Concerning Kabuasua—The Power of the Belief of Kabuasua]. Online: http://siraya.tnc.gov.tw/modules/tinyd0/index.php?id=86 (accessed December 2, 2009).

Feuchtwang, S. 2001. *Popular Religion in China: The Imperial Metaphor*. Richmond: Curzon Press.

Hefner, R. W., ed. 1993. *Conversion to Christianity: Historical and Anthropological Perspectives on a Great Transformation*. Berkeley: University of California Press.

Hsieh, J. 2006. *Collective Rights of Indigenous Peoples: Identity-Based Movement of Plain Indigenous in Taiwan*. New York: Routledge.

Huang, P. H. 1996. *A Theology of Self-Determination: Responding to the Hope for "Chhut Thau Thinn" of the People in Taiwan*. Tainan: Chhut Thau Thinn Theological Study Center.

Huang, S. 2003. "Accepting the Best, Receiving the Difference: Borrowing and Identity in an Ami Village." In *Religion in Modern Taiwan: Tradition and Innovation in a Changing Society*. Ed. by P. Clart and C. B. Jones. Honolulu: University of Hawai'i Press, 257–79.

Jordan, D. K. 1993. "The Glyphomancy Factor: Observations on Chinese Conversion." In *Conversion to Christianity: Historical and Anthropological Perspectives on a Great Transformation*. Ed. by Robert W. Hefner. Berkeley: University of California Press, 285–303.

Liu, H. 2001. *Nanying pingpu zhi* [Nanying Peipo Ethnography]. Xinying: Tainan County Cultural Affairs Bureau.

_____. 1998. *Liulang de tudi* [Vagrant Lands]. Taipei: Yuanmin Culture.

Sim, K. 2003. *Taiwan Xietong (Tai-oan Hiat-thong)* [Taiwanese Blood]. Taipei: Vanguard Press.

Stafford, C. 2000. *Separation and Reunion in Modern China*. Cambridge: Cambridge University Press.

Twu, S. 2002. *Nanying gongjie zhi* [Nanying Konkai Chronicles]. Xinying: Tainan County Government Cultural Affairs Department.

Yeh, C. 2006. *Zongjiao gaixin yu ronghe: Taizu xinyang yu shenming jiaohuan* [Religious Conversion and Syncretism: Interchange between Thai-tsou and Deities]. In *Constructing Siraya: Selected Conference Papers*. Ed. by Chuen-rong Yeh. Xinying: Tainan County Government, 199–220.

Yeh, S. 2000. *Xilaya moyi: Pan yinhua* [The Last Siraya Descendent: Gun-hoe Phoann]. Taipei: Vanguard Press.

LIST OF CONTRIBUTORS

Silke Bechler is a PhD candidate of the Graduate Program for Transcultural Studies, within the cluster "Asia and Europe in Global Context," University of Heidelberg, where she is working on her dissertation project, *Religion on Stage: The Vedic Sacrifice in New Public Spheres*. Her thesis focuses on religious flows between different cultures and their impact on the concept of religion in a globalized context. Among her research interests are traditional and modern ritual practices in India as well as in the Hindu diasporas and their appearance in new trans-cultural contexts.

Bei Dawei has doctorates in comparative religion from the California Institute of Integral Studies (CIIS) and philosophy from the University of South Africa (UNISA). An assistant professor in the foreign language department of Hsuan Chuang University (Hsinchu, Taiwan), his interests include Western esoteric traditions, New Religious Movements and artificial languages. His current project is a survey of English-language fiction about Taiwan.

Christian Etzrodt (PhD economics, University of Cologne; PhD sociology, Ritsumeikan University) is an assistant professor of sociology at Akita International University, where he teaches sociological theory, sociology of globalization, and the history of economic thought. He is the author of the books *Menschliches erhalten* and *Sozialwissenschaftliche Handlungstheorien*. His published articles have been on sociological theory and the sociology of globalization. He has published in several prestigious sociological journals including *Human Studies*, *Kölner Zeitschrift für Soziologie und Sozialpsychologie*, and *Zeitschrift für Soziologie*. His research interests include sociological theory, sociology of globalization and sociology of religion.

Thzeng Chi Hsiung (MA, Hyogo University of Teacher Education) is a professor of visual communication design at National Yunlin University of Science and Technology, Taiwan. His published books include *The Design Education of Bauhaus*, *The Reflection of Combine with Public Facilities and Art*, *The Colors* *of Science and Culture*, and *The Lost Colors in Chinese*. His published articles have been on basic design, cultural change and traditional visual communication design. He has published his work in such journals as the *Journal of Yunlin Institute of Technology*, *Journal of Science and Technology* and *Journal of Taipei Fine Arts Museum*.

Tiaukhai Iunn is currently a PhD student at St Andrews University, Scotland. He earned his MRes in social anthropology at the same university in 2008. Though his PhD program is in the School of Divinity, under the auspices of the Centre for the Study of Religion and Politics (CSRP), his research interest is Siraya religion.

Pei-Ru Liao studied for her PhD at the Centre for Interdisciplinary Gender Studies at the University of Leeds. Her thesis was entitled *Representation of Gender and Religion in Taiwanese Dramas: A Case Study of Da Ai Dramas*. The thesis aims to understand gender concepts in Taiwan, a Confucian society, and the interwoven relationships of gender, Confucianism and Buddhism. Her research also provides insights on contemporary Buddhism and Humanistic Buddhism by analyzing religious messages embedded in TV texts produced by one of the most powerful and influential Buddhist organizations in Taiwan.

Magdalena Karolak is an adjunct professor in the Arts and Sciences Department at Prince Mohamed bin Fahd University, Saudi Arabia. While teaching political science, history and anthropology courses, Magdalena has been working on her PhD in comparative linguistics. She is currently involved in three research projects related to the culture of the Gulf region. She has participated in a number of international conferences and published articles in the fields of cultural studies and linguistics.

Nikodem Karolak is a graduate student of Japanese philology at the Adam Mickiewicz University, Poland. His interests are foreign languages and their grammar systems, the history of film, and religion and its influence on politics. He is a laureate of the National Film Knowledge Contest (Warsaw, 2008).

Derrick M. Nault is founder, former president and current director of the Asia Association for Global Studies (AAGS), a scholarly organization based in Tokyo, Japan, as well as the editor in chief of the *Asia Journal of Global Studies* (AJGS), the association's official journal. In addition to assuming these duties, Nault has a PhD in history from Queen's University, Canada, and currently lectures in world history and development studies at the University of Calgary, Canada. His most recent publications are *Globalization and Human Rights in the*

Developing World, co-edited with Shawn L. England and *Development in Asia: Interdisciplinary, Post-neoliberal, and Transnational Perspectives*. He is currently working on a monograph on the history of human rights in the Global South.

Rab Paterson, the current president of the Asia Association for Global Studies (AAGS), teaches critical thinking, media studies, international affairs and digital literacy at the International Christian University, Tokyo University's Graduate School of Interdisciplinary Information Studies, and Dokkyo University's Faculty of International Liberal Arts. He holds a BA in Pacific Asian history and an MA in Pacific Asian studies from London University's School of Oriental and African Studies (SOAS). A doctoral candidate at London University's Institute of Education, he is presently conducting research on digital literacy and the mass media.

Girardo Rodriguez Plasencia is a PhD student at Ritsumeikan Asia Pacific University, Japan, where he completed his MA in Asia Pacific studies. He also holds a master's degree in anthropology from Havana University, Cuba. He is interested in the study of contemporary/alternative spiritualities in Japan and the globalization of Japanese New Religions. His current research explores the transplantation of Soka Gakkai in Cuba.

Cesar Andres-Miguel Suva (MA, University of Calgary) holds a teaching fellowship and is currently a PhD candidate in history at the Australian National University. His current research focuses on the Moro insurgency during the Philippine–American War. His broader interests include political conflict and identity construction in colonial Southeast Asia.

Chin Chia Tsai (MA, National Yunlin University of Science and Technology) is a student in the Design Doctoral Program at National Yunlin University of Science and Technology, Taiwan (R.O.C.). He was an exchange student in the Arts and Design Division (Doctorate Degree Course) at Kobe Design University, Japan. He is also a graphic designer in Pingtung City, Taiwan. His research interests include manga, mascot design and visual communication design.

Evangelos Voulgarakis (PhD, University of Kent, Canterbury) specializes in symbols of national and religious heritage in contemporary times. He has examined modern interpretations of ancient Greek democracy and drama for the purpose of social activism and conducted research on comparative religious rhetoric in relation to femininity and national identity. His doctoral dissertation is entitled *The Perception and Utilization of Symbols of American Heritage* *by the United States Neo-militia Movement and Its Critics.* Since 1999, he has taught American and British history courses in the UK, in addition to the history of English literature, Greek mythology and other courses on language-related subjects in Taiwan. He is a member of the editorial team of the *Asia Journal of Global Studies* (AJGS), the official journal of the Asia Association for Global Studies (AAGS).